About the editors

Melissa Hope Ditmore has investigated ethics in research, the effects of police raids on sex workers and trafficked persons, and violence against sex workers. She edited the *Encyclopedia of Prostitution and Sex Work* (2006). She is an author on the three reports produced by the Sex Workers Project. Her writing appears in *Development with a Body* (2007), *Trafficking and Prostitution Reconsidered* (2005) and *Affective Turn* (2007). Ditmore is a research fellow at National Development and Research Institutes (NDRI).

Antonia Levy is a PhD candidate and adjunct lecturer at the City University of New York. Her research interests include political sociology, gender and sexuality, social movements and activism, as well as visual sociology; her thesis focuses on the polyamory movement in Germany and the US. Her work as social justice activist centers around issues related to women's liberation and sexual rights, labor, as well as community media. Currently, she is a member of the PapertigerTV collective and a part-timer organizer for her union, the Professional Staff Congress at CUNY. She has been co-chair of several academic/activist conferences and workshops, including Sex Work Matters: Beyond Divides and the Second Annual Feminist Pedagogy Conference.

Alys Willman is a feminist economist specializing in gender, violence, and illicit markets. She is the author of *What's Money Got to Do With It? Commercial Sex and Risky Behavior in Managua, Nicaragua*, and numerous articles in both academic and grassroots publications. She has produced one documentary film, 'Mateando en la Gran Manzana, on Argentine immigration to New York. Ms Willman has worked in a dozen countries throughout Latin America with NGOs, the United Nations, and the World Bank. She holds a doctorate in urban and public policy from the New School University in New York.

To Patricia Clough,
without whom this book could not have been produced

Sex Work Matters

Exploring Money, Power, and Intimacy in the Sex Industry

edited by
Melissa Hope Ditmore, Antonia Levy, and Alys Willman

Zed Books
LONDON & NEW YORK

Sex Work Matters: Exploring Money, Power, and Intimacy in the Sex Industry was first published in 2010 by Zed Books Ltd, 7 Cynthia Street, London N1 9JF, UK and Room 400, 175 Fifth Avenue, New York, NY 10010, USA

www.zedbooks.co.uk

Typeset in Cumbria, UK by Long House Publishing Services
Index: John Barker
Cover designed by Alice Marwick
Printed and bound in Great Britain by Antony Rowe,
Chippenham and Eastbourne

Distributed in the USA exclusively by Palgrave Macmillan, a division of St Martin's Press, LLC, 175 Fifth Avenue, New York, NY 10010, USA

A catalogue record for this book is available from the British Library
Library of Congress Cataloging in Publication Data available

ISBN 978 1 84813 433 1 hb
ISBN 978 1 84813 434 8 pb
ISBN 978 1 84813 435 5 eb

Contents

Acknowledgements

Alys Willman and Antonia Levy would like to thank, first, Johannes Novy, who introduced us in 2004, leading to the beginning of the Sex Work Matters project the following year. We are grateful to the advisers of the 2006 Sex Work Matters conference for their many insights and invaluable help when organizing the conference in 2006: Patricia Clough, Sibyl Schwarzenbach, L. H. M. Ling, Melissa Hope Ditmore, and Robert Beauregard.

We also would like to thank our sponsors who generously funded the Sex Work Matters conference in 2006, and Patricia Clough for securing most of these funds: Center for the Study of Women and Society, CUNY Graduate Center; Barnard College Center for Research on Women; Department of Women's and Gender Studies, Rutgers University; Institute for Research on Women and Gender, Columbia University; Center for the Study of Gender and Sexuality, New York University; CUNY Center for Lesbian and Gay Studies; PhD Program in Sociology, CUNY Graduate Center; Woodhull Freedom Foundation; and The New School Office of Student Development and Activities.

We are most grateful to our families and close friends for their encouragement and infinite support during the various stages of this project. Particular thanks go to Diana Adams, Paula Boettcher, Megan Bourne, Steffi Dathe, Jen Gieseking, Julia Graff, Nathan Guisinger, David Halverson, Björn Kinne, Carl Lindskoog, Lily Ling, Janine Ludwig, Danny Malec, Jamie McCallum, Fabián Mosenson, Christine Mussel, Patrizia Nobbe, Michael Thompson, and Claudia Vettermann.

Melissa Hope Ditmore would like to thank Laura Agustín, Dan Allman, Max Barnhart, Andrea Berger, Patricia Clough, the Cooper family, Andrea Cornwall, Francis DiDonato, Deborah Gambs, Jean Halley, Anastasia Hudgins, Rose M. Kim, Juline Koken, Angus McIntyre,

Ananya Mukherjea, members of Prostitutes of New York, Barbara Katz Rothman, Tracy Quan, Sarah Steiner, Juhu Thukral, Patricia Venditto, Jo Weldon, Elizabeth Anne Wood, and Jeffrey Yamaguchi for their advice and support, which were indispensable when addressing the peculiar obstacles to producing this volume.

The editors of this volume would like to thank Tamsine O'Riordan of Zed Books for her insightful comments. We thank the contributors for their patience with this project, and their continued collaboration across time and space.

Permissions

An earlier version of Laura Agustín's 'The (Crying) Need for Different Kinds of Research' was published in *Research for Sex Work*, Vol. 5, June 2002, pp. 30–2.

Some material in Mindy Bradley-Engen's and Carrie M. Hobb's 'To Love, Honor, and Strip: An Investigation of Exotic Dancer Romantic Relationships' has previously appeared in M. S. Bradley (2007) 'Strippers, Wives and Girlfriends: Managing Stigma in Deviant Romantic Relationships,' *Deviant Behavior*, Vol. 28, No. 4, 379–406.

An earlier version of Kerwin Kaye's 'Sex and the Unspoken in Male Street Prostitution' was published in *Journal of Homosexuality*, 2007, Vol. 53, No. 1/2, 37–73.

An earlier version of Jo Weldon's 'Show Me the Money: A Sex Worker Reflects on Research into the Sex Industry' was published in *Research for Sex Work*, Vol. 9, June 2006, pp. 12–15.

Patty Kelly's 'Pimping the Pueblo: State-Regulated Commercial Sex in Neoliberal Mexico' uses selections from Patty Kelly (2008) *Lydia's Open Door: Inside Mexico's Most Modern Brothel*, © 2008 Regents of the University of California. Published by the University of California Press.

Foreword

Alys Williams and Antonia Levy

Like so many great – and not so great – literary and academic projects, *Sex Work Matters* was hatched in a coffee shop. One spring afternoon in 2005, the two of us sat lamenting the very few opportunities there seemed to be to meet others who were interested in research on sex work. We agreed that it seemed we were always being relegated to a panel on 'gender,' or 'poverty,' or 'deviance' in the conferences where we presented, as if our work was a topic of interest, but only marginal interest. Or worse, we were placed on a panel about trafficking and left to explain how our work was different, and how sex work in general is not trafficking by default, and so on.

From these mutual complaints the idea to organize a conference just on sex work was born, as a chance for us to see what kind of work was being done in different places, and to meet people we could learn from and work with. We wanted to bring sex workers, scholars, and activists (and those that fit more than one of these categories) together to explore the issues of most importance to them. We imagined a half-day affair with a handful of graduate students and activists from New York, or perhaps as far away as Washington, DC. We drew a bra hanging from a flagpole on the back of a napkin as our logo, and decided to keep on meeting. We were sure somebody would fund our great idea.

Nobody wanted to fund us or, at least, nobody with any money. Over the next eight months we tramped from one academic department and feminist organization to another, only to hear that there wasn't any money. Eventually we did convince the Center for the Study of Women and Society at the City University of New York (CUNY) Graduate Center that we were serious, and in one round of cappuccinos the director had brought the inter-university women studies consortium on board to the tune of $2,000. A few hundred dollars more from various financially strapped graduate student and lesbian, gay, bisexual, and transgender (LGBT) organizations, and some logistical support from the student activity office of The New School, New York, and we were on our way.

The day of the conference was an explosion in diversity and debate.[1] Presenters – 52 of them from thirteen countries – represented the experiences of sex workers, performers, activists, bloggers, students, teachers, parents, and partners. Discussions pushed the limits of current debates to address sex work in its broader context of power, politics, discrimination, and labor rights. The participation of many well-known academics, young and innovative scholars and activists, as well as long-time activists including Carol Leigh, Priscilla Alexander, and Robyn Few as panellists and active participants, created a stimulating and unique environment for exchange. Conversation was lively and candid, sometimes bordering on aggressive. The activists pointed out where the academics were way out of touch. The academics vowed to do more research in coordination with sex workers. Everyone agreed there needed to be more discussion and representation of class divisions in sex work by reaching out to street-based workers, and to sex workers in developing countries. This, of course, indicated the need for more funding for projects like this one – to have these groups actually present at the table – another strong point of agreement.

In the end, difficult questions were asked, and delicate issues discussed, and even scandalous things said. At the final roundtable, where 150 people crammed into a little conference room (standing room only) to discuss the main points of the day, several activists entered a heated debate about where the movement should go from here. And then, quietly, a female undergraduate from Brooklyn College stood up and asked a question that silenced the room. 'I don't understand the ultimate goal,' she said. 'I mean, what is it that you want for the future, say, for the unborn sex workers?' There was a long silence, and although some of the same activists jumped in to insist that yes, indeed, they were working for the unborn sex workers, so they could have better working conditions, the discomfort was tangible. From those who most celebrate sex work to the more pragmatic people in that room, who realize prostitution will always exist while demand exists, all seemed reluctant to entertain the notion of unborn sex workers, at least in the world as it is now. Is it that we all have a little abolitionist in us? Is it that the image of an unborn sex worker implies too much predetermination, even coercion? Can you support sex workers and still not be comfortable with the idea of a child, your daughter or son maybe, growing up to be one? Can you support sex workers and still believe there should be more options from which to choose? Could we imagine a world where sex work is a safe, even respected, employment option?

It is here, perhaps, that there is a starting point for future conversations and collaborations to address the challenges we face. This book finds its place within a growing, international movement for sex workers' rights and a broadening research agenda for the issues that affect them. The field of sex work is wide open to academics willing to engage in collaborative research with sex workers. Activists confront the task of teaming up with researchers in ways that advance a progressive agenda and combat social stigma, and help link the sex worker rights movement to broader social movements. A challenge also awaits funders, who have largely avoided projects that deal directly with sex work, to fund research and support activism addressing sex work in its social, economic, and political dimensions. We envision this volume as an important step toward addressing these challenges, and transforming them into opportunities.

NOTE

1 For more details on the program of the conference and participants, see the *Sex Work Matters* website www.sexworkmatters.net (Sex Work Matters, 2005).

Introduction: Beyond the Sex in Sex Work

Alys Willman and Antonia Levy

What do most of us really know about sex work? The media report regularly on the most sensational aspects of the sex industry: the rise of illegal trafficking networks, the looming threat of HIV/AIDS from a booming underground sex trade, and, of course, the occasional politician caught with his pants down. Offers for sexual services fill our email inboxes daily, and pack the classifieds of our newspapers.

In reality, much of what sex workers do is not glamorous, scandalous, or even necessarily dangerous. 'Sex workers' is a broad category that includes men, women, and transgender people employed in everything from erotic dancing to domination, from phone sex to street prostitution. What is often left out of the media, and research, is that people who work in prostitution and other forms of sex work are not only sex workers; they are partners, friends, and community members. The issues that most concern them are the challenges they face every day: managing money, juggling family and other intimate relationships, dealing with legal restrictions and policing, confronting social stigma, and challenges to them organizing collectively. Since the 1970s, sex workers have addressed these issues in their own writings and organizing campaigns, and have demanded more inclusive approaches to research and policy that affect them.

Still, despite the growing inclusion of sex workers in research, and the increasing visibility of the global sex worker rights movement, a critical reflection of the everyday concerns sex workers face is largely absent from current anthologies. In addition, even as more and more scholars, activists, and advocates engage the debates surrounding sex work, their efforts remain largely separate from one another. Students and younger activists are demonstrating a growing interest in the topic, as evidenced by their increasing involvement in activist organizations.

Artists, too, continue to challenge conceptual boundaries about sex work and ownership of the body in their work. Yet few forums bring these groups together.

This book is an attempt to do just that: to bridge the various divides that we have always noticed in the field of sex work, divides we experienced as obstructing the efforts of the sex worker rights movement. First and foremost, there is the longstanding, well-known and over-discussed divide among feminists themselves about the very nature of sex work: that is, whether it can and/or should be a woman's right (or a human being's right, for that matter) to choose this type of activity without this necessarily infringing on her/his integrity, violating her/his psychological wellbeing, and (in the view of some) damaging the reputation of all (wo)mankind. While we certainly don't want to resurrect this argument – the two extremes are usually so far apart that fruitful dialog is mostly impossible – we do recognize that this divide exists, and give space to identify and discuss concerns shared by both perspectives within the different chapters.

Added to feminist divisions are disciplinary divides among scholars of sociology, philosophy, political science, anthropology, and economics. Often, the main focus of writings in the humanities and social sciences remains either on deviance or the illegal aspects and negative consequences of sex work, or writings consist of isolated ethnographies on one particular facet in sex workers' lives, or the insistence is on human rights for sex workers while abstracting from other social and economic aspects of their lives. Economists, when they take an interest, are mostly narrowly interested in why female sex workers can earn more than women of their same skill level, and often more than men. Few dialogs bring these different approaches together, and as a result the overall understanding of the different dimensions of sex work remains fragmented.

The third, and most significant, divide is the deep division between academia and the activist community. This division is often decried as 'artificial,' as being maintained due to class, race, and gender issues, and as hampering the sex worker rights movement's efforts to become more acknowledged and accepted. Admittedly, this divide has been around as long as there have been sex workers and academics to produce it, and no project is going to undo that all at once. Still, we can stand on the shoulders of those who led previous efforts to move forward and voice different perspectives. The heroic feats of STELLA in Canada, the International Committee on the Rights of Sex Workers in Europe, or the

Desiree Alliance – all provide examples of what can be done with a lot of imagination, an inclusive environment, and, of course, a minimal level of funding.

This book is the product of conversations among sex workers, academics, activists, and those who fit all three categories. The contributions are organized into five sections. Section A presents new conceptual frameworks for understanding the sex industry. Here we include three selections by some of the most respected writers on this topic, challenging readers to explore the topic of sex work in new ways, especially its cultural, economic, and political dimensions. Barbara Brents and Kathryn Hausbeck open the section with a discussion of the ways mainstream culture and the sex industry are converging, with radical implications for sex workers and their allies. The past decade has witnessed an important sexualization of culture, in which diverse identities, practices, and values are more accepted, at the same time that the sex industry has expanded. These processes have intensified racial, gender, and class hierarchies in the sex industry, presenting an important challenge going forward. Laura Agustín takes up the issue of increasing diversity of realities in the sex industry, lamenting the fact that researchers studying migrant sex workers often find their funding opportunities limited to themes related to HIV/AIDS, 'trafficking,' or violence against women. She advocates for research from a migration perspective, for a better understanding of sex workers' varying experiences, and for more effective policy making. Juline Koken turns her attention to the portrayal of sex workers in academic scholarship, emphasizing the ways researchers often mirror the very virgin/whore dichotomy that feminists have sought to overcome. Her chapter illuminates the influence of competing ideologies in research on the emotional wellbeing of women in the sex industry, and proposes broader ways to make sense of women's involvement in sex work.

Section B, 'Managing Multiple Roles,' addresses the fact that sex workers are not only sex workers. Sex workers have families, friends, and neighbors, to whom they may or may not disclose their work. Maintaining boundaries between different areas of their lives requires complex strategies, and often involves multiple identities. Mindy Bradley-Engen and Carrie M. Hobbs describe the particular challenges that sex workers face in their intimate relationships, as they attempt to balance the expectations of their partners with the demands of their profession, including the social stigma attached to their work. The stories they present exemplify the power of this stigma, in that many strippers defend their profession, yet ultimately succumb to their partners' shaming and ridicule. Kerwin Kaye presents a rich ethnography of male street workers in San Francisco, highlighting the ways they balance sexuality and masculinity with the stigma attached to sex work, and the impact these strategies have on the relationships they form. The section concludes with Mashrur Shahid Hossain's candid account of the experiences of transgendered hijras in Bangladesh. Hossain describes how sex work can be used to reappropriate identity and power by a marginalized group. Because they fit into neither male nor female gender categories, hijras are often shamed and stigmatized for what they are not. As Hossain argues, sex work provides an outlet for many to exercise their sexuality and assert a normalcy that society denies them.

The book turns in Section C to the question of money in sex work, a subject long neglected in both the academic and policy literature. Around the world, the sex industry offers more money in fewer hours than most other jobs, and remains one of the few industries in which women outearn men of comparable skill level. Yet despite the general recognition that most sex workers are in it for the money, research has typically focused on the sex in sex work, rather than economic exchange. Economists, in particular, have shied away from analysis of the sex industry, primarily because reliable data are difficult to obtain. Alys Willman opens this section with an overview of what economics has to say about sex work, and the substantial gaps that remain in understanding the economics of swapping sex for money.

The following chapters are important steps in beginning to address those gaps. Jo Weldon gives a brazen account of her experiences with researchers during twenty years of work as an erotic dancer. Having been interviewed over the years by numerous researchers who press for details of any childhood trauma or sexual abuse, she wonders why no one has ever asked her about her financial mindset or motivations in working as an erotic dancer. From her perspective, researchers' focus on the sex in sex work – as opposed to the labor involved – has led to a distorted and misguided view of the sex industry; she argues for research into the financial psychology of sex workers.

The following chapter by Melissa Petro takes up this challenge. Drawing on her experience as a sex worker in Mexico while on a study abroad program, and numerous interviews with sex workers from around the world, Petro examines the influence of money in sex worker decisions at two key moments: entry into the sex industry, and the decision to continue in sex work. While most women purportedly enter the profession for economic gain, money is not the only reason women enter into sex work, and nor is it the only reason most stay. Once a woman has entered into sex work, the industry operates in a way that manufactures consent for continued participation, as the sex worker comes to understand sex work as 'work' and as she reconciles her identity with the identity imposed upon her by her profession. Together with Weldon's chapter, Petro's chapter shows how focusing on the importance of money can revolutionize the way we understand sex work, and draw important connections to other forms of labor.

Section D on 'Sex Work and the State' offers examples of the ways in which state policies and their implementation shape the sex industry in three locations. Patty Kelly's evocative description of Mexico's state-managed Galactic Zone brothels in Chiapas and the comparison by Anne Dölemeyer, Rebecca Pates, and Daniel Schmidt of two legal approaches to prostitution in Germany illustrate some of the ways in which local laws and policy shape the sex industry. Kelly interrogates the ways in which the Mexican state has retreated from economic life through the pursuit of open-market policies, at the same time that it reasserts its control over women's lives and bodies through the creation and regulation of brothels. Dölemeyer, Pates, and Schmidt contrast the implementation of prostitution policy in two cities in Germany, one adopting a law enforcement model and the other adopting a service provision model. The differences in implementation of the same federal law reflect variations in the conceptualization of sex work – as a legitimate business and as a social problem. Maggie O'Neill and Jane Pitcher conclude the section with a description of a participatory planning project in the UK Midlands. They document the discourse between police officials, sex workers, and other community members in a street prostitution area, and offer important lessons about the benefits and challenges of inclusive processes.

The chapters in the final section, 'Organizing Beyond Divides,' describe successful efforts by sex workers and friends and advocates working together. In her chapter, activist Giulia Garofalo reflects on the experience of the 2005 European Conference on Sex Work, Human Rights, Labor, and Migration, attended by over 200 sex workers and allies. This conference aimed to contribute to a movement led by sex workers and capable of challenging the trafficking debate from a perspective of human, labor, and migration rights. Garofalo discusses challenges facing the movement, especially in forming alliances with feminists, human rights groups, and groups working on migration and related issues. Where the sex worker rights movement will position itself within these broader movements, she argues, is still open to question. In the concluding chapter, Melissa Hope Ditmore discusses the lessons this book can offer the sex worker rights movement and the research and activist communities going forward.

Taken together, these chapters aim to go beyond the narrow discussions of sex in sex work, to understand the broader landscape of the sex industry and the movement for sex workers' rights. As a collaborative effort among sex workers and allied researchers and activists from different disciplines and movements, we hope it bridges some of the divides that frustrate the sex worker rights movement. At the very least, we hope it can inspire further activism, research, and alliances toward greater respect for sex workers, and for what they do.

A   Beyond Divides: New Frameworks for
     Understanding the Sex Industry

1 Sex Work Now: What the Blurring of Boundaries around the Sex Industry Means for Sex Work, Research, and Activism

Barbara G. Brents and Kathryn Hausbeck

We have been doing research on the sex industry and the legal brothels in and around Las Vegas for the past ten years. We have watched Las Vegas become the fastest-growing city in the United States precisely because it is a global tourist destination for the consumption of vice – sex and gambling, but especially sex.[1] As feminists we have struggled to understand this. It is tempting to see Las Vegas as unique, as the 'other' to 'normal' culture. However, the more we look, the more we see that Las Vegas is symbolic of broader cultural and economic shifts that have been transforming our sexual attitudes and the commercial context surrounding sex for the past fifty years. Understanding these broader changes is crucial for scholars, sex workers, and activists, as we struggle to make sense of sex work and the sex industry in the twenty-first century.

In this chapter we argue that the lines around the sex industry are blurring. The cultural and economic changes driven by global, late capitalism have created a consumption-driven, service-based economy that increasingly sells human interactions and emotional exchanges. The sale of personal service, leisure, spectacle, and tourism places more and more components of human relationships onto the market. This has contributed to two important trends. First, there has been a marked sexualization of culture where sexualized images are proliferating, and diverse sexualized practices, identities, and values are becoming more acceptable. The second trend is the mainstreaming of the sex industry. As the adult commercial sex industry expands, the more formal and upscale parts of the industry are increasingly organized and operated more like mainstream businesses. However, this mainstreaming often heightens the impact of social class inequalities.

The result of these two trends is that mainstream culture and the adult commercial sex industry are, in some important ways, converging.

This is happening most clearly in venues with more resources and capital, but the trend is clear. This convergence has radical implications for sex workers, sex work researchers, and their allies, and it presents both opportunities and challenges. Here we examine the research identifying these trends. We then discuss the opportunities and challenges these trends present for scholarship, activism, and the practice of sex work.

The sexualization of culture

'Sex ... has become the Big Story,' said sociologist Kenneth Plummer in 1995 (Plummer, 1995). The British scholar Feona Attwood argues that scholars are paying more and more attention to dramatic changes in social norms surrounding sexuality since the mid 1990s. Culture has become sexualized, as marked by

> a contemporary preoccupation with sexual values, practices and identities; the public shift to more permissive sexual attitudes; the proliferation of sexual texts; the emergence of new forms of sexual experience; the apparent breakdown of rules, categories and regulations designed to keep the obscene at bay; our fondness for scandals, controversies and panics around sex. (Attwood, 2006, p. 78)

This sexualization of culture is a central by-product of a large economic transformation that has occurred in recent years. Beginning in the years after World War II and accelerating in the 1970s, Western economies have changed from production-based (extracting raw materials and producing durable goods in rigidly organized large factories) to consumption-based (producing predominantly services, ideas, and cultural products by means of more independent workers in decentralized workplaces).[2] Most recently, entertainment, leisure, and tourism comprise a large and growing share of the service economy. Even non-tourist services are increasingly 'touristic' – that is, rather than selling products or services with specific outcomes, services sell experience, spectacle, fantasy, adventure, and escapism (Frank, 2002; Lash & Urry, 1994; Mandel, 1975; Rojek, 1994; Rojek & Urry, 1997; Urry, 2002).

Scholars argue that consumer economies have transformed culture, creating consumers driven to constantly create and re-create fragmented, flexible individualistic lifestyles (Gergen, 1991; Giddens, 1991; Harvey, 1989; Lash & Urry, 1994). In this context there has been an increasing commercialization of intimacy (Hausbeck & Brents, 2002; Hochschild,

1983, 2003; Illouz, 1997; Zelizer, 2005). Pleasure, sexuality, and the erotic have become central components of globalized late capitalist leisure culture (Bauman, 2003; Beck & Beck-Gernsheim, 1995; Giddens, 1992; Hawkes, 1996; Plummer, 2001; Plummer, 2003; Simon, 1996).

Several analysts of media culture argue that the increasing centrality of sexuality to consumer culture has created an ever-blurring line around what we used to consider 'obscene' (McNair, 2002; Plummer, 1995). Brian McNair argues that we have become a 'Striptease Culture', where sexual revelation, voyeurism, and sexualized looking are permitted and encouraged throughout the media and commercial culture. Others point to heightened public attention to scandals, controversies, and moral panics, which exemplifies a fascination with sexualized looking (Attwood, 2006). McNair describes a 'pornographication of culture' where the images and practices we used to call pornography are increasingly a part of urban upscale culture and popular advertising. The visual cultural landscape is replete with highly sexualized images employed to sell mostly non-sexual goods and services. Non-pornographic advertising, fashion, art, education, comedy, movies and television and their celebrities are all experimenting with representations and parody of porn. There is a style-based class element to this. 'Porno-chic's' pastiches of porn in avant-garde, upper-class cultural forms are hard, glossy images that play with porn, but are culturally validated as art. Hypersexual public images of seduction and eroticized objects are 'in.' And in fast-paced urban youth markets, flirtation, seduction, and sexual expression are hip and cool. This may not be very different from the quintessential teen experience of the past seventy-five years, but it is unique in that now there is a stylized upscale youth culture, both public and private, that routinely involves a broader range of sexual play, including multiple sexual partners, homosexuality, bisexuality, playful intimacy, partying, and even parts of the actual sex industry.

These changes are transforming norms surrounding sexuality. Over the past fifty years we have witnessed an increasing acceptance of women's sexual agency, sex outside of marriage, sexual pleasure, and homosexuality in the general population (Hawkes, 1996; Jackson & Scott, 2004; Roseneil, 2000; Seidman, 2003; Stacey, 1996). Giddens argues that a consumer culture has created a 'plastic sexuality' that has freed sex from reproduction and created much more gender-egalitarian intimate relationships. There is plenty of evidence in attitude surveys across the globe that the average citizen in late capitalist cultures is becoming more accepting of sexual pleasure and diversity. Various surveys in advanced industrial nations show a greater tolerance of premarital, heterosexual sex, casual sex and serial relationships since the 1980s, and greater tolerance of gay sexuality.[3] Even in the context of liberal trends, there are complications. There remain biases toward monogamy, and anxiety about the specialness of sex (Jackson & Scott, 2004).There is increasing polarization, often drawn along social class or ethnic lines, or urban/rural geographies, especially in the United States, over moral issues such as abortion, same-sex marriage, and tolerance of permissive sexual attitudes. The opposition to the sexualization of culture is smaller in number but often very active, and it does represent a religious and moral backlash in some circles against this sexualization of culture. These circles forestall liberalizing trends in social policy and law, and complicate the politics of sexuality. However, it is clear that sexual attitudes are in the midst of a major transformation.

Consumer economies also transform the nature of work. Far more workers are engaged in interactive service work that markets, packages, and sells human experiences, and emotions for profit, including sales, fast food, personal service, and a wide variety of jobs in leisure and tourist industries. More and more workers sell leisure, touristic forms of escape and experience, to consumers. Many aspects of interactive service work have become feminized and sexualized as women and men working in these jobs are subjected to an objectifying gaze inherent in selling emotional services (Adkins, 2002; Adkins & Merchant, 1996). Many scholars have analyzed the ways in which service and tourist industry workers do emotional labor, acting, and selling commodified human interactions (Hochschild 1983, 2003). What recent research finds is that today's service workers have become adept at emotional labor. Depending on the conditions of the job, workers are able to engage in a variety of strategies that allow them to perform different emotions and portrayals of their personality for customers without psychological harm (see Wharton, 2009). Sexuality is also increasingly a part of the performance for many service workers, from waitresses to fitness instructors and even corporate executives who subtly self-brand to manage sexual aesthetics (Wolkowitz, 2006). Thus, the performances of intimacy, connection, and sexuality are increasingly part of labor in the mainstream leisure economy.

Mainstreaming of the sex industry

How have these cultural and economic changes affected the sex industry, itself?[4] Changing attitudes and an increasingly sexualized culture have pushed more consumers to accept the consumption of sexuality as a legitimate market transaction. At the same time, neoliberal laws and policies that reduce constraints on business and encourage entrepreneurship have allowed sexually oriented businesses to proliferate (Brents & Sanders, 2010). The sex industry businesses and mainstream business are converging. This convergence includes a growth in the sex industry generally, diversification in formal sex industry businesses, corporate structures, partnerships with mainstream businesses, and shifts in marketing to appeal to expanded, often more upscale audiences. Not all aspects of the sex industry are affected equally, but trends are clear.

The global sex industry has grown tremendously since the 1990s. Exact numbers are hotly debated. Ten years ago the global sex industry was estimated to be worth 'at least $20 billion a year and probably many times that' (Economist, 1998). That same year another study estimated that the sex industry was between 4 and 13 percent of gross domestic product in Indonesia, Malaysia, the Philippines and Thailand (Lim, 1998). Researchers estimated the UK's massage parlors to be worth £534 million in 1999, and that lap dancing bars generated £300 million in 2002 (Moffat & Peters, 2004; Jones et al., 2003). There are estimates that in the United States the sex industry is bigger than the major national sports – football, baseball and basketball combined – generating as much as $12 billion in 2005 (Free Speech Coalition, 2006; ABC News, 2004; Ackman, 2001; Schlosser, 1997). Between 2,500 and 5,000 strip clubs operate across the US (ABC News, 2004). In 2005, the entire erotic dance industry in the US brought in approximately $2 billion (Spain, 2007).

The adult industries are more visible than hitherto in mainstream media culture. In the US, cable networks increasingly air adult content in 'specials' such as HBO's 'Real Sex', or series such as *G-String Divas*, *Pornocopia: Going Down in the Valley*, or reality TV shows based on various sex industry themes, like Showtime's reality TV series *Family Business* about adult film star Adam Glasser (Seymour Butts) and his family. HBO's *Cathouse* is a 'documentary' series about legal prostitution. HBO and Showtime are exceedingly low key about marketing these shows. Yet the *Cathouse* series was viewed by an average of 1.3 million viewers and

Pornocopia averaged 1.6 million viewers in 2005 according to Nielsen Media Research, higher than a number of highly advertised mainstream shows (Hibbard, 2005). Sex toys are gaining increasing respectability as stores appear on high streets in the UK (for example the Ann Summers chain) and the US, and adult videos are increasingly marketed toward women (Storr, 2003; Comella, 2008). Porn stars are becoming cult heroes. Pole dancing is taught in fitness clubs.

Mainstream businesses have recognized the profit potential from the adult industries and are getting involved, especially in adult video and strip dancing markets. Large communications and hotel chains reap huge profits from the pay-per-view porn business in hotel rooms (ABC News, 2004; Schlosser, 1997). Strip clubs have been opening chains and going public for a number of years.

This mainstreaming has a distinct class element. Sex industry businesses with the capital to do so are diversifying to attract upscale audiences. Gentlemen's clubs are redecorating and going upscale, expanding services, and opening on site restaurants targeting the lunch and dinner business crowd. In Antwerp, Belgium, a new upscale 'mega brothel' opened in a legal red-light district in 2006, decorated by superstar architects and designers (Castle, 2006). In the US, a legal brothel an hour's drive outside of Las Vegas added a non-brothel resort hotel to its site, and the corporation opened two strip clubs in Las Vegas. One is a traditional midsized strip club on the industrial corridor off the Las Vegas strip. The other is a large upscale ultra modern gentlemen's club that at 4 a.m. becomes a swank ultra lounge with $20 million state-of-the-art lighting and a unisex restroom. This level of capital investment was unprecedented in any company also owning a brothel.

Sex businesses of the past are nowadays under market-driven pressure to act, organize, and market themselves much more like mainstream businesses to compete in this environment. As the Adult Entertainment Expo, an industry trade show held in Las Vegas, has pointed out in its slogan for the past several years, 'It's Sexy. It's Powerful. It's Business!' These adult industry conventions hold workshops on marketing and consumer demand, as well as health insurance, investments, workplace rights, lobbying, website development, internet business practices, and self-branding for both business owners and workers (Comella, 2008).

There is also pressure, particularly for those sex businesses with high capital investment, to treat their employees better to compete with other service industries. For example, in legal brothels in the US state of

Nevada, many owners are under pressure to offer women more flexible schedules than in the past. The larger, more upscale brothels are changing rules that require workers to live on premises, providing more standardized work rules, and offering more incentives for quality labor (Brents & Hausbeck, 2007; Brents et al., 2010).

The mainstreaming of the sex industry takes place in an exceedingly diverse and unequal set of businesses. On the one hand, there is certainly more acceptance of and growth in businesses that are already legal, and have the capital to be more visible. Adult video stores, sex toy stores and even strip dancing, as they have remained legal businesses, are those experiencing the most mainstream embrace. Attitude polls show that a significant majority of the population is still against prostitution where it is illegal, though that percentage has been decreasing. The World Values Survey of attitudes in a variety of nations across the globe has found that in many countries, the number of people who said prostitution was never justifiable has declined. In the United States those who said it was never justifiable dropped between 1982 and 1999 from 65 per cent to 47 per cent (Ingelhart, 2004). Studies of the US find support of prostitution is more likely to come from men than women, whites than non-whites, older than younger, Western US more than the South, unmarried more than married, and those with more education rather than less (May, 1999). May argues that there is such a high correlation between acceptance of activities such as gambling and homosexuality, that it might be better to assess public sentiment about legalizing prostitution without directly asking that question.

There is also certainly more acceptance of the industry to the extent that it represents upper-class, stylish, urban images. That 'your Dad's wank magazine' has been transformed into 'a trendy style magazine about sex and the zeitgeist,' as the marketing literature of UK's *Penthouse* put it (McNair, 2002), is as much about a class transformation as it is about the liberalization of sexual attitudes. As is obvious from the above, the pornographication of culture is about upscale, trendy culture. Criticisms of the sex industry businesses, especially prostitution, center on classed images: images of seedy strip clubs attracting lower-class criminals, or lower-class, drug-addicted, often minority streetwalkers.

The 1998 article in the *Economist* referred to above described a dual effect of the growth in global demand for sex. The market for sex is in upscale venues – audiences with financial resources, businesses with capital, and workers with enough social capital to pass among the upper class themselves. Smaller, more informal businesses are seeing prices drop and workers without the social capital being treated more poorly. The acceptability of the sex industry is as much about social class, race and ethnicity as it is about liberal attitudes toward sexuality.

Implications for sex workers, sex businesses, scholars, and activists

OPPORTUNITIES

This convergence of sex industry businesses and mainstream business has major implications for sex workers (including workers in all aspects of the industry, legal and illegal, formal and informal), activists (any who lobby for worker rights and liberalization of sexual markets), and scholars. Work in the sex industries, while stigmatized in ways unlike other jobs, has elements that are very similar to mainstream work. As such, it makes little sense for scholars to continue to examine sex work as if it were unlike other forms of work. Comparing sex work to existing research on other forms of interactive service work and labor management relations in late capitalist societies can help dispel stereotypes, and help further sex worker rights.

For example, while we have in the past been concerned with what it means to sell such a basic part of our humanity as sex, we are living in a world where more and more services that have been parts of human relationships are being bought and sold (Zelizer, 2005). Yet service workers are daily faced with performing prescribed emotions, and evoking these in customers, negotiating issues of authenticity in exchange, as their very identities seem compromised and challenged. Research is showing that sales people and service workers are becoming increasingly adept at managing multiple, flexible presentations of self to meet customer expectations (Holyfield, 1999; Sharpe, 2005). Recent research has examined similarities in the experience of commodifying emotions between these workers and sex workers including exotic dancers (Barton, 2006; Frank, 2002; Montemurro, 2001; Wood, 2000), and prostitutes themselves (Agustín, 2003; Brewis & Linstead, 2000c; Brewis and Linstead, 2000b; Brents et al., 2010; Chapkis, 1997; Lever & Dolnick, 2000; Sanders, 2005a; Sanders, 2005b; Seppa & Michelle, 2003). When research compares various elements of sex work to other forms of work, it finds that those who are able to control their work conditions, have job autonomy, and have access to resources are better able to combat any psychological or physical harm involved in doing emotional and sexual labor.

Research on late capitalist leisure and touristic practices can help us better understand customer and worker relations. Rather than seeing empowerment and exploitation as mutually exclusive, we can examine the elements that determine each. In a culture where consumers regularly purchase intimacy and emotion, the purchase of sex is changing its meaning. How the consumption of sexuality fits into this flexible narrative then becomes important – not just for the women and men whose identity rests on the sale of their sexuality, but also for the type of sexuality that is sold (Bernstein, 2001; Frank, 2002; Prasad, 1999). For good or for ill, maintaining aspects of one's sexuality as consumable and marketable goods becomes part of the standard repertoire for many workers and consumers. As customers and workers become more adept at negotiating these exchanges throughout industry, the impact of the stigma attached to selling intimacy is likely to decline as the resources available for dealing with the ill effects will increase.

Given the growing similarities between the adult sex industry and other service industry businesses, analyses of the sex industry benefit from adopting frameworks and conceptual tools that scholars have long used to make sense of the broader service industries and fields of consumption. With the convergence of public and private spheres where all patterns of human interactions are exchanged in the marketplace, the question is no longer 'Is sex really work?' Now the question is how we make sense of these kinds of labors in the current global cultural and economic context.

In this context of convergence, sex work activists have had numerous successes in changing laws. Since the 1970s many countries have revised laws on prostitution, the most stigmatized form of sex work. New Zealand decriminalized prostitution; several states in Australia as well as Nevada in the US legalized prostitution during that time. Iceland, Germany, Switzerland, Austria, and Denmark have all recently liberalized prostitution laws. The Netherlands and parts of Australia removed bans on brothels, Austria and Germany have granted sex workers social security and equitable taxation. The US has remained outside the norm in doing little to revise its laws outside of Nevada (Outshoorn 2004, 2005). The research on the experiences of sex workers in Nevada, Australia, the Netherlands, and Germany show, however, that legalization alone does not always change the stigma associated with prostitution (Arnot, 2002; Brants, 1998; Vanwesenbeeck, 2001; Wonders & Michalowski, 2001; Brents et al., 2010). But legal changes coupled with broader cultural changes can matter.

Convergence brings more opportunities for building alliances. With increasing legitimation, especially for workers in the formal and legal sectors of the industry, there are more possibilities for building coalitions with a broad range of individuals and organizations. Success in countries other than the US has come in using alliances opened up by this convergence between the sex industries and mainstream work. Common issues can be made more explicit between sex workers and other interactive service workers and their unions, activists, and businesses that depend on sexual markets.

Alliances can be built within the sex industry as well. As some sex work sectors become more mainstream, the stigma that causes erotic dancers to distance themselves from adult film actors, who distance themselves from escort workers, who distance themselves from street prostitutes, etc., might lessen. Certainly the fact that some workers work legally while others work illegally makes for serious complications in organizing. However, we believe that increasing legitimation for many workers can be capitalized on to further legitimation for others.

In addition, growth and profitability in the sex industry mean potentially more resources for organizing. Those parts of the sex industry able to profit from growth and mainstreaming can provide an important resource base for sex worker activists and organizations. Certainly most of the profits in formal, high-capital businesses go to owners. However, to the extent that activists can highlight commonalities between owner interests in a more tolerant climate and workers' interests in rights, perhaps owners will provide resources for organizing. Likewise independent prostitutes, for example, have more opportunities for income with the internet and can fund organizing.

Finally, while few politicians are yet willing to offer public support for the sex industry, opportunities for coalitions and support do exist. Sex workers and activists, especially those with social capital, have partnered with supportive politicians and do much behind the scenes, including offering research, alternative viewpoints and positive policy examples. Many politicians will attend to the demands of mobilized voters. Sex workers with social capital and political savvy are increasingly able to take advantage of increasing media interest to frame important issues carefully, especially in consultation with sympathetic politicians.

As the larger and more formal sex businesses become increasingly structurally integrated with 'legitimate' businesses, their economic and political power increases. Integration makes it harder for local governments to close or increase sanctions against profitable businesses.

Businesses can increase their own legitimacy by being good corporate citizens, donating to charitable causes, participating in civic events. Likewise, legal businesses can make legitimate campaign contributions to politicians. Because of the stigma, sex industry businesses must be ready for increased public scrutiny of these donations. In Las Vegas, illegal campaign contributions by a strip club owner resulted in a high-profile FBI probe that landed several politicians in jail. It is likely that some politicians may turn contributions down if donations are made public. But business can increasingly offer legitimate input into the political system.

CHALLENGES

Convergence also brings several distinct challenges. The more liberal attitudes toward sex that we see in consumer culture are complicated to unravel. The struggle over where and how to define appropriate sex and appropriate relations between intimacy and commerce continues albeit in a new social, cultural, and economic context.

The 'culture wars' around homosexual rights, gay marriage, abortion, and teen sexuality have brought numerous social movements and new alliances to the fore. One such alliance has been between some anti-sex feminists and the Bush administration who were mobilizing global discourses on sex trafficking. For years international organizations have struggled to deal with sex trafficking, often bringing a variety of perspectives on sex work to the table. However, in the US, the Bush administration had funded – and heavily – only those feminists and activists who support abolitionist perspectives on prostitution. They had managed to push policies that prevent harm reduction programs and restrict condom distribution, and HIV/AIDS education in other countries. The geopolitics of terrorism created a global culture of fear and spawned repressive laws. These laws are increasingly used against sex workers, and curtail funding for activists. In the US, the Bush administration provided research funding only for scholarship opposing prostitution. Although this administration is no longer in power, many of these groups have retained funding and in public circles are very vocally opposing legitimate sex industry research. The anti-trafficking/anti-prostitution lobby is working across the UK and Europe. If it becomes successful in framing prostitution generally as a trafficking issue, that might make politicians even more wary of publicly supporting reforms.

On the other hand, the left has long criticized both the alienation that renders basic human relations commodities on the market and the structural inequalities that create conflicts between workers and owners, and among different races, ethnicities, and genders. The reason selling sex has moved more mainstream is not simply that our attitudes are changing, but that it is profitable. Mainstreaming happens in the areas that have the most resources – economic, legal and cultural. Just as in capitalist economies generally, this creates a hugely stratified system for the sex industries, stratified both between workers and owners and between a dual labor market within sectors. Mainstreaming also benefits workers with the most social capital – education, training, and other resources that allow them to look and act like their upper-class or aspiring-upper-class customers. The amount of capital it takes to compete in the mainstreamed world makes it less and less possible for small businesses to survive. It also makes it less possible for workers without economic, legal and cultural resources to survive. Large business owners use their economic and social capital to influence policy primarily for their benefit, often to the detriment of worker rights and power. While we may see an improvement in working conditions for certain sex industry workers where stigma is reduced, we have no reason to expect that sex workers will fare better than mainstream workers in fighting large capital.

Much of the stigma associated with sex work is wrapped up in social class and ethnoracial inequalities, and this is unlikely to change with the kind of convergence we are seeing. The sex industry becomes more mainstream as it looks and feels more 'normal,' that is, more upper class and white. Upscaling happens because it appeals to a more moneyed customer. That street prostitution is the most stigmatized and most dangerous business is precisely because it is the poor and minorities who conduct the work. High-class escorts have more social capital and more resources to get the highest-paying clients and work under the safest and most autonomous conditions. Classism and racism continue to encourage stigmatization of these workers while valorizing those with the most cultural and economic capital. While opportunities for making sex work businesses more mainstream increase, such changes are likely to leave workers without resources behind.

And while gender inequality, some analysts argue, is changing in the arena of sexuality, it is still the case that women are far more structurally disadvantaged than men in the workplace generally, and particularly within sex work. It is a distinct challenge to do research and promote laws that protect women, as a class, when they need protecting. And researchers and activists face the distinct challenge of seizing the opportunities of convergence while still creating a space for critique of marketplace liberalism and its capitalist, patriarchal, sexist, racist, classist, and ethno-centrist practices.

Because of the vast inequalities within sex work, convergence creates as many challenges as opportunities for organizing. Divisions often fostered by stigma, as well as by race, class, gender, and sexual orientation, have caused problems for sex work organizing in the past. Increasing inequality may deepen these divisions. Several scholars who have studied the sex worker rights movements argue that problems such as a shortage of resources and committed activists have plagued the movement. Mobilization of sex workers, particularly prostitutes, is difficult – fear of police surveillance and harassment, discouragement from pimps and other managers, repercussions from family members, few pre-existing networks and lack of a subculture or sense of community all work against mobilization. Whilst alliances with groups within the different components of the sex industry and outside of it are more possible now than ever before, mistrust still plagues the movement (Weitzer, 1991). Yet at the same time, sex workers rights organizations have managed to shift the debate in many arenas, and to increase cultural support for the idea of the sale of consensual sex and sexuality between consenting adults (Jenness, 1993).

Conclusions

We began with the observation that Las Vegas as a global destination for the consumption of sex was really emblematic of larger changes happening in the world economy. The lines around the sex industry are blurring, in Las Vegas and in urban cultures across the globe. The continuing convergence between mainstream culture and the sex industries seems inevitable in globalized consumer culture. The implications of this are far-reaching. Understanding the sex industry as a central component of late capitalist culture and economy is important for both activists and scholars. Scholars need to do more work situating the sex industry as part of the central shifts of our age, and they can use the conceptual tools we use to examine other cultural shifts, workplace relations, identity management, and social policies in late capitalism. Laura Agustín argues that we ought to move research on commercial sex out of the narrow framework of individuals and personal motivations and into a framework of cultural and economic studies that relate knowledge about commercial sex to findings on other economic, social and cultural concepts. This approach, she argues 'would look at commercial sex in its widest sense, examining its intersections with art, ethics, consumption, family life, entertainment, sport, economics, urban space, sexuality, tourism, and criminality' (Agustín , 2005c).

NOTES

1   The marketing of sexuality has been central to Las Vegas's appeal to tourists. However, unlike in many Asian or European resort centers, prostitution in Las Vegas is not marketed and Las Vegas resort industry would not consider itself a sex tourist destination in the narrow sense of the term. Prostitution itself is not legal in the city and is not tolerated by officials. Nevada's legal brothels are central to Las Vegas's image, but they play a minor role in the economy. However, the glamor, spectacle and fantasy sold both in the resort corridor and in off-resort strip clubs and ultra lounges do heavily market sexuality, creating a city based on increasingly blurred lines delineating what has traditionally been called the sex industry.

2   There is a great deal of debate over labels describing these economic and cultural changes, as well as debate over the universality of the changes. In this chapter we use the term 'late capitalism' to refer to the general economic and cultural trends we describe. We rely on the works of several authors including Agger (1989); Bauman (2000); Bell (1976); Gergen (1991); Giddens (1991); Harvey (1989); Jameson (1991); Lash and Urry (1994); Mandel (1975); and Toffler (1990).

3   The US General Social Survey shows increasing acceptance of premarital sex and homosexual sex between 1972 and 2004 (Davis et al., 2006). Gallop polls show that in the US in 1977, 56 percent of the population believed homosexuals should have equal rights to job opportunities; by 2004, 89 percent believed they should. As recently as 1992, 38 percent of the population felt homosexuality was an acceptable alternative lifestyle; 54 percent believed it was in 2004. The World Values survey of post-industrial countries found similar trends elsewhere toward sexual liberation (Ingelhart, 2008). The US Supreme Court repealed sodomy laws in 2003, and since 1999 same-sex unions in some form have been legalized in a number of European countries, Canada, South Africa, and a few US states.

4   We define the sex industry as all legal and illegal enterprises that sell explicit sexual fantasies, sexual products, sexual services and/or sexual contact, for profit. It includes prostitution, pornography, strip dancing, phone sex, internet sex, adult video industries, and a host of other sexual services.

2 The (Crying) Need for Different Kinds of Research

Laura Agustín

In October 2001, while on a trip to Australia and Thailand, I met five Latin American women with some connection to the sex industry: the owner of a legal brothel and two migrants working for her in Sydney, and two women in a detention center for illegal immigrants in Bangkok. These five women were from Peru, Colombia and Venezuela; they were from different strata of society; their ages were very different. They also all had very different stories to tell – stories I heard not while doing formal research but while accompanying people from helping projects.

The brothel owner now had permanent residence in Australia. Her migrant workers had come on visas to study English which gave them the right to work, but getting the visa had required paying for the entire eight-month course in advance, which meant acquiring large debts. The madam was very affectionate with them but also very controlling; they lived in her house and travelled with her to work. She was teaching them the business; the outreach workers from a local project did not speak Spanish.

Of the two women detained in Bangkok, one had been stopped at Tokyo airport with a false visa for Japan. She had been invited by her sister, who had been an illegal sex worker but now was an illegal vendor within the prostitution milieu. The woman had been deported to the last stage of her journey, Bangkok; there she had been in jail for a year before being sent to the detention center. The second detained woman had been caught on camera in a robbery being carried out by her boyfriend and others in Bangkok, after travelling around with them in Hong Kong and Singapore; she had just completed a three-year jail sentence before being sent to the center (and she also had completely false papers, involving a change of nationality). Both detained women were waiting for someone to pay their plane fare home, but no one was offering to do this, since the women's degree of complicity in their situations disqualified them from aid to victims of trafficking, and not all Latin American countries maintain embassies in Thailand. Only one person from local non-governmental organizations (NGOs) visiting the detention center spoke Spanish.

How can we understand these stories?

Given the very different stories these women have to tell, labeling them either 'migrant sex workers' or 'victims of trafficking' is incorrect and unhelpful to an understanding of why and how they have arrived at their present situations. The placing of labels is largely a subjective judgement dependent on the researcher of the moment, something like the attempt to make complicated subjects fit into a pre-printed form, and is not the way women talk about themselves. The following descriptions illustrate this complexity.

While the two new migrants in Sydney seemed accepting of the work they had just begun doing, there was clearly ambiguity about the significance of the language course on which their visas were based, and their debts did not leave them much choice about what jobs to do. The migrant to Japan had believed she would not have to sell sex, but her own family had been involved in getting her the false papers, and she was suffering considerable guilt and anguish. The woman caught in the robbery seemed to have sold sex during her travels, but without any particular intention or destination being involved; nor did she give the matter much importance. The total number of outsiders implicated in their journeys and their jobs was large; nationalities mentioned were Pakistani, Turkish and Mexican. The need for research to understand how all these connections happen is urgent, but funders are unlikely to finance research that does not fit into one of the currently acceptable theoretical frameworks: 'AIDS prevention,' 'violence against women,' or 'trafficking.'

These frameworks reflect particular political concerns arising in the context of 'globalization,' and they are understandable. Elements of the stories of people such as those I have described may share features with typical discourses on 'trafficking', 'violence against women,' and 'AIDS,' but these are prejudiced, moralistic frameworks that begin from a political position and are not open to results that do not fit (for example, a woman who admits that she knew she would be doing sex work abroad and willingly paid someone to falsify papers for her).

The desires of young people to travel, see the world, make a lot of money, and not pay much attention to the kind of jobs they do along the way are not acceptable to researchers that begin from moral positions; neither are the statements by professional sex workers that they choose and prefer the work they do. Ethical research simply may not depart from the claim that the subjects investigated do not know their own minds.

Why do we do research, anyway?

A theoretical framework refers to the overall idea that motivates services or research projects. For service projects with sex workers this framework might be a religious mission to help people in danger, a medical concept of reducing harm, or a vision of solidarity or social justice. Most projects with sex workers focus on providing services, not doing research, though often the line between them is not easy to draw.

Service projects accumulate a lot of information over time, but it seems as though the only thing governments want to know about is people's nationalities, how old they are, when they first had sex, and whether they know what a condom is. Many NGO and outreach workers would like to publish other kinds of information, research other kinds of things. But where, how? If their research proposal does not reflect one of the existing research frameworks regarding migrant prostitution – 'AIDS prevention,' 'trafficking,' or 'violence against women' – it will be hard if not impossible to find funding.

Some of my own research concerns people who work with sex workers. There is a small minority that is really only interested in preventing infections and is therefore satisfied to produce graphics on rates of sexually transmitted diseases (STDs) per nationality. But even many people interested only in epidemiology are frustrated, because so much research continues to focus on street workers and reproduce the same information over and over again. And to study women like the ones I met in October 2001, none of the frameworks mentioned above is at all adequate. AIDS prevention and their health may be important to these women, but no more than to anyone else, and no one has done violence to them. So that leaves 'trafficking,' but not only did they participate in the planning of their trips, they enjoyed parts of them and were willing to do sex work in order to visit places like Tokyo and make the kind of money they could not earn anywhere else.

Now if these women were framed as travelling to work and see something of the world at the same time, it would at least be possible to tell their stories. On the way, quite a number of injustices, most of them structural, would be revealed, and researchers could be satisfied to have brought them out. But also the aspect of these women's lives that we never hear about would be brought out: their leading role in their own life stories, complete with making decisions about taking risks in order to get ahead in life – their agency.

Research without prejudice

The goal of research is to answer questions that will help societies understand themselves better, and these questions cannot avoid existing within some kind of framework. For example, interviews with sex workers about their lives can be carried out within a frame of 'life histories,' the goal being to publish voices that have been marginalized before. Or interviews with police can attempt to show how they perceive their jobs, inside a criminological frame. There can be ethnographies of brothels (anthropology), surveys on how sex club owners view the business (urban studies), comparative work with people before they work in the sex industry and after (labor studies, psychology), investigations on how small family-and-friends networks function to facilitate migrations (sociology). The list of possibilities is endless, and all would be useful for improving our understanding of the sex industry and the people who work in it.

However, whatever 'field' the frame belongs to, we do not need more research imposed by people who believe they know best how other people ought to live and who have already taken a moralistic position before research is begun. An example is the statement, 'We began this work from the perspective that prostitution itself is violence against women' (Farley et al., 1998, p. 406). On the contrary, we need a lot of research undertaken by people who are very close to sex workers' lives, or who are sex workers themselves, but who will above all commit themselves to recording honestly all the different and conflicting points of view and stories they run into during the research.

Migration as a research framework

In my view, migration studies is the research frame that makes most sense for thinking about the five women I met in October 2001, as well as for the great majority of those I've met who work in sex, domestic and 'caring' services (for children, the elderly and the ill). When I lived in the Caribbean, it was common to talk to people who were thinking about going abroad to travel and work as migrants, and these are the same people who are working now in Europe, Australia, Japan. By locating these women as migrants rather than 'sex workers,' whether exploited or not, it is possible to include them in the growing body of research on diasporas, globalization, immigration law and international relations. A migration framework allows consideration of all conceivable aspects of people's lives and travels, locates them in periods of personal growth and risk-taking, and does not force them to identify as sex workers (or as maids, or 'carers,' for that matter).

The publication of research that looks at migrant sex workers' lives in a myriad of ways would eventually affect how society at large considers these people. It would inevitably reveal that a minority suffer from disease and violence, while the majority can be seen as resourceful entrepreneurs or pragmatic workers trying to make their way within government policies and structures that are all against them. Harm reduction and other social projects could concentrate on supporting such people at a specific stage of their lives but could also expand into different areas and not be forced to continue to work uncomfortably inside stigmatizing frameworks (those that construct all migrants as victims of trafficking or risk groups for the transmission of disease). It's worth a try.

3   The Meaning of the 'Whore': How Feminist Theories on Prostitution Shape Research on Female Sex Workers

Juline A. Koken

Whilst social scientists have amassed a large body of research on women in prostitution in the decades spanning the latter half of the twentieth century to the present day, the majority of this research frames prostitution as a social problem in need of control or eradication. Hence, research on prostitution as deviance, vector of disease, and symptom or sequelae of psychopathology or trauma comprises the focus of nearly all literature on prostitution (Vanwesenbeeck, 2001). However, the feminist movement and the burgeoning prostitutes' rights movement that have gained momentum over the past two decades introduced a new framework for viewing prostitution into social scientific literature: that of prostitution as labor or *sex work*.

This chapter provides a brief overview of the ways in which feminist positions on prostitution have come to shape social scientific research on female sex workers from the 1990s to the present.

The debate on agency and sex workers' physical and emotional health crosses national boundaries and involves questions of culture, social policy, public health, and human rights. As a complete review of this literature is far beyond the scope of this chapter, here the focus will be on the ways in which feminist positions on prostitution influence research on the psychological wellbeing of women working in this industry. This literature includes theories of trauma and victimization in the lives of sex workers, as well as research which explores the ways in which women work to maximize profit and minimize the risk of harms within sex work. For the purposes of this review the terms *prostitute* and *sex worker* will be used to refer specifically to persons who engage in direct paid sexual contact with clients. The term *prostitute* will be used in reference to writings by feminists who reject the phrase *sex work*, and also on occasion to reference the stigma associated with prostitution. The term *sex work* will refer to all other writings cited here.

Examining agency and researcher positionality

Feminist theorizing on female sexuality within patriarchal society has taken up the question of the meaning of women in prostitution as a contested symbol of female sexual agency within a male-dominated culture (Scoular, 2004). Yet while arguments regarding the potential for, or impossibility of, agency within sex work have dominated feminist discourse on the meaning of women's participation in sex work, very few authors provide definitions of 'agency' or 'sexual agency' in their arguments. Historically, the term *human agency* has been used to reference a philosophical concept which is often juxtaposed with *structural determination* or *natural forces* (Bourdieu & Wacquant, 1992). Human agency may be conceptualized as the power of groups to enact change through democratic process, but more often references an individual's power to make choices regarding his or her actions within given circumstances. Thus, agency is not 'free will'; an individual may possess free will but lack agency (Bourdieu & Wacquant, 1992).

Feminist theorizing on women's sexual agency encompasses a diverse array of perspectives. Mohanty (2004) asserts that women's agency has been defined too narrowly in the past, and that in order to recognize the agency of marginalized persons a broader conceptualization of agency must be used. This view posits that women – particularly women workers – are not merely to be viewed as exploited under patriarchy and capitalism. Rather, women's agency must include what Mohanty terms 'oppositional agency,' wherein women's efforts to resist subjugation are recognized as agentic (Mohanty, 2004). However, radical feminists such as Dworkin (1997), while providing no explicit definition of women's agency, appear to view women's agency very differently from feminists such as Mohanty.

Thus whores embody the essence of women's sexual objectification to some (Dworkin, 1997), while at the other end of the agentic spectrum, whores are positioned as gender/sexual outlaws defying taboos of female sexuality (Califia, 1988). In other words, the feminist debate on sex work revolves around the question of whether it constitutes a form of voluntary sexual labor or involuntary sexual objectification. Hence, feminist positionality on the meaning of women's sexual economic behavior is reflected in the terms used to reference it.

Traditional empirical methodology stresses the fundamental importance of objectivity in research. However, a large body of feminist

29

scholarship, particularly 'standpoint theory' (Harding, 1991), questions the assumption of researcher objectivity, instead viewing the researcher and the research itself as a product of the socio-historical moment. Standpoint theory argues that social scientists are human beings who have been socialized to have values and beliefs, and that these values and beliefs (or 'positionality') – as well as the larger political and economic climate in which the research is formulated – shape every aspect of the research process. Which questions are considered to merit research, which group should be sampled and where, and even how data will be interpreted may all be guided by the researcher's standpoint on the meaning of prostitution or sex work.

Following the adoption of standpoint theory in much of feminist scholarship, the inclusion of position statements has become increasingly popular in feminist research and theoretical writings. Position statements clarify for the reader the assumptions underlying the research project and help locate the research findings within a broader theoretical framework. It should be noted, however, that even in the absence of a clearly delineated position statement, all researchers have beliefs/assumptions about the meaning of sex work/prostitution, and these should be taken into account when evaluating the findings of the research.

Hence, the question of how sex workers fare flows from a diversity of feminist perspectives on sex workers' agency. Two broad positions have emerged in research on sex work (Doezema, 2002); these may be characterized as the 'anti-prostitution' stance and the 'pro-sex work' stance. The following are examples of each position, as stated in publications by two well-known researchers:

- anti-prostitution position: '... prostitution itself is violence against women ... [there is a] need for asylum and culturally relevant treatment when considering escape or treatment options for those in prostitution' (Farley et al., 1998, p. 406);

- pro-sex work position: '... sex work is, on principle, considered legitimate work, not violence. At the same time, it is acknowledged that the illegal status of sex work and its consequences do violate the civil and workers' rights and integrity of sex workers' (Vanwesenbeeck, 2001, p. 243).

These examples of position statements only hint at the diversity of perspectives espoused by social scientific researchers on sex work. By reviewing recent social scientific research on sex work, I aim to demonstrate that researcher positionality has come to play a major role in shaping discourse and research on sex work.

Terms of debate

The ongoing feminist debate concerning individuals who provide sexual services to paying clients can be glimpsed in the changing social representations of this activity and those involved in it – from *prostitutes, prostituted women* to *sex work* and *commercial sex workers,* or even *whores.* These terms are by no means equivalent in meaning. The choice of terminology acts as a positioning device, as the meanings embedded in these phrases locates the speaker on a political and epistemological spectrum (Shah, 2004).

The term *prostitute* was once seen as a standard 'neutral' term used in research and scholarly writing. For example, the Dutch researcher Ine Vanwesenbeeck titled the book describing the findings of her studies *Prostitutes' Well-Being and Risk* (1994), using *prostitute* as a simple descriptor of a person who engages in paid sex. However, some researchers feel that *prostitute* has become a pejorative label loaded with the stigma attached to those who engage in prostitution (Koken et al., 2004; Weitzer, 2005). In addition, many researchers feel that the term too often implies a conflation of the person with the work (Pheterson, 1990), overlooking the behaviors and choices which are made by individual human beings, not *categories* of persons (think of the distinction sometimes drawn in HIV transmission research between risk *behaviors* and risk *groups*).

In response to the neglect (or rejection) by many researchers and some feminist theorists of the *labor* performed by prostitutes, and springing from a burgeoning feminist prostitutes' rights movement, the term *sex worker* was coined in 1980 by the activist Carol Leigh, also known as 'Scarlot Harlot' (Leigh, 1997). *Sex work* and *sex industry* are useful phrases in that they emphasize the labor/employment aspect of paid sex; at the same time, they are umbrella terms which encompass a diversity of persons who provide a variety of erotic services. Thus, a *sex worker* may be employed as a phone sex operator, porn star, dominatrix, stripper, etc., but not necessarily as a *prostitute,* in that the person may not engage in direct sexual contact with a paying client. It should also be stated that many of the individuals working in these jobs may not always self-identify as sex workers, even if their work is considered such by others.

31

The inclusive meaning of *sex work* was and continues to be a deliberate strategy to organize women, men and transgender persons from a variety of sex-related professions under the category 'sex worker' for the purposes of finding common ground and building political alliances (Kempadoo, 1999). The new term soon appeared in the titles of feminist anthologies, such as *Sex Work: Writings by Women in the Sex Industry* (Delacoste & Alexander, 1987), and *Global Sex Workers: Rights, Resistance, and Redefinition* (Kempadoo & Doezema, 1998). Books such as these signified a shift in the social representation of prostitution both by persons inside the industry and academics writing from the 'outside.'

While the term *prostitute* was increasingly rejected in favour of the newer phrase *sex work*, during this same time period (the late 1980s to late 1990s) some feminist sex workers also worked to reclaim the old epithet *whore*, seeking to rid the term of the stigma associated with prostitution and claim pride in their identification with it. The reclamation of the 'whore' label was a political project similar to the movement by gay and lesbian activists to reclaim previously pejorative terms such as *dyke*, *queer* and *faggot*. To this end, salvos such as *A Vindication of the Rights of Whores* (Pheterson, 1989), *Whores in History* (Roberts, 1992), and *Whores and Other Feminists* (Nagle, 1997) were published. Note the reference to the classic feminist work by Wollstonecraft *A Vindication of the Rights of Woman* (1792) in the title of one book and the use of the label 'feminists' in another. The deliberate referencing of feminism in the titles of these works served as a symbolic claiming of sex workers' right to claim membership in the feminist community. That this right was contested illustrates the tension that arose between various feminist groups during the 1980s and 1990s, a period characterized by some as the era of the 'feminist sex wars' (Chapkis, 1997). During this period, a rift deepened between feminists opposed to prostitution and those who advocated that sex work could be chosen employment.

A photo featured in one of these books, *Live Sex Acts* (a photo taken by sex worker/activist Annie Sprinkle and printed in Chapkis, 1997, p. 181), plaintively illustrates the position of women caught in the crossfire of the feminist sex wars: those who identified both as feminist and sex worker simultaneously. In the snapshot, porn actress Marlene Willoughby is shown holding a protest sign which reads in part 'Support your local pornstar! Ms. Magazine hear our side ... We're your sisters too!' Meanwhile, the author of this book, Wendy Chapkis, was jeered by anti-prostitution feminists such as Ann Simonton:

Chapkis, who admits to never prostituting herself, has become Santa Cruz's celebrity apologist for pornography, sadomasochism, prostitution, and other patriarchal ideals. She does this successfully by waving flags of sexual freedom and choice. (Simonton, 1992, p. 8, as excerpted in Chapkis, 1997, emphasis mine)

In this statement Simonton's use of the phrase 'prostituting herself' acts as a flag for her position against prostitution and other 'patriarchal ideals.' Chapkis, a lesbian feminist sociologist who was new to this debate, writes of the sting of finding herself rejected by some of her feminist 'sisters' for her sex work advocacy, and of developing her own nascent consciousness around the meaning of sex work:

> Sex workers, I was discovering, often wear their outlaw status in a way that reminds me of my own defiant attitude toward having a mustache or being lesbian. The '*queerer*' I became, the more I found myself admiring and identifying with politicized *whores* ... Still, it seemed improbable to me that in the United States in the 1990s, feminists could possibly continue to see each other as the biggest problem around. (Chapkis, 1997, p. 4, emphasis mine)

In this telling recollection, Chapkis aligns her *queer* self with the *politicized whores* she has encountered, deliberately manipulating words that formerly served as symbols of lesbian and female sexual oppression in a manner which defied the position of anti-prostitution feminists who did not see Chapkis as their 'sister.'

The call to hear the views of sex workers and sex worker advocates was widely disseminated in the academy, if not always attended to. However, in the decades since its inception, the term *sex work* has increasingly gained acceptance and is now commonly used in research and theory on sex workers. When Ine Vanwesenbeeck published a literature review in 2001, it was titled 'Another Decade of Social Scientific Work on Sex Work: A Review of Research 1990–2000.' *Sex work, sex workers*, or less commonly, *commercial sex workers*, have become widely used terminology in academic writing and are considered by many to be more 'politically correct' phrases than *prostitutes/ prostitution*. This is true even among researchers who do not profess a specific 'position' on the issue of paid sex, as can be seen in a recent issue of the *Journal of Psychology and Human Sexuality*. The special issue, titled *Contemporary Research on Sex Work* (Vol. 17, No. 1/2, 2005), features eleven articles, nearly all using the term *sex work* or some close approximation in their titles, although few explicitly incorporated feminist theory into the work. Only one article used the more traditional prostitution in the title, and it is difficult to discern any significant differences underlying this article in comparison with others in the volume. Thus, since its inception in 1980, the term sex work has shifted from a highly politicized positioning device to a relatively accepted 'standard' phrase replacing prostitution.

However, feminists who view prostitution as inherently forced and by definition violence against women (Barry, 1995; Dworkin, 1997; Farley et al., 1998; Giobbe et al., 1990) view the term sex work as inappropriate and inaccurate. If, as these theorists posit, prostitution is a form of 'paid rape' and cannot by definition be chosen, then sex work is an unacceptable term.

> In that one word – work – the sexism and the physical and psychological violence of prostitution are made invisible. A battle is being waged by those who promote prostitution as a good-enough job for poor women against those of us who consider prostitution an institution that is so intrinsically unjust, discriminatory, and violent that it can't be fixed. (Farley, 2005, paid editorial in the *Nation*)

Hence publications by authors who share this position continue to use the terms prostitution, survivors of prostitution, or prostituted women. The small addition of the 'd' following 'prostitute' serves to imply coercion by a third party (or patriarchal system); adding 'women' specifies that the authors are concerned specifically with females, excluding male prostitutes from consideration.

Theorists on all sides of the prostitution/sex work debate have also used the words 'trafficked' or 'trafficking' with varying implications. Of these, two broad opposing positions can be identified: first, there are those who view prostitution as inherently forced and as a result view all prostitution as a form of trafficking. Political organizations working to abolish prostitution, such as the Coalition Against Trafficking in Women (CATW), and Women Hurt In Systems of Prostitution Engaged in Revolt (WHISPER), exemplify their stance against sex as work through the use of the words 'prostitution' or 'trafficking'. The second position posits that prostitution may be chosen labor, although forced prostitution and exploitative working circumstances do exist and should be handled from a labor rights perspective (Ditmore, 2005a). In this view, trafficking is defined through the inclusion of deception and coercion, and may not be specific or limited to sex work.

Feminist theory and sex work research

As can be seen from the terms of debate described above, the most commonly and hotly debated point among feminist theorists on paid sex concerns whether it may ever be considered chosen labor – or if it is inherently forced. This debate has been a veritable minefield ever since the 'feminist sex wars' of the 1980s and 1990s, and continues to be so (Chapkis, 1997; Sanders, 2005a). While many researchers, activists, and sex workers have expressed increasing frustration with being 'forced to choose' their position in this dichotomy (Doezema, 1998), this debate on agency has influenced what questions receive attention in sex work research, chosen by whom and about whom, and what for some remains 'unknowable' or excluded from the field of debate.

The question of how sex workers fare emotionally, physically, and in their larger social context flows from a diversity of perspectives on sex workers' agency, and these perspectives influence resulting research questions, samples, and data interpretation. Even the notion of grouping diverse populations such as homeless adolescents, highly paid independent escorts, and trafficked migrant women under the overarching heading of 'prostitute' has been questioned as poor scientific practice (Agustín, 2005d; Pheterson, 1990). It has also been suggested that sex work is not unique as work that is sexual and gendered by nature (Chapkis, 1997; Sanders, 2005a), but rather may be thought of as part of a broader group of service occupations such as massage therapy, cocktail waitressing, or being a flight attendant. Socialist feminists as far back as Emma Goldman have even placed paid sex on an economic continuum that features prostitutes at one end and women who marry for money at the other (Goldman, 1917).

It is useful to focus specifically on women who engage in the exchange of sex for money for a few important reasons. First and foremost, as mentioned previously, such women are in violation of the powerful social taboo against 'whoring.' As such they are vulnerable to potentially extreme consequences such as social marginalization, arrest, violence at the hands of clients, lovers or law enforcement officers, and infection with sexually transmitted infections (Thukral & Ditmore, 2003; Thukral et al., 2005; Vanwesenbeeck, 2001). While currently all forms of sex work could be said to be stigmatized, prostitution in particular remains in varying degrees around the globe the most legally and socially persecuted form of sex work. Additionally, the advent of the HIV pandemic has brought increased attention to prostitution (Vanwesenbeeck, 2001), as the struggle by feminists on all sides of the sex work debate has brought attention to the issue of trafficking (Ditmore, 2005a). Whilst HIV infection, violence against women, and forced servitude are not specific or limited to prostitutes (Ditmore, 2005a; Doezema, 2002; Nathan, 2005; Pheterson, 1990), the fact that so much research and policy has remained focused on this particular group of women (and not on the men who also work in prostitution), and almost solely on the harms that may or do befall them, indicates that 'whores' retain their iconic status as victims or pariahs. Whores have come to symbolize the 'problem' of female sexual agency in patriarchal society that many feminists struggle to understand and improve.

Feminist theories on sex work influence policy on trafficking

If, as Ronald Weitzer asserts, 'In no area of the social sciences has ideology contaminated knowledge more pervasively than in writings on the sex industry' (Weitzer, 2005, p. 934), it may also be argued that nowhere has the treatment of sex work in social policy been more contaminated by religious and feminist dogma than it has in the debate on trafficking. The nexus of the feminist debate on sex work can be clearly seen in the struggle over the definition of trafficking, whom it includes and excludes, how trafficked persons are viewed in the law, and how US policies on aid to foreign nations and non-governmental organizations (NGOs) treat the subject of sex work (Ditmore, 2005b; Doezema, 2002; Nathan, 2005). The anarchist Emma Goldman, who noted wryly in 1917 that 'Our reformers have suddenly made a great discovery – the white slave traffic' (Goldman, 1917, p. 171), would find herself in familiar territory today, as journalist Debbie Nathan writes in the Nation,

> government press releases and the news are rife with accounts of 'sex slaves' – even though the limited evidence that exists suggests sex work is not the most common type of forced labor, and even though most immigrants who work as prostitutes do so voluntarily. (Nathan, 2005, p. 27)

To this, the anti-prostitution feminist Melissa Farley replies, 'Pornographers, johns and pimps are given aid and comfort by the likes of Nathan' (Farley, 2005).

Ironically, anti-prostitution feminist groups have joined forces with right-wing religious organizations in a 'moral crusade' against trafficking. As Ronald Weitzer points out:

The single-issue focus of most of these feminist groups – targeting the
sex industry exclusively – trumps all other issues and facilitates their
willingness to work with right-wing groups. The same dynamic characterized radical feminist involvement in the anti-porn coalition of the
mid-1980s. (Weitzer, 2007, p. 449)

Through this alliance, anti-prostitution feminists gained insider access
to federal policy makers in the Bush administration and inserted their
agenda into federal anti-trafficking policy (Ditmore, 2008; Weitzer,
2007). The allegiance with these radical feminist groups benefited the
Bush administration as well, by allowing the latter to frame their efforts
as 'pro-woman' policy making and as a reflection of their interest in
'women's issues' globally, in spite of their increasing crackdown on
women's reproductive rights and access to family planning, both in the
US and internationally (Ditmore, 2008).

Two articles written by feminist lobbyists who were present during
the crafting of the United Nations Protocol on Trafficking, 'Who Gets to
Choose? Coercion, Consent, and the UN Trafficking Protocol' (Doezema,
2002) and 'Trafficking in Lives: How Ideology Shapes Policy' (Ditmore,
2005a), describe the contentions among various feminist lobbying
groups during the debate on defining trafficking. As described above in
the 'Terms of debate' section of this chapter, two basic opposing positions were presented at the negotiations over the trafficking protocol.
Lobbyists for CATW represented one feminist stance. Their position
holds that all sex work is a form of trafficking; according to this
perspective prostitution may never be a chosen occupation. The group
for which Ditmore and Doezema lobbied, the Human Rights Caucus,
which represented the International Human Rights Law Group as well
as the Asian Women's Human Rights Council, advocates for the
analysis of sex work as labor. As such, sex workers are persons who are
entitled to the same rights, and may be subject to the same exploitative working conditions, as workers in many other industries.
Additionally, the Human Rights Caucus maintained that a violation of
consent was necessary to the definition of trafficking (Ditmore,
2005a; Doezema, 2002). A statement endorsed by the Human Rights
Caucus in 1999 reads in part: 'If no one is forcing her [a female sex
worker] to engage in such an activity, then trafficking does not exist
… The Protocol should distinguish between adults [who may give
consent] and children [who by definition cannot]' (cited in Doezema,
2002, p. 21).

Ditmore argues that the abolitionist position presented at the nego-tiations for the UN protocol on trafficking is problematic when

> Prostitution as a condition is assumed to be so inherently intolerable that no rational person could freely choose it for themselves; therefore if anyone appears to have chosen it for themselves, it can only indicate that they are either not rational, or they are victims of coercion or deception, that is to say, victims of trafficking. The perils of such an argument lie precisely in the way that it opens the door to a paternalistic interpreta-tion of 'what is best for women.' (Ditmore, 2005a, p. 13)

The abolitionist view held by groups such as CATW presents a problem for women who assert that their entry into sex work was chosen. The position of these groups may cause them to be reluctant to hear the testimony of any sex worker who argues that their experience within sex work was not the unrelenting nightmare imagined by women such as Melissa Farley, who seems only able to imagine experiences such as that of a sex worker who is forced to 'smile and say you like it when some foul-smelling man your grandfather's age comes on your face' (Farley, 2005).

The schism between abolitionist feminists such as members of CATW and those representing the Human Rights Caucus has deepened to the point that many sex worker activists complain that there is

> Reluctance to believe sex workers by some [abolitionist] feminists ... a misrepresentation of sex workers and sex work experiences in feminist discourse and ... an active exclusion of sex workers and their positive experiences of sex work from feminist spaces. (Fawkes, 2005, p. 22, emphasis mine)

In other words, the reality of some experiences is rendered impossible, 'unknowable,' and excluded from the field of discourse by the 'prostitu-tion as violence against women' views espoused by some feminists. The political implications of the abolitionist perspective have been wide-spread and are potentially damaging to the work done by organizations as diverse as Doctors without Borders, the Thai sex worker advocacy group EMPOWER, and many other organizations that work with sex workers (Ditmore, 2005b).

The conflation of prostitution with trafficking may be seen in recent US government policy regarding the distribution of US aid money to NGOs (Ditmore, 2005b). Following the UN protocol debates in 2000, in 2003 a new policy was introduced by the Bush administration which imposed limitations on which NGOs might receive aid monies from the US. The stipulation was outlined in a statement released by US Secretary of State Colin Powell, which read in part: 'Organizations advocating prostitution as an employment choice or which advocate or support the legalization of prostitution are not appropriate partners for USAID anti-trafficking grants and contracts' (Powell, cited in Ditmore, 2005b, p. 1).

The creation of this policy resulted in the crafting of an 'anti-prostitution pledge,' which all NGOs receiving US aid are currently required to sign. Many NGOs have found this pledge to be in conflict with their work with sex work advocacy groups, and as a result they find themselves in the difficult position of breaking such ties, or refusing needed aid money. In 2005, Pedro Chequer, the director of Brazil's HIV/AIDS program, announced that Brazil would refuse to sign the anti-prostitution pledge, thus turning down $40 million in US aid. Chequer objected to the pledge, stating, '… we can't control [the disease] with principles that are Manichean, theological, [and] funda-mentalist' (quoted by Phillips and Moffett in the Wall Street Journal, 2 May 2005). Brazil, which has been seen as a model for its public health programs fighting the spread of HIV and providing free treatment to all who need it, has a well-organized and vocal sex worker rights move-ment. Collaboration between sex worker organizations and the Brazilian government would violate the stipulations of the Bush administration's anti-prostitution pledge; Brazil's refusal of the US monies was viewed as a victory by many sex worker advocacy groups worldwide.

In 2006, the US-based non-profit groups Alliance for Open Society International, Pathfinder, and DKT International won a court injunction against the application of the anti-prostitution pledge for organizations working in the US, on the basis that it was a violation of the First Amendment right to freedom of speech (Masenior & Beyrer, 2007). However, the 'gag rule' still applies to work done by these and other aid organizations internationally, and several have expressed confusion regarding the interpretation of the pledge; others argue that it restricts them from doing needed work with sex workers and other populations vulnerable to HIV infection (Masenior & Beyrer, 2007). In April 2008, the President's Emergency Plan for AIDS Relief (PEPFAR) was reauthor-ized with the anti-prostitution language intact; a disappointment for many sex work advocates (Clemmitt, 2008).

The election of Barack Obama to the presidency in November 2008 and the beginning of a new, and presumably more progressive, adminis-tration brought hope to many sex worker advocates. At the time of writing, the first year of Obama's presidency is coming to an end, and it remains unclear how his administration will change its approach to sex work and HIV-related policies. The anti-prostitution 'pledge' enacted as part of PEPFAR has been found unconstitutional as applied to aid agencies in the US; however, it remains in effect as part of USAID efforts internationally. While it is unclear if the Obama administration will alter this or other policies concerning sex work, trafficking, and the global HIV pandemic, sex work advocates, activists, and academics continue to lobby for improved sex work and HIV policy.

Moving beyond 'consent' v. 'force'

While the notion of consent remains a point of contention among feminists in the debate on sex work, increasingly many feminists who view sex work as possible chosen labor are expressing frustration with the limitations of this focus. Feminist sex worker activist Jo Doezema likens the present-day fixation on 'consent' in debates on trafficking as a mirror to the early-twentieth-century panic concerning 'white slavery.' Persons who were engaged in sex work at that time, particularly those who migrated to the US from other nations, were divided between forced, and therefore innocent, victims of 'white slavery,' and 'immoral women' who chose prostitution and had 'fallen' from the graces of mainstream society (Doezema, 2002). Women who chose prostitution were likened to 'sewers, cesspits and refuse dumps' (Roberts, 1992, p. 223) and thus were viewed as needing regulation. Doezema writes: 'Regulationists argued that state regulation was the only way to control venereal disease. "Innocent" women and girls needed protection from immorality; however, once fallen, it was society that needed protection from the immoral woman' (Doezema, 2002, p. 22).

This distinction between forced (innocent) and consenting (immoral) women reflects the long-standing dichotomy in Western culture between virgin and whore, good girl and bad girl (Doezema, 1998; Kempadoo, 1999). Ultimately, a great deal of social policy distinguishing between chosen and forced prostitution reflects this dichotomy, criminalizing consenting sex workers and aiming to protect (and exempt from legal persecution) victims of force. Thus one group of women is seen as not deserving of the same civil rights and legal protections as the other.

Notions of choice are also complicated when located within the context of a gendered, racially stratified and class-stratified global economy.

Noting the participation of many poor women in prostitution, Melissa Farley states: 'Do women consent to prostitution? Do they say to themselves, hmm, what job should I choose: computer technician, lawyer, mechanic, restaurant manager – no, I really want to be a prostitute?' (Farley, 2005). The options available to women (and men) at the lowest ranks of the economic ladder, particularly immigrants and persons of color, are few; hence it is not surprising that many studies of sex workers have identified 'money' as the primary motivation for entering sex work (Vanwesenbeeck, 2001). Deciding between poorly paid factory or domestic work, retail industry jobs, and higher-paying sex work may constitute a rational choice, but it is one that is clearly constrained and may arguably be seen as a 'forced choice' for some. This is one point on which many feminist positions find common ground (Chapkis, 1997; Ditmore, 2005a).

However, if it is important to note the role of economic position when examining the choices made by women who enter prostitution, it should be noted that not all women employed in sex work live in poverty (Bernstein, 2007a; Chapkis, 1997; Thukral et al., 2005; Vanwesenbeeck, 2001). Can we, as Janelle Fawkes asks, believe them when they say they chose their work (Fawkes, 2005)? Or do relatively privileged women sex workers suffer from 'false consciousness,' only thinking they have made a choice? Decrying the refusal by some feminists to believe that sex workers could be anything other than a victim, Pat Califia argues 'the anti-porn movement has done at least as much as the "male system" to make "whores" seem vile in the popular imagination' (Califia, 1988, p. 18). In the same vein, the sex-worker-turned-feminist-historian Nickie Roberts writes 'To put it bluntly, the feminist movement has failed the prostitute, and failed her badly' (Roberts, 1992, p. xi). Creating a dichotomy between poor (innocent) prostitutes and more economically privileged (unfeminist) sex workers undermines feminist dialog on female sexual agency and smacks of a nasty combination of puritanism and classism as well.

Distinctions made in the feminist discourse concerning trafficking or sexual slavery and voluntary sex workers have tended to nurture disturbing comparisons between 'Third World' and 'First World' sex workers, echoing the larger division of women into categories of poor/innocent/victims (Third World) and immoral/patriarchal collaborators/privileged (First World) (Kempadoo, 1999). This distinction is hard to maintain when the number of large, well-organized sex worker advocacy groups that have achieved prominence and notable successes in developing nations are considered. In Cambodia, large numbers of street-based sex workers successfully protested and ended an unethical HIV vaccine trial (Tenofovir, 2006). In Calcutta, India, the Mahila Samanwaya Committee has implemented large literacy campaigns for sex workers and been a vital force in the fight against the spread of HIV (Kempadoo, 1999). In Thailand, the group EMPOWER has achieved similar success in their fight for recognition as a political voice as well as an instrument for fighting the HIV epidemic. Several groups in Brazil, as noted previously, have worked with government health officials in the fight against HIV. These are only a few examples of local sex workers organizing in developing nations and provide clear evidence that sex workers in developing nations do not always share the view of First World feminists such as Farley and the CATW that they are primarily victims. It should be noted as well that these organizations may be restricted in their activities if they choose to accept USAID funding under the current PEPFAR policy.

Researching the wellbeing of sex workers

The questions of which sex workers, if any, possess agency, who may be believed, and which women are in need of study have permeated research on how female sex workers fare emotionally and physically in their work. The stigmatized and legally marginalized position in society held by sex workers complicates this study, and sex workers as a group constitute a 'hidden population' (Lewis & Maticka-Tyndale, 2000; Thukral et al., 2005). Perhaps due in part to the public visibility of street-based women, they have been and continue to constitute the majority of sex workers sampled in research (Parsons, 2005; Thukral et al., 2005; Vanwesenbeeck, 2001). As such, the questions of generalizability and sample representativeness of the larger population of sex workers pose a challenge for all research on sex work (Weitzer, 2005). Women, men, and transgender persons across the globe work in a variety of settings: from the street to bars, brothels, massage parlors, escort agencies, and independently on the internet; yet sex workers who work indoors continue to be underrepresented in research (Sanders, 2005a; Shaver, 2005; Thukral et al., 2005; Vanwesenbeeck, 2001; Weitzer, 2005).

The more tolerant legal and social climate of the Netherlands provided the setting for one of the first methodologically rigorous and large-scale investigations of the wellbeing of female sex workers. In

1994, Ine Vanwesenbeeck broke new ground in this field with the publication *Prostitutes' Well-Being and Risk* (Vanwesenbeeck, 1994), which described the findings from two studies of female sex workers in the Netherlands who worked in a diverse array of settings, from the street to upscale brothels. In this publication Vanwesenbeeck does not offer a 'position statement' regarding her perspective on prostitution. Instead, she describes three different feminist positions she has observed on sex work: (1) all prostitution is violence against women, (2) all women must negotiate their sexuality within a larger hetero-normative, male-dominated context in which women are at an economic disadvantage, and (3) female prostitutes are gender outlaws who break sexual taboos and may potentially experience sexual liberation as such. Vanwesenbeeck does not place herself in any of these three feminist positions.

Following prior research, Vanwesenbeeck (1994) theorized that wellbeing (physical and emotional) in sex work is related to historic, personal, and contextual factors. The confluence of these factors, including job satisfaction, is theorized to shape the wellbeing of the woman working in prostitution. Vanwesenbeeck's research is notable for the attention it pays to class, and to the variations of class within prostitution. Noting that prior research of non-sexworker populations had shown an association between living in poverty and higher rates of psychological problems, as well as utilization of ineffective coping strategies, Vanwesenbeeck predicted that she would uncover similar rates of poor outcome among her sample – especially when taking into account the loss of status that accompanies entering prostitution. Additionally, prior research on prostitution indicated that most prostitutes lived in poverty, and thus were vulnerable to the physical and emotional health problems faced by poor people who were not prostitutes.

The two studies presented in Vanwesenbeeck's 1994 publication sampled 187 current and former prostitutes recruited through snowball sampling, newspaper advertisements, and outreach to women in their working environments. Across both studies, distribution of work venue is similar to a 'normal curve,' which seems to reflect the distribution of venues in the Netherlands at the time of sampling. Women completed a questionnaire measuring wellbeing, childhood sexual abuse, partner abuse, and violence on the job; coping styles, frequency and type of drug and alcohol consumption, safer sex practices, working practices, and current or former work venue.

Ultimately, the results of the two studies uncovered a diversity of experiences among women working in sex work in the Netherlands. While approximately one fourth of the women sampled were experiencing mental health problems such as anxiety, depression, and substance abuse, another 25 percent of the sample scored higher on measures of emotional wellbeing than the average non-sexworker comparison sample. The remaining 50 percent of women sampled scored somewhere in between. Perhaps unsurprisingly, the women who were most likely to score in the lower 25 percent on measures of wellbeing were also the most likely to be working in the least-paid, most dangerous venues for sex work, such as on the street, or in brothels where third parties allowed women little control over their working conditions. Women of color and migrant women were also more likely to be working in these venues. Ex-prostitutes from Study One scored at the bottom of the sample on measures of wellbeing, raising the possibility that women who were poorly suited to the work were most likely to leave it.

In contrast, women who worked towards the top of the pay scale in sex work, and worked independently, were most likely to score in the top 25 percent of measures of wellbeing. These women were also more likely to be native Dutch, had higher educational attainment, and a better standard of living overall. Vanwesenbeeck's respondents reported significantly higher rates of childhood abuse when compared with Dutch population studies of childhood sexual abuse; however, past experience of such abuse was not predictive of current levels of wellbeing.

The findings of these two studies call into question the notion that prostitution is inherently traumatizing, and certainly that all prostitutes develop pathology as a result of their work. Notably, in her later review of research from 1990 to 2000, Vanwesenbeeck does include a position statement at the beginning of her manuscript. She states that she will approach the review

> from a pro-sex work feminist frame of reference, meaning that sex work is, on principle, considered legitimate work, not violence. At the same time, it is acknowledged that the illegal status of sex work and its consequences do violate the civil and workers' rights and integrity of sex workers. (Vanwesenbeeck, 2001, p. 243)

Vanwesenbeeck's study stands out from most previous studies of sex work in two key ways: first, she sampled a cross-section of women at all levels of the business; second, the questions she posed of her sample allowed for a diversity of responses. Whatever her feelings may

have been concerning prostitution at the start of the study, her methodology did not limit her participants to a narrow range of reportable
experiences.

For abolitionist feminists opposed to the position expressed by Vanwesenbeeck in her 2001 review, research on sex work often begins with
a search for the negative factors that 'forced' women into prostitution.
Prior traumatic life experiences are often investigated as factors that are
assumed to have molded the psychology of the victim, in effect creating
a 'potential prostitute personality.' Examples of this can be seen in
psychodynamic literature, which retrospectively investigates the prevalence of childhood sexual abuse in prostitutes, theorizing that prostitution may be viewed as negative sequelae of such abuse (Abramovich,
2005).

Anti-prostitution researchers have often posited the theory of 'repetition compulsion' as an explanation for involvement in prostitution by
persons with a history of childhood sexual abuse (Farley et al., 1998;
Farley, 2005; Simons & Whitbeck, 1991). According to this theory,
persons working in prostitution are 're-experiencing' their original
trauma through their work in prostitution, while at the same time
attempting to 'take control' psychically over the situation and thus
remove themselves from the position of the victim. Repetition compulsion behaviors are frequently thought to be symptomatic of pathologies
such as borderline personality disorder and post-traumatic stress
disorder (PTSD), both of which researchers such as Farley (Farley et al.,
1998) and others argue act simultaneously as a cause *and* an effect of
involvement in prostitution. Notably, this analysis glosses over the role of
the economic situation of the prostitute as a potential motivating factor
for entering prostitution. Additionally, any positive or even neutral
experience within prostitution is cast beyond what may be found in the
research; as the researchers view the possibility of such experiences to
be impossible, they remain literally unknowable.

A 1998 investigation of violent experiences and PTSD carried out by
Farley and others (Farley et al., 1998) follows the 'repetition compulsion' theory of prostitution. The authors begin the article by stating:

> We began this work from the perspective that prostitution itself is violence
> against women. The authors understand prostitution to be a sequelae of
> childhood sexual abuse; understand that racism is inextricably connected
> to sexism in prostitution; understand that prostitution is domestic
> violence, and in many instances slavery or debt bondage; and we also

understand the need for asylum and culturally relevant treatment when considering escape or treatment options for those in prostitution. (Farley et al., 1998, p. 406)

Following this, they describe the findings of a survey of violent experiences and PTSD in a sample of 475 mainly street-working prostitutes in South Africa, Thailand, Turkey, the US, and Zambia. The survey assessed physical and sexual assault on the job, lifetime history of victimization on and off the job, and included performing in pornographic films (voluntary or coerced participation was not measured, due to the authors' belief that voluntary participation in pornography was impossible) in their definition of violent experiences. Women were asked whether they wished to leave prostitution and what they needed in order to leave the work, whether they had ever been homeless, if they had physical health problems, and if they had a problem with drugs or alcohol. Finally, respondents also completed a scale assessing symptoms of PTSD.

Interviews for this study were conducted in a variety of settings, such as homeless shelters, workplaces, and drug treatment clinics; the surveys were administered by a variety of local personnel. Like Vanwesenbeeck's original Study One, Farley's respondents included persons who currently or formerly worked as prostitutes (or, as Farley states, 'were prostituted'). The sample was racially diverse and respondents ranged in age from 15 to 61 years. One strength of this study is the large sample and many sampling sites.

Farley's study found that the majority of women (and of the few men and transgender prostitutes sampled) had experienced sexual violence in their work, and 67 percent met criteria for PTSD. High rates of violence (73 percent beatings; 62 percent rape) were reported, although Farley does acknowledge lower rates of violence among the 25 brothel-based respondents in South Africa. Nearly half of the sample (46 percent) had 'had pornography made of them,' and 92 percent expressed desire to leave prostitution. Unsurprisingly, given the street-based sample, very high rates of homelessness were also reported.

However, there are several major limitations to this study, including a methodology that varied from country to country, making comparison of data across nations problematic (Weitzer, 2005). Irregularities in data analysis also raise questions of author bias. Thai respondents were removed from analysis of PTSD rates (after differences were found between sites – Thai women scored lower on this measure) because they completed questionnaires 'in a large group.' Also, the sample was highly specific, comprised mostly of persons who were homeless and working on the street, or former prostitutes who had 'escaped' prostitution. The inclusion of former prostitutes in the sample also raises the possibility that such women skewed the findings, as happened in Vanwesenbeeck's (1994) study, which also included former prostitutes. Also, the formatting of the questions ('have you ever ...' as compared to a time-limited 'in the past year, have you experienced ...') may have led to higher rates of reported violence and homelessness than have been found in other studies, such as Vanwesenbeeck's (Vanwesenbeeck, 1994).

In spite of the limitations to generalizability imposed by the sample collected by Farley and her colleagues (1998), the authors make broad claims such as 'Our data show that almost all those in prostitution are poor' (Farley et al., 1998, p. 421). Thus poverty is cast as a finding of the research, and not an artifact of the sampling strategy (the authors argue that sampling non-street-based prostitutes proved too difficult to implement, and thus, with the exception of a small group of brothel-based prostitutes, few non-street-based women were included in the sample). However, other studies carried out during this time period, such as Vanwesenbeeck (1994), and Chapkis (1997), were able to recruit brothel-based and independently employed women who worked indoors. Also, as Vanwesenbeeck's 1994 data show, working venue plays a crucial role in the wellbeing of women in sex work.

By limiting their sample, Farley et al. could also be said to have limited their findings; yet, these limits are not addressed in the authors' claims regarding the generalizability of their findings. As Farley and her colleagues define prostitution as violence against women, it may have been in their interest to exclude from their sample women whose experiences or perspectives might conflict with this viewpoint. Additionally, the study protocol included only questions about the harms potentially associated with prostitution. In fact, following the release of her 1998 study, Farley was asked in an interview 'Do you encounter women who say they like this work?' To this Farley replied, 'Women don't say that to me because of the questions I ask' (Farley, quoted in the August 1998 issue of the online magazine www.mergemag.org). Thus Farley chose to limit her partici-pants to a narrow range of reportable experiences, lending support to Weitzer's (2005) assertion that Farley's data was limited by 'ideo-logical contamination.'

Beyond trauma: exploring sex workers' coping strategies

If the questions posed by Farley and other abolitionist feminists limit the range of data to the harms possible in prostitution, then questions of how sex workers work to maximize the benefits of their labor are left to feminists who view prostitution as sex work. Studies of how sex workers maintain their emotional wellbeing within their work, of how they manage the impact of their work on their personal life, and of how they draw boundaries between work and private life become possible and relevant only when sex work is considered a matter of choice and not equated by definition with violence. Thus a great deal of research on sex work as emotional labor, identity management by sex workers, and stigma resistance strategies utilized by sex workers flows from the 'sex work as labor' position.

In 1997, feminist sociologist Wendy Chapkis broke new ground in sex work research with the publication of her book *Live Sex Acts: Women Performing Erotic Labor* (1997). This work was the result of several years of ethnographic research in the United States and the Netherlands, and weaves together qualitative interviews with women in a variety of sex industry professions. Chapkis, who had some experience in sex work advocacy prior to the publication of the book, clearly aligns herself with the 'sex work as labor' position. Like Vanwesenbeeck's (1994) earlier research, she inquired about both positive and negative aspects of the women's experience as sex workers, and also sampled women from a variety of venues (unlike Farley's majority street-based sample). While Chapkis's position on sex work differs significantly from the abolitionist perspective, she deliberately included in her sample women who had been victims of coerced trafficking as well as women who had worked on the street, out of a desire to include as diverse a variety of perspectives as possible. Additionally, Chapkis writes in her introduction that she made a conscious effort to include quotes that she did not agree with, in order to avoid the danger of the author being the 'ventriloquist's dummy' of the interviewee. In these ways, whilst Chapkis clearly stated her own position on sex work, she did not limit her data to only those experiences or viewpoints that confirm her perspective on prostitution.

Drawing on feminist social psychologist Arlie Russell Hochschild's (1983) theory of 'emotion work' and 'emotional labor', in which gendered service jobs are viewed as necessitating the production or appearance of 'appropriate' emotions, Chapkis (1997) explored the ways in which sex workers managed their emotions on the job. To this end, Chapkis sampled fifty sex workers, political activists, trafficked women, dominatrices, and others involved in the industry (such as brothel staff and law enforcement officers). Participants completed open-ended qualitative interviews, which Chapkis conducted in Dutch or English, depending on the participant's preference. The qualitative interview data was then examined for themes and fit with Hochschild's (1983) theory of emotional labor.

The women Chapkis interviewed described a variety of techniques which aided them in drawing boundaries between their work lives and personal lives; these skills enabled them to give the client a pleasurable experience without feeling that they had sold a 'private/personal' part of themselves in the process. Sex worker Jo Doezema states: 'Now it is true that there are parts of myself that I don't want to share with my clients. But drawing boundaries in my work doesn't mean that I am in danger of being destroyed by it' (Doezema, as quoted in Chapkis, 1997, p. 75).

This perspective offers an alternative to the view held by anti-prostitution feminists (such as Barry, 1995; Dworkin, 1997; and Pateman, 1988) who state that prostitution is selling one's self and an abuse of one's personal integrity. The question of interpreting women's reported experience arises here in noting that what to one person may be 'drawing boundaries' (an emotionally healthy coping strategy) may be viewed as 'dissociation' (a pathological response to victimization) by another. One sex worker interviewed by Chapkis, Cheyenne, expressed frustration at the ways in which her skills might be misinterpreted by outsiders because of the stigma associated with being labelled as a 'prostitute':

> I know how to maintain my emotional distance [from clients]. Just like if you are a fire fighter or a brain surgeon or psychiatrist, you have to deal with some heavy stuff and that means divorcing yourself from your feelings on a certain level. You just have to be able to do that to do your job. But if you're a prostitute who can separate herself from her emotions while you're working everybody condemns you for it. I don't get it. (Cheyenne, quoted in Chapkis, 1997, p. 79)

In the way described by Cheyenne, the stigma attached to prostitution colors the lens through which outsiders interpret experiences. One wonders how Cheyenne's experiences would have been viewed by a person who equates prostitution with violence. Chapkis acknowledges that emotion work can lead to burnout or feelings of being alienated from one's 'true' emotions, and argues that this relates not to sex work by definition, but to the control one has over one's working conditions, and other personal factors such as previous life experience, social support, etc. This perspective is justified given Vanwesenbeeck's (1994) earlier research finding that venue of work and other socioeconomic factors were related to wellbeing in sex work.

There are some limitations to consider when reviewing Chapkis's (1997) work. Her sample was mainly collected in the cities of Santa Cruz, San Francisco, and Amsterdam – three of the most socially and sexually permissive cities in the world; many well-known sex work activists participated in the interviews. However, as stated previously, Chapkis was careful to include women whose participation in sex work was coerced, as well as women who espoused beliefs she did not share. In this way Chapkis attempted to reduce any bias towards 'positive' findings that may have been present.

In the years following Chapkis's (1997) publication, the study of sex work as emotional labor has become increasingly popular. The work of Joanna Brewis and Stephen Linstead (2000a, 2000b) and, more recently, Teela Sanders (2002, 2004b, 2005a) builds and expands upon previous work by Hochschild (1983) and Chapkis (1997), exploring the performance of emotional labor by female sex workers in the UK. These works seem uniquely a product of the time period in which the research was conducted – following decades of hotly contested 'forced' versus 'choice' debate among feminists (this is not to say that the debate is fully resolved), the foundational notion of 'sex as work' reached a degree of theoretical development and acceptance among many feminists and the larger community of social science researchers. The question of sex work as emotional labor is no longer one of 'choice' versus 'force', nor of 'victimization' versus 'wellbeing'; the theoretical assumptions underlying this burgeoning field of sex work literature seem to be 'now that we are here as workers, selling leisure time and sensual/sexual services to clients, how may we maintain our safety, a healthy sense of boundaries between personal and working life, and take care of ourselves emotionally?' To this end, the work of Brewis and Linstead explores the 'liminal space' wherein professional sex occurs:

> The fact that they [sex workers] are selling something which has not been fully commodified and which is usually associated with the private

sphere, governed as it is by values of intimacy, love and affect ... means that the *place* where prostitution happens, whether actual geographical location, part of the body or symbolic location ... is also crucial to the prostitute's sense of self, to their self esteem. (Brewis & Linstead, 2000a, p. 89, emphasis original)

This space emphasizes the 'work/personal' divide that is needed to main-tain psychological boundaries while performing activities with clients that involve a combination of physical intimacy and emotional distancing.

Brewis and Linstead's (2000a, 2000b) two-part article reports an analysis of their own earlier qualitative research as well as reviewing qualitative studies carried out in the UK by other authors. Ultimately, strategies that appeared consistent across the samples described by Brewis and Linstead include the use of substances to alter consciousness during work (this strategy appears to have been more prevalent among the street workers sampled), and more symbolic ways of maintaining emotional distance, such as the construction of a work persona complete with different name, affect, and mode of dress.

The main 'problem' Brewis and Linstead (2000a) locate in their sample is not that a divide between work and private life is needed, but that this divide requires constant internal policing to maintain properly. Their argument does not depart significantly from Chapkis's (1997) exploration of emotional labor, but the overarching theme of Chapkis's work (sex workers are rational agents who should be listened to, respected, and viewed as co-feminists) contrasts with the less political, less entreating tone of Brewis and Linstead (strategies employed by sex workers to maintain their psychological integrity are worthy of study as exemplars of ways in which sexuality and self are constructed and enacted in 'late modernity'). Chapkis's work seems to have played an important role on the front lines of the social scientific discourse concerning sex work – she needed to publish *Live Sex Acts* and be smeared as the 'celebrity apologist for prostitution' in order to lay the less-contested groundwork upon which Brewis and Linstead strode just a few years later.

Following Brewis and Linstead's (2000a, 2000b) exploration of boundary maintenance among sex workers, Teela Sanders (2002, 2004b, 2005a) entered the field with her ethnographic study of female sex workers in Britain, the majority of whom worked indoors. Over a ten-month period in the years 2000 to 2001, Sanders conducted over 1,000 hours of on-site observation, and interviewed 45 indoor female sex workers in Birmingham, UK. Sanders's inclusion criterion was that women sex workers must be over the age of eighteen, British citizens, and self-described as voluntary participants in sex work. Sanders also interviewed professionals involved in sex work, such as madams and brothel staff. Women ranged in educational attainment and employment skills: 34 out of 45 had few job skills and left school at age sixteen; however 11 out of 45 had some or completed college and skill degrees (nursing, hairdressing) and of these 8 had left mainstream employment for the greater flexibility offered in sex work. Describing her sample, Sanders notes:

> Unlike the typical patterns of prostitutes' histories that are reported in the literature, the participants I have based this set of arguments on were not scarred by abuse, violence by clients, financial exploitation from male partners or recurring patterns of arrest. They tended to define themselves as 'career girls' or 'working girls', expressing entre-preneurial attitudes and business acumen. (Sanders, 2005a, p. 324)

Here Sanders was likely offering a direct response to earlier work by Farley (1998) and other anti-prostitution feminists.

Sanders argues that emotional labor constitutes both an effective business strategy for gaining and maintaining clientele, as well as a strategy for self-preservation while performing the intimate inter-actions required by sex work. In addition to the strategies described by Brewis and Linstead, Sanders argues that condoms act as symbolic barriers between the worker and her client, providing emotional distance in the moments when maintaining personal boundaries becomes most challenging. Thus condoms are not only tools, which prevent unintended pregnancy and infection with sexually transmitted disease, they prevent 'the client entering their minds, stealing their thoughts and affecting their personal relationships' (Sanders, 2002, p. 564). Unfortunately, Sanders reports that for many of the women she interviewed, associating condom use with work sex resulted in the reverse association for personal sex – here a sexual encounter with a lover must be condomless in order to allow for intimacy during the sex act.

Later work by Sanders (2004b, 2005a) elaborated on additional strategies utilized by female sex workers (all of whom worked indoors) in order emotionally to manage self-presentation to the client while working to maintain a coherent sense of self outside of work. In her 2004 work, Sanders explores the use of humor by sex workers to build alliance between workers, maintain distance between the self and the client (especially when making jokes of which the client is unaware), and maintaining the 'appropriate' and desirable emotional presentation of a 'happy hooker'. Sanders's (2005a) work '"It's Just Acting": Sex Workers' Strategies for Capitalizing on Sexuality' coalesces her earlier work on emotion management as a business strategy employed to create the most marketable personas in order to attract the desired clientele while maintaining personal boundaries in the process.

In her 2005a piece, Sanders also responds to Brewis and Linstead's and others' assertion that sex work requires the 'consumption' of the female body. Rather than singling out sex work as uniquely requiring of women's sexuality in the workplace, Sanders places prostitution on a continuum of sexualized service work performed by women. She asserts that while female sex workers operate within a gendered, hetero-centric profession, they also work to manipulate male sexuality for their own profit. (Sanders posits that equating prostitution with force and victimization overly simplifies the realities of sex work: 'Theory that locates power and influence only with male customers or the wider structures that determine economic relations leaves female sex workers theoretically devoid of agency, responsibility and rationality' [Sanders, 2005a, p. 336]). Prostitution therefore can be seen as merely one example of a service profession (like waitressing, nursing, or being a flight attendant) that is gendered, and requires intimate interaction and displays of 'appropriate' appearance and emotions.

While Sanders's research represents the most important research on the coping strategies of sex work since earlier work by Chapkis (1997) and Vanwesenbeeck (1994), her research findings are constrained by several limitations. First, while Sanders asserts that her participants were not the traumatized, victimized, drug addicted women most often described in research on sex work, her methodology did not measure PTSD or depression. The sample was comprised of women who identified as voluntary sex workers and who were legal adults and British citizens. Thus, this was a group more likely to be coping well, if the 1994 work of Vanwesenbeeck is any indication. And finally, the majority of the sample worked indoors. This 'bias' towards indoor workers helps to balance the majority of literature on street-based women, yet it precludes generalization to this group.

The research of Sanders (2002, 2004b, 2005a), Brewis and Linstead (2000a, 2000b), and Chapkis (1997) together form a qualitative body of literature that has thoroughly explored sex work as a form of service industry work (akin to nursing or being a flight attendant). These studies have identified coping strategies utilized by indoor female sex workers to manage sex-work-related stigma as well as cope with the demands of performing emotional labor on the job. Along with the earlier research by Vanwesenbeeck (1994), this body of literature provides firm evidence that women's experiences with sex work are diverse, and it refutes the assertion of anti-prostitution feminists who argue that sex work is inherently traumatizing.

Sex work and mental health: comparing sex workers to non-sexworkers

If sex work is not inherently traumatizing, the factors that shape women's positive and negative experiences within it have only just begun to be explored. As described previously, research by Vanwesenbeeck (1994) provided evidence that work venue plays a major role in women's expressed satisfaction with their work as well as their emotional well-being in sex work. Personal and contextual characteristics of sex workers and their working environments, as well as factors which may be unique to sex work over and above service work, have just begun to be studied. Two studies comparing the emotional health of sex workers to non-sexworkers (Romans et al., 2001; Vanwesenbeeck, 2005) constitute important contributions to this developing area of research.

A small study carried out in New Zealand by Romans and colleagues (2001), a group of researchers who advocate that sex work is legitimate employment, aimed to test the assumption that women employed in sex work would fare poorly on assessments of mental health when compared to a community sample of age-matched women. The sample consisted of 29 female sex workers who were recruited from the New Zealand Prostitutes Collective, a sex work advocacy and support group. The majority of the women were employed in massage parlors; one woman worked through an escort agency, and two worked on the street. Data collected from a large-scale survey of women's health in New Zealand, adjusted to match the age range of the sex worker sample (18 to 40), provided the comparison group. Sex workers were compared to the community sample on measures of social support, self-esteem, and psychiatric symptomology (as measured by the GHQ-28, the General Health Questionnaire, as well as the IBM, or Intimate Bond Measure). Physical health, history of sexual assault or other violent experiences, and demographic characteristics were also assessed.

The findings of the Romans et al. study (2001) indicate that many of the difficulties encountered by the female sex workers sampled relate to the stigma associated with sex work as well as the economically and socially marginalized position of sex workers generally. The sex workers did not differ significantly from the comparison group on measures of social support, self-esteem, psychiatric symptomology, and overall physical health, although they did drink and smoke cigarettes at higher rates than the comparison group. Sex workers were also equally likely to be partnered, and to express comparable levels of relationship satisfaction, as the women in the comparison group.

Unfortunately, disturbing differences between the sex work and the comparison sample did emerge on the measures of interpersonal violence. Sex workers were more likely to have been the victim of physical abuse and sexual assault than were the comparison sample (59 percent of sex workers as compared to 20 percent of the comparison group). However, the majority of the assaults were not perpetrated by clients – sex workers experienced violence at the hands of partners and sometimes strangers, much as non-sexworking women do. It is difficult to determine what unique factors specific to sex workers left them more vulnerable to abuse than the non-sexworking comparison group, but it is likely that they relate to the economically and socially marginalized position of the sex work sample relative to the community as a whole.

The results of the Romans et al. study lend further support to the earlier work of Vanwesenbeeck (1994), indicating that while female sex workers constitute a stigmatized and marginalized population, sex work is not inherently traumatizing in itself. Rather, the circumstances in which some women work, which may be characterized by violence, coercion, or poverty, present a serious threat to the mental health of some sex workers. In spite of this, the sex workers sampled by Romans and colleagues, as well as those who participated in Vanwesenbeeck's (1994) research, did not suffer from poor mental health at the rates which might be expected given the marginality of many sex workers – and many appear to fare well.

The findings of Romans and her colleagues (2001) present a contribution to the study of the wellbeing of female sex workers, yet their generalizability may be limited by the small sample size (only 29 sex workers) and the potential characteristics of the recruitment site. While all non-random samples present challenges to generalizability, it is possible that the members of the New Zealand Prostitutes Collective who constituted the sex work sample may differ from sex workers who do not take part in this support and advocacy group. In spite of these limitations, the research of Romans et al. (2001) provides evidence that sex work is not experienced as traumatic by all sex workers, although sex workers appear to be more vulnerable to violence on and off the job than non-sexworking women.

If sex workers as a whole are not more poorly emotionally adjusted than non-sexworkers, much more remains to be understood concerning the uniquely stressful characteristics of sex work in itself. Previous research by Chapkis (1997), as well as work by Brewis and Linstead (2000a, 2000b), explores the potential for the performance of emotional labor to result in negative psychological adjustment or burnout as a result of sex workers' coping skills being pushed to the limit. Burnout, a work-related psychological syndrome characterized by feelings of emotional exhaustion, by feeling a lack of personal competence, and even by depersonalization, has been identified as a potential downside to the performance of many forms of labor. Those who are employed in service industry jobs, or work in the 'helping professions,' appear to be particularly vulnerable to burnout as they are required to perform high levels of emotional labor (Maslach et al., 2001). Vanwesenbeeck's most recent research (2005) aims to untangle the uniquely stressful charac-teristics of performing emotional labor in sex work, and the additional strains placed on the worker due to the stigma and social marginality associated with sex work.

Vanwesenbeeck (2005) utilized two comparison groups to assess differences between the sex workers she sampled: female health pro-fessionals (mostly nurses) and persons seeking counselling for work-related burnout. The non-sexwork comparison groups are particularly apt given Vanwesenbeeck's aim of identifying the unique stressors of sex work (which has been argued by many researchers to involve the selling of one's 'self' [Barry, 1995; Farley et al., 1998]) apart from those asso-ciated with performing emotional labor *per se*. Some researchers have drawn comparisons between service work professions and sex work, arguing that sex work should be viewed on a continuum of service work professions which are gendered and sexualized by nature, such as cocktail waitressing or being a flight attendant (Chapkis, 1997; Sanders, 2005a). This perspective lends support to Vanwesenbeeck's inclusion in the comparison group of female health professionals. Additionally, the non-sexwork group of professionals seeking counselling services for treatment of work-related burnout provide a comparison group of individuals who presumably are struggling with the emotional downsides of their work, although they are not sex workers and thus may be presumed to be a less socially marginalized group, as well as less personally taxed by their jobs, which do not require sexual labor.

Based on prior studies of trauma and poor emotional adjustment among female sex workers Vanwesenbeeck hypothesized that sex workers would score higher on measures of burnout when compared to the professionals in the comparison groups. Further, she predicted that burnout would be associated with contextual factors, such as working circumstances and social support. Finally, Vanwesenbeeck predicted that for sex workers, cynicism (depersonalization) would be found to be a protective factor, rather than a negative outcome.

The sample comprised of 96 female sex workers, all of whom worked indoors (in the Netherlands street-based sex work is uncommon). Women worked in a variety of circumstances, from independent escorts to trafficked migrants working for a third party. The sample was ethnically diverse, and comprised native-born Dutch women as well as many women who had migrated to work in the Dutch sex industry, the Netherlands being a nation where sex work is legal. There was also a diversity of educational attainment and socioeconomic background among the sex-working sample. All told, Vanwesenbeeck made a concerted effort to include as diverse a sample of female sex workers as possible, in an effort to provide a counterpoint to previous research, which as we have seen had focused on relatively narrow subgroups of female sex workers, such as street-based women who were frequently dealing with issues of violent family or home life, homelessness, substance abuse, and mental illness (Farley et al., 1998; Pheterson, 1990; Simons & Whitbeck, 1991; Weitzer, 2005).

Using a structured interview protocol, Vanwesenbeeck assessed burnout using a slightly modified version (translated from English to Dutch, and with wording changes to make the scale specific to sex work) of the Maslach Burnout Inventory. This scale measures three aspects of burnout: emotional exhaustion, depersonalization, and personal competence. In addition to the measure of burnout, the interview assessed other stress symptoms such as sleeplessness, headaches, lack of appetite, and anxiety. Also assessed were women's experiences of harassment and violence on the job in the previous year, perceptions of stigma and problems in personal life due to sex-work-related stigma (namely, being rejected by a friend or loved one, demeaned, or subject to discriminatory treatment when accessing services), and motivations for entering sex work. Working environment factors were also assessed, such as support from management and colleagues, number of hours worked and clients seen per week, amount of money earned, and degree of control over interactions with clients.

Like Vanwesenbeeck's earlier research (1994), the findings of her 2005 study shed light on the complex web of personal and environmental factors which shape women's experience of sex work. Vanwesenbeeck (2005) found that, overall, sex workers' scores on emotional exhaustion and personal competence did not differ from the female health care workers, and were much more positive than those of the patients in treatment for work-related burnout. However, sex workers scored higher on depersonalization than the health care workers, although their scores did not differ significantly from those of the comparison group in treatment for burnout. While the findings of this study suggest that sex work is not always detrimental to the wellbeing of the individual, factors that are associated with negative mental health outcomes among female sex workers emerged upon analysis of women's working circumstances and personal history. Sex workers' scores on stress symptoms were distributed along a curve, with a quarter of the sample experiencing them often, a quarter seldom/never, and the remainder of the sample in between. Almost one quarter of the sample reported having been the victim of violence in the past year, and 54 percent of the women had experienced work-related stigma. In spite of these indicators of significant stress among some of the sex workers sampled, the majority of the women (70 percent) reported that they 'hardly' or 'almost never' used drugs.

When compared to the rates of violence reported by Farley and colleagues (1998), the rate of reported violence among female sex workers in Vanwesenbeeck's sample is relatively low, especially when considering that this study included some trafficked sex workers in the sample. A recent study of indoor female sex workers in New York (Thukral et al., 2005) reported rates of on-the-job violence and substance use that were similar to those reported by Vanwesenbeeck (2005), lending support to the validity of Vanwesenbeeck's findings. It is likely that the disparity in rates of victimization and drug use across these various samples is due to the unique characteristics of street-based sex work, which comprised the majority of the sample utilized by Farley et al. (1998).

The rates of stigma and violence reported in Vanwesenbeeck's study (2005) continue to reflect the marginalized position occupied by female sex workers, even in a state which has legalized sex work. However, the majority of the women who took part in this study reported that they entered the sex industry voluntarily. Further, most of the women sampled expressed high levels of control over interactions with client and enjoyed high rates of social support on the job from managers and colleagues.

Among Vanwesenbeeck's (2005) sample, statistical regression showed that four variables predicted the highest levels of burnout: lack of social support by management, high rates of experienced stigma in private life and lack of personal support, lack of choice in working (that is, being trafficked or forced into sex work), and negative work motivation (that is, feeling that one had little choice in entering sex work, although not coerced by a third party). Additionally, rates of depersonalization were related to the experience of violence on the job, lack of control over sessions with clients, and perceived stigma in one's private life.

Overall, Vanwesenbeeck's (2005) work, as well as her earlier research (Vanwesenbeeck, 1994), demonstrates that the wellbeing of sex workers relates more to their working circumstances than it does to sex work itself. Additionally, work by Chapkis (1997) and Sanders (2002, 2004b, 2005a), indicates that many female sex workers are able to create successful coping strategies to manage the emotional demands of the job while minimizing the impact on their lives of sex-work-related stigma. Taken as a whole, these studies indicate that venue matters; that sex work can be chosen work, and that sex work does not present a uniquely traumatizing form of labor when it is chosen and working circumstances are good.

Sex work as middle-class occupation and leisure activity

Recent research on independent female sex workers in the US, as well as on those employed in legalized brothels in Nevada, has shifted the focus to sex workers who do not fit within the trope of the traumatized, poor, under educated street-based sex worker. Increasingly, researchers have begun to frame sex work as falling within the scope of 'leisure activities' (Bernstein, 2007a; Brents & Hausbeck, 2007), which are often provided by relatively middle-class workers to upper-middle-class clients. The ethnographic work of Elizabeth Bernstein (2007a, 2007b) explores the experiences of a small sample (n=15) of relatively privileged women employed in the indoor sex industry between 1994 and 2002. These women, Bernstein argues, may have enjoyed race and class privilege, but they still found themselves largely shut out of the high-paying tech and financial industry jobs that their male counterparts had access to. Such women often had college degrees and experience in mainstream employment, yet elected to enter sex work because of the relative freedoms available through self-employment and higher-paid sex work. Bernstein argues: 'Given the gendered disparities of postindustrial economic life, the relatively high pay of the sex industry (compared to other service industry jobs) provides a compelling reason for some women from middle class backgrounds to engage in sexual labor' (Bernstein, 2007a, p. 475).

The internet eased this transition further through the proliferation of erotic websites where women could solicit potential clients directly, eliminating the need for a third party such as a madam or agency. In this period, Bernstein observed the increasing 'professionalization' of sex work through the appearance of websites and how-to manuals offering advice to women just entering the escorting business (Bernstein, 2007a).

Like the women described by Chapkis (1997) and Sanders (2002, 2004b, 2005a), the middle-class women interviewed by Bernstein (2007b) framed their work as both an emotional and an erotic service. These women strove to provide a seemingly authentic intimate relationship with their client, which is popularly known as 'the girlfriend experience' or GFE (Bernstein, 2007b). The GFE service expands the boundaries of sex-for-money so that it becomes an exchange into one that encompasses a show of caring, affection, and even love. Sex workers providing GFE to clients may engage in kissing, receiving 'sexual pleasure' (or performing pleasure), and other activities requiring a high level of emotional labor. In fact, Bernstein argues (2007b) that middle-class sex work, or 'postindustrial sexual commerce', is distinguished from more traditional notions of selling sex by the diversity of emotional and sexual services on offer and the emphasis on the sex worker's own pleasure in the work (real or performed).

The calm discussion of 'postindustrial sexual commerce' featured in Bernstein's work (2007a, 2007b) provides further evidence that feminist research on women's experiences in sex work has significantly expanded beyond earlier divisions regarding women's agency in sex work and the debate over the meaning of prostitution. From earlier research intended to demonstrate empirically the diversity of sex workers (Chapkis, 1997; Vanwesenbeeck, 1994) to more recent work exploring the emotional nuances of the experience of performing sex work (Bernstein, 2007a, 2007b; Saunders, 2002, 2004b, 2005a), the available 'frames' for sex work research have increased significantly. Recent media coverage of sex work (Clemmitt, 2008) in the US provides a glimpse of the increasing recognition among researchers, advocates, and policy makers that women's experiences in sex work defy broad generalization and reduction to two-dimensional stereotypes of victimhood.

Linking methodology with ideology

As previously noted, research on the emotional labor of *sex work* builds on the foundation of the concept that the worker is by definition engaged in legitimate paid labor, albeit labor that is socially marginalized and potentially risky. When reviewing the works discussed in this chapter, trends in methodology arise across works that seem to be associated with the ideology held by their author/s. Researchers such as Farley and colleagues, who begin with the stance that *prostitution* is violence against women, collect samples that are almost entirely comprised of current or former street-based women (Farley also stated in a 1998 interview that she prefers to interview women who have 'escaped' prostitution). Additionally, Farley admits to limiting the responses that interviewees may share with her, as she maintains control over the interview process by deciding which questions will be raised, and limiting these questions to ones concerning victimization.

In contrast, work which aimed to explore sex as work which may be characterized by a diversity of experiences, sought out a diversity of sex workers for its sample. Vanwesenbeeck (1994, 2005) began this trend, and following her work researchers such as Chapkis (1997), Brewis and Linstead (2000a, 2000b) and Sanders (2002, 2004a, 2005b) sampled diverse groups of women, the majority of whom worked indoors. The addition of qualitative methodology utilized by Chapkis, Bernstein (2007a, 2007b) and Sanders (2002, 2004b, 2005a) also expands the range of reportable experiences that sex workers may share. While Chapkis was careful to probe for positive as well as negative experiences within sex work, Brewis and Linstead and Sanders simply asked in effect 'How do you get by?' Their work did not foreclose the possibility that participants would report personal struggles and even serious emotional harms within sex work (and such experiences were reported by some participants), but notably it did aim to identify women's strengths and skills within their work. Sex workers here are not simply victims, also not 'liberated' women who have escaped patriarchy – but they are fully realized and agentic human beings performing work inside a complex web of personal and social contexts.

Future directions in sex work research

Ultimately, if sex work is to be treated as a form of labor like other income-producing strategies, the larger cultural and economic context of sex work must be more comprehensively attended to in research and social policy on the subject. Just as the ideological positions of researchers have shaped the course of sex work research, researchers and policy makers are further constrained by the moralistic assumptions driving which questions are deemed worthy of funding. Laura Agustín, a sociologist and cultural studies theorist, critiques the dominant focus on sex workers and clients – a focus which excludes the supporting businesses and cultural context in which sex work is performed (Agustín, 2005d). This narrow focus, argues Agustín, is itself driven by the limitations of the ideologies held by funding agencies, policy makers and researchers themselves:

> These reasons [for funding research on sex work only as a health or social problem], however, both derive from moralistic attitudes and lead back to them, since as long as moralism informs research policy, the research that might enlighten it cannot be done. (Agustín, 2005d, p. 7, italics in the original)

Thus, if the 'prostitution as sex work' position is to be followed to its conclusion, sex work research must be expanded beyond the narrow focus on women, prostitution, and the underlying moral attitudes, which have led to this limited analysis. What would such research look like? Agustín suggests a cultural studies approach which would expand researchers' level of analysis beyond the sex worker/client dyad to include the business proprietors, the supporting industries, the cultural context of sexual commerce, the impact of migration patterns and policy, and the ways in which sex work is situated within the tourism and leisure industries (Agustín, 2005d).

Conclusion

If the Whore remains a contested symbol of victim/outlaw/laborer to various feminist 'camps', it should also be remembered that one of the long-standing projects of feminism has been to fight the sexual double standard and the virgin/whore trope. Sex work continues to confront all feminists with difficult issues of the meaning of women's participation in sexual commerce within a patriarchal society. The feminist scholar Jane Scoular formulates a 'moderate' position which moves beyond the 'prostitution is violence against women' perspective and brings the role of social norms and reproduction into the 'sex work as labor' framework: 'Sex work may be more usefully viewed with ambivalence given that it is an activity which challenges the boundaries of heterosexist, married monogamy but may also be an activity which reinforces the dominant norms of heterosexuality and femininity' (Scoular, 2004, p.348).

Thus, so long as our culture remains stratified along lines of gender and racial and ethnic disparities in education and employment opportunities, and so long as political and social pressures guide women to remain within the bounds of a conservative heterosexual model of sexuality and gender, sex work will continue to reflect these inequalities even as it remains a rational or even desirable choice of work for many women. As sex worker activist Margo St James stated in 1982, 'A blow job is better than no job. In trying to stop abuses in prostitution, one should not try to put the women out of work because the job is all they have' (St James, as quoted in Pheterson, 1989, p. 21).

The view that pornography and the sex industry generally could provide pleasure to female consumers and enjoyable work to female workers certainly remains controversial from a feminist perspective, but it should be noted that more than twenty years after Califia wrote that the anti-porn movement had helped to 'make "whores" seem vile', women have become increasingly involved in the production and consumption of sexual products, such as pornography (Milne, 2005) and sexual services (Kempadoo, 1999). Several woman-owned and -operated porn companies, such as the well-known Femme productions, and others, have arisen in recent years, as women creating porn with an explicitly woman-centred, feminist perspective gain a foothold in the larger adult industry (Milne, 2005).

In the United States and many other nations, sex work remains criminalized, fostering working conditions which are often exploitative and unsafe (Lewis et al., 2005; Thukral & Ditmore, 2003; Thukral et al., 2005; Vanwesenbeeck, 2001). Even forms of sex work that are legal in the US, such as stripping, often take place in work environments where labor laws are bent, broken, or ignored entirely (Thukral et al., 2005). Decriminalization of prostitution has been proposed by many researchers, activists, and organizations which provide services to sex workers (Chapkis, 1997; Fawkes, 2005; Pheterson, 1989; Thukral et al., 2005) who argue that laws which criminalize sex work do not make the work safer, do nothing to end prostitution, and further marginalize and stigmatize sex workers.

However, decriminalization alone will not be enough to end the stigma against sex work and the harassment, discrimination and violence that sex workers confront too often, as these problems persist even in nations that have legalized or decriminalized sex work, such as the Netherlands and the UK (Brewis & Linstead, 2000a, 2000b; Vanwesenbeeck, 2001). A larger transformation of gender relations and cultural values surrounding sexuality, as well as a revolution in labor rights and distribution of resources, is necessary to effect large-scale change in the sex industry and in the condition of those who work within it.

B Managing Multiple Roles

4 To Love, Honor, and Strip: An Investigation of Exotic Dancer Romantic Relationships

Mindy S. Bradley-Engen and Carrie M. Hobbs

Conventional sex roles in many cultures across the world foster the assumption of exclusivity; that is, partners assume they are the exclusive recipients of romantic affection and sexually related activity. This assumption includes nudity and sexual arousal. Within a feminist ideology, heterosexual relationship norms may be understood as a regulation of women's sexuality by their male partners (Bartky, 1990; Singer, 1993). That is, involvement in heterosexual relationships provides males with exclusive sexual access to their female partners. This exclusivity affirms male power and virility. Based on this perspective, one may argue that although monogamy may be generally assumed for both partners, this expectation is especially strong for females. Subsequently, a violation of this norm by women is considered particularly humiliating and/or emasculating to their male partners. For a man, being unfaithful may reinforce his sexual mobility, while being involved with an unfaithful partner makes him a cuckold (Bartky, 1990).

By definition, the occupation of exotic dance violates heterosexual relationship norms. Nudity, seduction, and sexual arousal are the job expectations in this line of work. The term 'counterfeit intimacy' has been used to characterize the work of exotic dance and the interactions between dancers and customers (Enck & Preston, 1988). Research consistently finds that dancers routinely feign arousal and romantic interest in exchange for money (Ronai & Ellis, 1989; Chapkis, 1997; Frank, 2002). In a society that promotes the 'normalcy' of monogamy and the exclusive sexual privilege of partners, dancers sell this image of sexual accessibility.

Thus, it seems obvious that women in sex work careers face some formidable obstacles when dating. Dancers' work seems to commodify heterosexual romantic relationships: women flirt, seduce, undress for, and pretend to be attracted to a predominantly male clientele. Yet, these job responsibilities are problematic for maintaining genuine romantic relationships. By objectifying her body and appearing sexually available for customers, a dancer violates the larger social norm of exclusive sexual privilege of her partner. Thus, a dancer must not only manage the negative image of her occupation, but also negotiate relationship expectations in order to accommodate relationship norm violations.

Dancers may avoid being faced with the stereotypes of their profession in a number of ways. For example, they may only disclose their 'true' occupation to a close circle of 'insiders,' or may avoid those whom they perceive will regard them negatively (Philaretou, 2006; Thompson & Harred, 1992; Thompson et al., 2003; Skipper & McCaghy, 1970, 1971). Such tactics allow them to manage the negative images of their jobs as they negotiate between their deviant and conventional social worlds. These management strategies may be effective at managing the stigma associated with acquaintance and familial relationships. However, many techniques, such as hiding one's occupation, are implausible in romantic relationships. Whereas it may be easy to lie to one's child's teacher or neighbors about sex work employment, it is not feasible to hide a stripping career from one's boyfriend or husband for very long.

Current studies on exotic dance have explored the perspectives of dancers, customers, and staff. To date, there are no current studies on the romantic partners of strippers or other members of the strippers' social world. This ignores the interactions of erotic laborers with other actors in their lives. These women are not merely sex workers; they are wives, girlfriends, mothers, daughters, fiancées, and lovers. It is likely that these relationships have a substantial impact on the way dancers perceive themselves and their work. These relationships are often the most salient and meaningful in their lives, and thus perhaps exert the most powerful influence in how they do their job, how they think about their occupation, and how they perceive themselves.

What impact does involvement in a deviant career have on relationship quality and duration? How do exotic dancers maintain relationships within the larger social stigma associated with their work? This chapter investigates the process of partnering and dating among exotic dancers. Furthermore, it looks at the stigma dancers experience in romantic partnerships and the strategies they employ when seeking romantic partners.

68

Methods

Information comes from over three years of field observations and interviews (on-site and through phone and email) with approximately 37 female dancers and 19 current or former partners of dancers, all male.[1] Participants (dancers and their partners) were recruited on a voluntary basis through on-site verbal requests and through referrals from other participants. Dancers ranged in age between 18 years old and approximately 40 years old (N = 37). All of the romantic partners were male, ranging in age from about 25 to 55 years old (N = 19).

With the consent of club management, the first author also engaged in purely observational research, often spending time socializing with dancers in their dressing rooms. Every effort was made to observe the actual interaction between dancers and their male partners. Because most dancers are transported to or from work by their partners, the majority of observations involving romantic partners were conducted at the club, at the beginning or end of a shift.

Findings

Dancers were questioned regarding their previous relationships, as well as the relationships in which they were currently involved. Additionally, dancers were asked to describe the characteristics of the type of partner they desired. Dancers were asked, 'Describe the partner you would like to have,' and 'What do you think would make an individual be a good/ ideal partner for you?' Dancers were urged to discuss their previous relationships, focusing specifically on why these relationships ended, and to talk about the most common issues and strengths in their current partnerships.

At the time of the interview, over half of the dancers were currently involved in romantic relationships. Of these, four reported that they were married or engaged, and six indicated that they were in serious, long-term dating or cohabiting relationships.[2] Roughly 35 percent of the women described their relationship as 'dating.' Although all dancers indicated they had had previous relationships, approximately 38 percent of the women were currently single.

DANCER RELATIONSHIP IDEALS

Nearly all the dancers gave comparable responses when describing their ideal relationship. Similar to the current literature on non-deviant relationships, such qualities as financial security, honesty, monogamy, sense of humor and attractiveness were identified as desired partner characteristics.[3] When asked about their ideal partner, both alone and in groups, many women enumerated these character-istics. Overall, dancers appeared particularly concerned with two qualities: being treated with respect, and financial security. Financial stability/ambition was the first response and was given by nearly all the dancers. Most seemed particularly exercized over this issue. In addition, nearly all dancers fervently expressed the importance of being treated with respect and appreciation. Even though other characteristics such as attractiveness were mentioned, a great deal of time was spent discussing the importance of financial responsibility and appreciative treatment. These two traits dominated both individual interviews and group discussions, solicited the most counterexamples, and appeared to be the most emotionally contentious. As Shanna, who has danced for two years, stated, 'Well, first his ass can't be broke. Nigga better have a damn job cuz I ain't supporting him ...' Similarly, Tia, a dancer for over five years, said, 'My guy? He'd better keep a damn job – do something with himself, rather than sit on the damn couch all day. Cuz I'm for real. I need a man who can do for himself and do for me ... I won't put up with any bullshit from a man.'

In addition to the importance of financial stability, dancers consis-tently stated that being treated well was a primary concern. Tia stated '... and he better do right by me. I can't put up with no bullshit ...' Other dancers gave similar responses, including 'he'd treat me right,' 'he'd be good to me,' and 'treat me like a lady deserves to be treated.'

DANCER RELATIONSHIP REALITIES

Further discussion revealed why these women appeared particularly concerned with issues of financial security and kind treatment: nearly all dancers reported having had several relationships in which both of these qualities were lacking. Whereas other traits were mentioned, the characteristics of respectfulness and financially responsibility prompted emotionally intense and lengthy discussion. Importantly, these traits were also associated with the disclosure of repeated counterexamples. A recurrent theme revealed in both observation and interviews was a pattern of abusive, exploitative, degrading, or stressful romantic relationships for women involved in exotic dance.

Dancers regularly indicated having been the sole provider in their relationships, 'taking care of a man.' Ironically, such partners seemed to condemn the dancer's occupation, while reaping the financial gain: Tia stated, 'he'd always give me shit about dancing … but never had any trouble spending my money.' Savannah, who danced regularly for five years, describes her partner: 'He'd make me feel like crap about dancing, but who paid for our trip? Me. He never paid a cent for the whole week [of vacation]. But "I don't want you to work" [sarcastically]. Yeah, right. When are you gonna pay the bills?'

Approximately 54 percent of dancers reported similar experiences, in which they were made to feel guilty about their occupation while simultaneously being the sole or primary financial provider.[4] Both observations and interviews reveal a consistent pattern of dancers working to compensate for the intermittent employment of their partners.

Dancers regularly reported incidents in which the profits they made from dancing were used to pay the child support, court costs, or other financial burdens of their partners. In addition, many indicated that their romantic partners were verbally or psychologically abusive, using insult specifically related to the dancer's occupation. Often, this abuse took the form of using the occupation as an insult, in effect equating the occupational title to that of 'slut' or 'bitch.'

Many dancers reported constant feelings of guilt associated with their work. Yet these feelings appeared to be triggered by their partner's actions. Although not all of these actions were overt, these tactics were strong sources of guilt and shame, and became particularly stressful for the dancers.

Partners' tactics include pouting, sulking, or withdrawal. These behaviors appear to occur in relation to dancing activity. These behaviors were displayed immediately prior to or after the woman participated in dancing, in order to invoke guilt or shame associated with her career. Whether strategically or emotionally motivated, such behaviors were specifically related to the social stigma of sex work. For example, one dancer described her two-year relationship thus:

> Every fight, he'd throw my fuckin' job out there. 'Well at least I'm not grinding on some guy's lap. You're out there practically jerking guys off. How am I supposed to feel?' And shit, what can I say to that? He would be totally cool about my job, but then throw it in my face when he needed to get one up on me. I just got so sick of defending myself.

71

Dancer interviews illustrate a consistent pattern, in which the use of a dancer's occupation is used by her partner to provoke feelings of guilt and establish or maintain partner control. Comparable to their experiences in the larger social environment, dancers must continually confront stigmatization in their romantic relationships. That is, within their relationships, intentionally or unintentionally, dancers are made to feel 'deviant' or immoral.[5] Whereas romantic relationships are often considered a source of comfort and support, for many dancers these relationships become an additional source of shame and ridicule. One dancer described her partner's behavior thus:

> He would refuse to touch me at all until I had a shower. He'd always make this face like he was disgusted and say – you smell like a strip club. And he wouldn't even give me a hug or kiss until I'd had a hot shower and scrubbed my entire body. It's like I was dirty. I'd always feel so dirty, even though I knew he was just doing it to make me feel bad and quit. But I'd feel like shit anyway ...

The techniques previously described are unique in that they are specifically related to a partner's occupation. Indeed, in any relationship partners may be unsatisfied with characteristics related to a partner's occupation (spending less time at home, making less money). Yet control techniques in dancer relationships are inherently related to the occupation itself, in that being involved in this career is shameful or identifies them as 'bad,' and thus deserving of poor treatment.

All of the dancers interviewed stated that there was 'nothing wrong' with their occupation. They openly expressed their disdain for 'conventional thinking' and argued for freedom and control over their sexuality. They spoke openly about their desire and their right to have partners that both understand their occupation and treat them with respect; their ideal relationships that are not financially or emotionally abusive.

Yet their descriptions of their actual relationships suggest that partner guilt and manipulation techniques are effective to some extent. Given that nearly all dancers reported having these experiences in their current or former relationships; it appears that dancers are repeatedly unsatisfied with their romantic relationships. Moreover, this dissatisfaction is directly related to their involvement in exotic dance. Women in exotic dance are working in both a relatively lucrative and a relatively deviant career. Thus, the structure of this career (and other sex-related occupations) uniquely provides opportunities for relationships with partners that further stigmatize them and financially exploit them.

EXPLAINING RELATIONSHIP STRESS

Understanding how the relationships of exotic dancers become so troubled necessitates an investigation of partners' perceptions. To this end, the current study draws on information from interviews and informal conversations with 19 current or former partners of dancers (see methods above).[6] All conversations with partners were conducted one-on-one, either outside of the club setting, in an isolated location in the club, or over the telephone. This was done to ensure the confidentiality of responses and to avoid any influence by the dancer or other individuals on the partners' responses.

During these conversations, partners were asked to talk about themselves, their occupation, and other demographic information. In addition, partners spoke about their current or former relationship, characterized their current or former partner, and discussed their feelings regarding exotic dance. The following paragraphs compare the women's and men's responses to the questions regarding what impact, if any, dancing had had on their relationship.

Whereas many dancers reported being verbally abused with the 'dancer insult,' they frequently admitted feeling shame and guilt. That is, rather than attributing the negative comments they heard to their partner's character, dancers often instead responded by accepting this negative assessment. When asked why they responded in this manner, many dancers appeared to sympathize with their partner's position.

Sarah, a dancer for almost two years, stated, 'I know it has to be hard on him. I can see why a guy would have issues.' Raquelle, who has danced for three years, said, 'I can see it's a job and it's no big deal, but most guys just won't get that. They can't see that. All they see is their woman on top of some other dude.'

Thus, one recurrent theme in exotic dancer relationships is differential role-taking. That is, dancers can take the role of the generalized other, and indeed sympathize with the concerns and perspective of their partners. In other words, they can imagine what their partners must feel like.

Interviews and observations with dancers provide substantial support for differential role-taking. The following field note describes such an example:

Nikita describes a stressful interaction with a customer, in which he kept touching her, and himself, inappropriately. She says something like,

'I look back during my lap[dance], and he's touching his dick ... he fuckin' came [ejaculated] on me ...' Her boyfriend, Dan, gets angry. He makes a face to indicate that he is disgusted with her. He says something like, 'I can't fucking believe you,' and storms outside. Nikita goes after him, apologizing.

This observation illustrates the contradiction between the requirements of erotic labor and the societal norms of female sexual exclusivity and male sexual privilege. Specifically, in performing her occupational duties, Nikita arouses another male. This violates her partner's expectation of sexual ownership. Dan, rather than sympathizing with her negative experience, condemns her for the behavior of another male, her customer. That is, he feels betrayed, as if she violated his sexual ownership rights by allowing herself to become victimized. To Dan, her sexuality belongs to him, and she is required to maintain his exclusivity at all costs. Thus her sexual violation becomes not about her, but an affront to his masculinity and sexual privilege.

This example also demonstrates Nikita's role-taking behavior. She begins by describing a situation that is stressful and upsetting to her. However, she quickly becomes apologetic to her partner; she is apologizing for her own victimization. In doing so, she is empathizing with her partner's distress rather than experiencing her own. She discussed her negative experience, seeking sympathy and comfort. Yet she received none of these from her partner. Rather, her partner's concerns become the focus of her attention. She must now deal not only with her own stressful experience, but with the additional burden of soothing her partner.

Furthermore, observations such as this reveal a relative lack of dancer role-taking among partners. Dan, rather than taking the perspective of the dancer and sympathizing with Nikita's degrading and stressful experience, becomes enraged at his partner for her apparent 'deviant' behavior. Thus, although dancers often took the role of the partner, and were able to imagine the feelings and perspective of the men with whom they were involved, their partners appeared either unwilling or able to accomplish this. Excerpts from an email interview with Brad, a former partner of an exotic dancer, express the males' lack of identification with the role of their female partners: 'I just couldn't get over it. No guy wants to be the chump who's [whose] girlfriend is grinding naked all over other guys all night. I look like a sucker ... I'd just feel like she was wronging me. I should be the only one to see that [her naked body].'

These and similar comments from male partners demonstrate that these men identify with the perspective of *clients*, not *workers*. Rather than taking the perspective of the women performing job tasks, men often see through the eyes of customers. As a result, both are competing consumers of her sexuality. For partners, customers are seen as trespassers, and women are seen as enabling or enticing others to consume property which does not belong to dancers, but to their partners. For some partners, access to a dancer's body and eroticism is the exclusive right of her partner; it is not hers to display, use, or sell. Thus, when women engage in exotic dance, partners feel violated, and disgrace dancers for selling what they see as their possession. The lack of reciprocated emotional support and the perception of inequitable power distribution could be the reason for the persistent relationship dysfunctions experienced by those in exotic dance.

The work of exotic dance involves anticipating the needs, concerns, or desires of others; having the ability to 'take the view of the other' and anticipate what a potential customer may want is a lucrative strategy and may be essential in dancer careers. Thus, it is not surprising that dancers become very adept at seeing the perspective of the generalized other. Their partners, in contrast, may or may not have occupations that require this skill. Interviews with partners suggest that many, when discussing the employment of their partner, either cannot or will not engage in role-taking behavior; they can only or will only see the role of the customer. Because he identifies with the other male patrons, dancing for the romantic partner becomes a challenge to his masculinity:

> I felt like she was cheating on me. I mean, who wants to see their girlfriend putting her boobs in another guy's face? And he gawking and staring at her. He's treating her like a whore and she's ok with that? Yeah, yeah, it's like no big deal to her, but I get a lot of shit about [he gets teased by his friends].

DANCER RELATIONSHIP MANAGEMENT

How do women negotiate the apparently contradictory demands of the role of stripper and the role of girlfriend/wife? Ultimately, many women simply 'gave in,' and conceded to their partner's control tactics. Although, as previously mentioned, dancers initially refuted negative characterizations of their careers and outwardly stated that they were not doing anything wrong, most did not condemn their partners' actions as unjust or unduly deserved. Rather, they seemed to accept condemnation as unavoidable, rationalized their partners' behavior, and accommodated the stigmatization. Nearly all of the former dancers interviewed reported that these tactics and romantic difficulties were influential in their decision to terminate their careers, accepting the perspective of their partners. Others accommodated their partners by working intermittently or even hiding their involvement.

Sarah, married to an accountant, says of her decision to exit the profession: 'I would love to dance. But he always gave me so much shit about it. I know if I do it again it'll be a fight. So it's not worth it. If he wasn't here, I'd be dancing. Sometimes I think about going and doing it when he's outta town and I won't get caught.'

In this way, these women succumb to the 'shaming' of their partners. Interestingly, they quit or hide their occupations out of guilt and a desire to avoid 'feeling badly.' Although they may personally enjoy what they do and perhaps take pride in their work, they nonetheless feel shameful. Perhaps these women subscribe, at least to some degree, to the assessment put forth by their partners, or at least sympathize with the perspective of their partners. Erin, a dancer for over five years, describes a common phenomenon:

> They all say they're cool with you being a dancer. That's when they're trying to get you to fuck them. But then the minute things are going great they want you to quit. It's like the second they say 'I love you' they get possessive and jealous and all the sudden what you're doing [dancing] is bad.

In other words, many dancers enjoy their work. Yet, they feel guilty about enjoying their work because of the larger social stigma surrounding strippers. This macro-level stigma is played out on a micro level through dancers' relationships with their partners. Metaphorically, partners act as the social mirror, continually confronting dancers with the larger social stigma surrounding their work. While some dancers continually struggle between their work and relationship expectations, others find resolution. Some resolve this conflict by accepting the negative characterizations of stripping and disassociating from that identity – that is, hiding or terminating their careers.

MODIFYING PARTNER CRITERIA-SELECTION OF 'INSIDERS'
Whereas many women involved in exotic dance accommodate their partner's use of the 'dancer insult' and perceive negative treatment or relationship stress as inevitable because of their occupation, other dancer

utilize a different strategy in order to manage romantic involvements while maintaining sex work careers. Essentially, many women simply modify their criteria for selection of a romantic partner. Some 20 of the 37 dancers interviewed stated that they often selected 'insiders.' Many of these dancers reported intentionally selecting a partner for his capability to see a dancer's perspective and to avoid the stigmatization of dancing. Of the men interviewed, eight were currently or previously involved in the exotic dance or sex work industry.

In addition to the partners that participated in the study, many dancers indicated that they were, at one time or another, involved with bouncers, deejays, bartenders, club owners, male dancers or other staff members. Some of this is because these people are around and accessible. Dating in the workplace is not a feature unique to dancers. However, dancers seem particularly motivated to seek someone 'in the business' in order to avoid the negative experiences associated with 'outsiders.' Dancers avoid the stigma associated with sex work by intentionally seeking relationships within the sex industry. These partners (fellow workers) share the 'inside perspective'; these partners share the dancers' perspective regarding their work.

In the strip club, many behaviors and discussions by dancers and staff are intended to appease the clientele, whereas more genuine feelings and behavior are reserved for display before a limited number of similar others. Similar to Goffman's (1959) conceptualization of 'front stage' versus 'back stage,' dancers frequently put forth an image in front of customers, while acting very differently among their fellow dancers and club staff (Spivey, 2005). Dancing involves quite a lot of both front-stage and back-stage behavior, and those who witness or engage in back stage behavior seem to regard themselves as privileged relative to those who do not. This could be a coping mechanism adopted in response to the stigma outsiders attach to the dancer's devalued master status: the creation of a safe haven amongst insiders to gain much needed self-acceptance.[7]

Because they themselves are often involved in the 'back-stage' behaviors associated with strip clubs, fellow dancers, bouncers, deejays, and management are more likely to see the genuine feelings and behaviors of the women involved in exotic dance. As 'insiders,' these men view customers with disdain and distance themselves from the role of the customer. They come to view exotic dance similarly to the dancer – they regard dancing as work: 'My wife is totally hot. She's a sexy chic [chick]. I told her it's totally cool. I want her to go and have fun. It's not like she's fucking around or something. It's hard work. Why would I have a problem with it?' (Jon, a former dancer). Another stated, 'Dude, it's fine. I got no issues. It keeps her in shape and lets her get her frustrations out. Besides, we got kids to feed and this job lets her work only a night or two a week. Shit, I'd do it myself if I could. I danced a couple times. But dudes don't make shit' (Johnny, a deejay at a strip club).

The selection of fellow 'insiders' is a useful strategy to avoid the career-specific control tactics often experienced when dancers are involved with non-deviant partners. 'Insider' partners share a similar 'worldview' with dancers. Whereas non-deviant partners identified with the customers, 'inside' partners repeatedly identified with dancers, and distanced themselves from customers.

While this strategy is effective at avoiding stigmatization, it is not without disadvantages as well. These relationships are positive in terms of how males regard their dancer partners, yet these partners (just as in their relationships with 'outsider' partners) struggle over issues such as age, financial security, drug dependency, and criminal involvement. Men involved in sex work consistently make less money than women. Bouncers, deejays, and bartenders in this study were no exception. These women trade objective qualities (money, attractiveness, and sobriety) for acceptance of the dancer's deviant career.

MODIFYING PARTNER CRITERIA: THE SELECTION OF 'LOWER-QUALITY PARTNERS'

The popular culture generally agrees that attractive and sexy women have an advantage when it comes to dating. Furthermore, the literature on relationships lends support to the belief that attractiveness increasing the number of available and interested partners as well as increasing the objective quality of partners. That is, those who are more attractive have higher-quality partners available to them (Chapdelaine et. al., 1999; Johnson, 2005). One might conclude from that notion that exotic dancers, who are generally considered to be attractive (to at least some extent, it is a job requirement), would have their pick of partners, and thus form relationships with men they perceive to be of high quality. In contrast, the literature on exotic dance finds that dancers experience considerable stigma in their interactions with the larger social world. In addition, this implies that dancers may confront stigma when seeking romantic partners.

As previously stated, many of the women interviewed dismissed the negative stereotypes associated with dancers. However, when pressed, many women admitted to having mixed feelings about the morality of their jobs. Dancers frequently stated that they could understand how others thought dancing was acceptable for particular 'types' of women (single women, women without children, young women, women in college, etc.), but not appropriate for others (wives, mothers, affianced women). Ironically, many of these same women were the latter 'type' of women. Moreover, these 'mixed' feelings seemed to related to the interpersonal relationship roles they identified with. In other words, these women experienced moral role conflict. They struggled with their desire to take pride in their work and their internalized guilt about not meeting the expectation of potential high-quality partners regarding how a 'good' wife or girlfriend should behave.

One way many women resolved this conflict was by seeking partners who would not place those expectations on them. Seeking partners without such expectations allowed these women to engage in their vocation with less condemnation. That is, many dancers specifically selected partners based on their desire to avoid stigmatization, rather than based on partner-specific attributes (attractiveness, intelligence, financial security, etc.). Perhaps women from a variety of stigmatized groups (with particular professions or characteristics, that is; Harris, 1990) accept lesser partners than maybe they deserve – equivalent in terms of status, but lesser on some dimensions. Indeed, research finds that partner selection is strongly related to the availability of alternatives, as well as an individual ideal (Crawford et al., 2003). Finding a mate a matter is not simply of what type of partner one may 'deserve,' but of what is the best available, given one's options.

What makes this circumstance unique is the burden of the internalized 'deviant label.' That is, women who, were it not for their profession, would otherwise have their choice of very high-quality partners appear often to select poor quality partners. Approximately one third of male partners were significantly older than the women with whom they were romantically involved. The average age of dancers was 25.5 years, while the average age of partners was 34.8 years. Many partners had drug, alcohol, or health problems.

Over half of the partners interviewed were unemployed or intermittently employed. Employment among male partners was not related to age. However, whereas most dancers reported dating significantly older partners, few had financially stable partners. In fact, most dancers were the sole or primary providers in the relationship. While the class background of dancers was not specifically addressed in the study, all of the women interviewed were working in highly lucrative careers. Thus, they shared a common socioeconomic status, and they all expressed their desire for financially secure partners.

These partners were qualitatively less attractive, older, and less financially stable than the women with whom they were involved. Thus, it appears that many dancers are willing to accept partners with fewer objective attributes than themselves.

Perhaps the label 'dancer' lowers these women's 'partner attraction status,' in that they perceive, at least to some degree, that these 'low-quality' partners are the best they can get if they want to find partners who will accept their profession. Although they may objectively be 'lower' in terms of attractiveness, financial stability, drug dependency, age, and so on, these partners become equalized by being in a normative profession but accepting of a deviant-status partner. In this way, many dancers sacrifice other aspects of preference for acceptance of the deviant label and their ability to maintain power and continue in their career without internalized shame.

Several dancers demonstrated their willingness to accept 'lower-quality' partners in exchange for the continuation of their dance careers, or in an effort to minimize the stigma of exotic dance. This appeared to be particularly the case for dancers who had been involved in dancing for long periods of time. As one dancer explains,

> I'm not trying to sounds like a snotty bitch, but I know he'll at least treat me right and not give me any shit about dancing. He's a lot older than I am, and, I mean, I'm not trying to be mean, but I'm like the best looking girl he'll get. It's like he's lucky to get me, and he knows it. So he knows better than to rag me [complain] about dancing.

Angel, a dancer of five years, gives a similar account of her romantic choices:

> I'd rather be an old man's sweetheart than a young man's fool. Every time I was with a guy who was young and hot and had money, he'd treat me like shit. It was like, 'She's a dancer. She's a slut. I can treat her like shit. That's all she's worth.' So, my old man now, he's a biker and shit, and maybe he ain't all that to look at, but he sees me like this hot chick who's outta his league. He calls me a dancer, not no stripper.

Rather than modifying their criteria, many women simply did not become romantically involved. Of the 37 women interviewed, roughly 38 percent were single, with no current involvement. Many of them describe their singlehood as inevitable. These women perceive that their career precludes them from having successful relationships with high-quality partners. As one dancer, Jade, states: 'I just can't deal with the bullshit ... so why bother? [and in response to the question *'What do you mean by bullshit?'*] Y'know ... the crap. Sooner or later it comes back to what I do [dancing]. So it becomes more hassle than it's worth.' Similarly, Savanna, a long-time dancer said: 'Every guy wants to fuck a dancer ... but no guy wants to *marry* one.'

In this sense, the label 'dancer' became accepted as marking a deviant status. Statements such as these suggest that dancers often do subscribe to similar ideals to those of 'higher-quality' potential partners (of financially stable, attractive, successful, 'typical' men) and society at large, and accept the typification of women and the stereotyping of women's roles. This finding suggests the old adage, 'Party with the bad girl, but marry the good girl.' This suggests that although these women may overtly attempt to manage stigma by rejecting the negative stereotypes about dancers, these women, at least to some extent, feel that they are 'bad girls' and that good, moral women don't engage in this behavior. Thus, they accept condemnation and either avoid romantic involvement altogether or seek out individuals who are their 'equals.'

Discussion

Our study found that dancers are frequently involved in poor romantic relationships, and that their careers are a significant source of romantic stress. Thus, there appears to be a paradox, in that women involved in an industry that selects and rewards participants based upon attractiveness, and who therefore are themselves generally attractive, often have low-quality partnerships. Based upon appearances, these women would seem to be able to have any partner of their choosing; yet they are often in poor-quality, abusive, exploitive, or troubled relationships.

Dancers often reported that romantic involvement is a significant source of stress, and is strongly related to their occupations. Women in this occupation have serious difficulties balancing their partners' expectations and the demands of their work. Additionally, interviews suggest that some of this relationship stress is related to differences in role-taking behaviors, or the inability of male partners to take the perspective of workers.

Moreover, we describe the variety of interpersonal and intrapersonal adaptation patterns employed by dancers and their partners to confront relationship norm violations. While many dancers explicitly rejected male dominance of female sexuality and conventional relationship norms, many reluctantly admitted to subscribing to gender-specific norms regarding heterosexual relationships and male exclusive sexual privilege. That is, dancers often strongly believed that their occupation was not genuinely intimate, and thus should not be an issue in their relationships. Nevertheless, many of these same dancers also indicated that they often accepted guilt or ridicule from their male partners. Yet rather than blaming their partners, many dancers regarded this negative treatment as an inevitable product of their occupations. Examining partner and dancer descriptions of relationships, this study found stigma management techniques which aid in or hinder relationship persistence.

More broadly, this study suggests that 'deviant' females may be perpetually denied the opportunity to 'marry up'. Once a woman is labelled deviant, this label carries over into other aspects of her life beyond her employment. She is a stripper at all times, whether at work or not, especially when dating. In other words, although dancers may have no shortage of potential casual dates or lovers, they have few, if any, available 'high-quality', long-term partners. Consequently, dancers often adjust their relationship strategies to increase the likelihood of long-term commitment by seeking out what they acknowledge to be 'lower-quality' partners, feeling that this is a sacrifice they must make in order to negotiate both a relationship and a deviant career. Despite seemingly explicit changes in popular culture, and the ostensible de-stigmatization of sex work careers, popularized by the media and the glamorization of sex workers, the times have not truly changed. With the increasing number of women becoming involved in sex work careers, and the 'mainstreaming' of the sex work culture, more women may be potentially limiting their long-term relationship opportunities. Thus, although significant strides have been made to de-stigmatize sex work careers, the stigma of sex work is perpetuated in male perceptions of romantic relationships.

The current study was limited to heterosexual relationships. While bisexual and lesbians are represented among sex workers, the majority of women we encountered are ultimately seeking male partners; thus, we could not obtain a sufficient number of lesbian, bisexual, and transgendered dancers and/or partners for adequate comparison. Ideally, we would have liked to compare heterosexual relationships to same-sex and other sexual-minority relationships among strippers; however, the data simply did not allow this. Although some dancers performed same-sex acts for shows or upon customer request ('girl–girl shows'), all but one of the women interviewed sought heterosexual romantic relationships. Currently, we can only speculate about the negotiations of sexual-minority women and their partners. We suspect they face an entirely different set of challenges.

Previous literature has examined socio-demographic characteristics of partner selection such as race and ethnicity (South, 1991; Spanier & Click 1980). However, consistent with much of the previous literature on dancers, the majority of women involved in the current study were white. Indeed, there is limited research that addresses potential differences in sex work correlates across women of color, and the current study is similarly limited. We simply did not have sufficient ethnic variation for inter-ethnic comparison.

Additionally, social psychological literature suggests that, when choosing a partner for marriage, men and women will self-select people of a similar class or with shared occupations (Dinitz et al., 1960; Williams et al., 1999). However, women make class-based decisions when they date, while men typically make partner selection based on physical attractiveness (South, 1991).

Our study did not fully explore potential class-related outcomes for two reasons. First, our study was specifically focused on the women's stigma management strategies as they relate to dancing. Certainly there are a number of reasons why women select partners; we could only feasibly explore one aspect. Second, women from a variety of socio-demographic backgrounds are involved in exotic dance (Sweet & Tewksbury, 2000; Ronai & Ellis, 1989; Burana, 2001). That is, involvement in stripping is not necessarily class-based. The current study did not differ in this regard; women interviewed had a variety of socioeconomic backgrounds prior to their entry into exotic dance. Thus, it appears that at least some of the challenges these women experienced in partner selection were profession-based, rather than class-based.

Importantly, this study points out that the difficulties of those involved in stigmatized occupations extend beyond their interactions with their larger social environment. The 'deviants' are frequently involved emotional, physically, and psychologically with 'non-deviant' others. Thus, this study highlights the importance of partners in sex work advocacy. Sadly, despite the many successes of sex work activist organizations, most activism has been limited to political and legal action. While continuing these efforts is certainly important to create macro-level social change, these findings call for micro-level advocacy as well. The existence of organizations specifically created for intimates of other stigmatized groups, such as Parents, Families, and Friends of Lesbian and Gays (PFLAG) and Al-Anon (for family and friends of alcoholics), demonstrates the necessity of getting partners and intimates involved in confronting the stigma of 'deviant' groups, and that stigmatization is not limited to outside the home. Helping partners come to terms with and become supportive (if not outspoken advocates) of these occupations is an essential step toward improving the quality of life for sex workers.

NOTES

1 Most men (n=15) were current or former partners of the dancers participating in this study. However, some male participants (n=4) were current or former partners of dancers who declined or were unable to participate in this study.

2 The characterization of a relationship as 'serious long-term or cohabitating' is based on the dancers' perceptions of the relationship as 'long-term,' rather than on a specific time criterion. The actual length of such relationships ranged from approximately two to twelve years.

3 Many answers were consistent with ideal partner attributes in general, and as such are not unique. Therefore, they are not presented. Typically, in addition to their concern over respect and financial security, most dancers made such statements as ' a good sense of humour,' 'he should be attractive.' One dancer stated, 'He'd be Brad Pitt with a sense of humor, and good in bed.'

4 Some 20 of the 37 women interviewed stated that they had been involved or were currently involved in a relationship in which they were shamed by their partner but provided the sole or primary financial support.

5 Many people may consider the label 'deviant' as synonymous with 'bad' or 'immoral.' However, among sociologists, the term 'deviant' is used to identify behavior that exists outside conventional norms (Thio, 1998; Becker, 1963). Following this tradition, we utilize the term to distinguish sex work as a stigmatized profession, not to infer any negative evaluation of sexual labor.

6 Five of the partners were recruited through previous contact; I had already known these individuals through my previous involvement in exotic dance research. The remaining fourteen partners were previously unknown to me and were recruited specifically for this study.

7 Many of the male insiders stated that they also selected dancers. This finding suggests that males involved in exotic dancing too may experience stigmatization in their relationships (see Tewksbury, 1993).

5 Sex and the Unspoken in Male Street Prostitution

Kerwin Kaye

Although the overwhelming majority (around 80 percent) of male prostitutes work through agencies or by placing their own ads (Allman, 1999; Leigh, 1994), most studies of male prostitution focus upon young men who work on the street.[1] Remarkably, these studies seldom identify the dynamics of poverty and street-level violence as important elements of their examination. Investigations of male sex work – few though they are – tend to follow studies of female prostitutes in focusing almost exclusively upon sexual aspects of 'the life.' While these studies might make reference to the notion that poverty forces individuals into prostitution, they generally do not discuss the other consequences of this poverty, and the manner in which it shapes both social networks on the street and conflict within those networks.

Meanwhile, studies which do examine the dynamics of male street life typically do not examine questions of prostitution or other issues related to sexuality. A dominant theme within this literature consists of specifying the social mores of the most violent participants within street society, particularly gang members and drug dealers. Many of the contemporary classics of urban ethnography such as works by Anderson (1990, 1999), Bourgois (1996), Jankowski (1991), Venkatesh (2000), Wacquant (2003), and Williams (1992) direct attention toward the most aggressively masculine men on the street. Ethnographies within this genre typically fail to document situations in which the masculine identity of young urban men is compromised, or situations in which these men act against locally hegemonic versions of masculinity, leaving only the image of the 'young tough.' To the limited extent that sexuality is considered within these narratives, the imagery is heterosexual and tends to reinforce an iconography of male domination, as in Anderson's (1990) analysis of black male interest in 'sexual conquest,' Williams's (1992) narration of male-controlled sex-for-crack exchanges, or

Bourgois's (1996) description of gang rape among urban adolescents.[2] The focus upon the most macho and terrifyingly brutal aspects of street life is perhaps understandable given the socially problematic nature of the behaviors described, as well as the power these men exercise within the street environment. However, in the absence of a more fully developed literature documenting less violent aspects of urban males' lives, these masculinized ethnographies run the risk of reinforcing an image of underclass men as dangerous, hypermasculine reprobates.

Not surprisingly, then, there is little crossover between the literatures that explore male prostitution and those that examine the dynamics of men's life on the street. The texts do not cite one another, and even more interestingly, their various protagonists – the sexualized male prostitute victim and the hypermasculine drug-dealing gang member – do not appear together. An artificial divide exists between these two sets of writings, despite the simple facts that (a) men prostituting on the street encounter and participate in a masculine economy of violence and threat which shapes their daily interactions; (b) many men prostituting on the street form loose cliques which might engage in a variety of illegal acts; and (c) at least a few male gang members also engage in prostitution (the practice was even relatively commonplace throughout the 1950s and 1960s; see Allen, 1980; Kaye, 2003; Reiss, 1987 [1961]). Mass media representations of young men on the street similarly present two divergent foci, one upon the sexualized victim status of the (white) prostitute, and another upon the non-sexualized predator status of the (non-white) gang member, drug dealer, etc. The dissimilar nature of these images relates directly to the political projects of the dominant culture which, in a very general way, seeks to 'rescue' and thereby reintegrate deviant white youth, while controlling and excluding deviant youth of color. Given the rapid ascendancy of prisons in contemporary society, it is not surprising to find that reports on 'youth' in general tend to emphasize the violence of youth of color, even though actual youth crime rates are declining (Males 1996, 1999). At the same time, the desire to rehabilitate 'lost' white youth can be seen both in the state focus on providing services for (implicitly white and middle-class) runaway youth, and more generally in the sympathetic portrayal and victim status usually accorded to runaway teens. Thus, the political aim of reintegrating runaways into middle-class trajectories has the effect of authorizing certain discourses regarding male prostitution while marginalizing or completely disallowing others.

The point in identifying these divergent trends within the representation of race and gender on the street is not to suggest that the lives of male street prostitutes exactly resemble those of male gang members, that 'boy prostitutes' are really 'angry young men.' Given the punitive treatment young men of color receive as actual or potential 'gang-bangers,' this could hardly be considered a useful goal. Nor is the point to suggest that male street prostitutes should not be considered sexually exploited victims, as they are most commonly portrayed within both the popular and social scientific literature. Rather, my aim is to highlight the larger political projects which inform not only portrayals created by service agencies and researchers, but also those created by male street-based sex workers themselves. Ultimately, my aim in this regard is three-fold: to illuminate the tropes which have been utilized in the portrayal of male prostitution; to point toward the material and political interests which have shaped those depictions; and to bring forth imagery which has been left out by the dominant tropes.

Directing attention to questions of power and ideology draws out the important fact that hegemonic representations of male street prostitutes are not made by the street workers themselves, but by individuals who work at various service agencies, as well as by journalists and researchers who perform their work through these organizations. In shaping a particular vision of male street prostitution, service providers implicitly define their own status and role within the environment. Seen in this light, the narratives which surround male street prostitutes are often only peripherally related to the experiences and concerns of the sex workers; instead, these narratives act as a useful means through which the authors situate themselves within the social field, both within the street and especially within society as a whole.

The narratives which surround male street prostitution deploy a variety of discourses in contradictory ways in order to achieve their particular effects. One of the central questions around which the narratives cluster concerns the issue of 'agency.' Given the status of free choice within ethical (that is, social) debate, it is not surprising to find heated controversy concerning the agency, or lack thereof, of participants engaged in various disputed practices (Flax, 1995). In establishing that a given population does or does not exercise agency, one makes implicit judgments regarding the status of the activities that define that group. The result of this situation makes the subjectivity of male prostitutes a contested ground of representation, with various sides attempting to 'prove' that street hustlers do or do not exercise agency.

Consequently, male street prostitutes are most typically portrayed as being young (vulnerable/powerless/naïve), drug dependent (emotionally enslaved), sexually abused (emotionally unstable and incapable), economically desperate (powerless), and white, middle-class and perhaps even straight (innocent/worthy of rescue). Alternatively, they might be portrayed as being of age (powerful) and in search of sexual excitement and community (gay and empowered). A third narrative, more noticeable in the past than today, represents male street prostitutes as being of age (powerful), black, latino, and/or working class (dangerous), and lawbreaking (dangerous).

In their voluminous and detailed work concerning male prostitution, West and de Villiers (1993) label these three different depictions of male street prostitutes as 'desperate,' 'homosexual,' and 'dangerous.' In the first depiction, correctly identified by West and de Villiers as dominant within the academic (and social service) literature, male prostitutes are described as runaway youth who turn to prostitution as a last resort. In the second, young men are said to move into prostitution by choice, as a means of exploring their own sexual identity as developing gay men. Finally, male street prostitutes are sometimes envisioned as 'amoral delinquents' who threaten and rob their clients. While West and de Villiers suggest that these three types actually exist on the street, I contend that the various portrayals have as much to do with the political agenda of the authors as they do with actual street life. Each of these portrayals highlights certain facts while underplaying others, implicitly identifying its own problems and suggesting its own solutions in the process (providing services, challenging heterosexism, and facilitating incarceration, respectively). Far from being neutral descriptions, then, these representations of 'life on the street' implicitly serve to advance various types of political claims.

With male gang members and other violent street criminals, for example, journalistic depictions commonly create support for the idea that the individuals involved are in total control of their behavior, thereby justifying any sort of punishment which might follow. The predominant discourse which surrounds male prostitution today, on the other hand, actively disavows the presence of agency. While the assertion of masculine agency facilitates punitive incarceration, the denial of agency in the case of young male prostitutes accomplishes a different series of tasks: it (1) denies the relevance of the participants' experience of a given practice, (2) encourages the adoption of external evaluations of these practices, and (3) justifies control over the lives of participants, ranging from return to one's family to allegedly protective types of custody in extremely rule-bound shelter and treatment facilities. Thus, whereas virtually none of the 'non-masculine' or subordinating experiences of gang members are explored, only these elements are examined in most depictions of male street prostitutes.

This narrative approach runs the risk of reinforcing conservative notions of familial benevolence and of simplistically equating street life with danger, a perspective that fundamentally fails to address why many youth would choose to leave their homes, or why many parents push their children out of their homes. Unsurprisingly, Christian social service organizations tend to incorporate more fully an approach that works to 'restore' a normatively middle-class and family-based lifestyle (see, for example, McGeady 1994, 1996; Ritter, 1988), but academic portrayals often hold 'the family' over and against 'the street' as well (for further critique, see Brock, 1998). At a different level, the image of 'sexually vulnerable youth' may serve to reinforce the fetishization of innocence which partially fuels the sexual market for youth (see Kincaid, 1998).

These ideational difficulties have concrete effects in terms of the nature and distribution of services. While familial restoration or place-ment in a highly controlled treatment facility may serve the needs of some participants, the exclusionary focus on sexual victimization leaves many agencies unable to offer relevant assistance to participants who do not see themselves in such terms. Such representations, then, work to limit the type of help that is available to those on the street, particularly services that are based upon the potential for ongoing prostitution and participation in street life (precisely the premise of 'harm reduction'). Services based upon a model of rescue also tend to result in what is informally known within the service community as 'skimming': the removal of the easiest-to-serve (read: middle-class and obedient) individuals from the street, while leaving disobedient, drug-using, and otherwise 'trouble-causing' individuals without significant aid. Bringing forth new representations of male street prostitution, there-fore, may promote alternative services which are relevant to those whose needs fall outside what is offered by most programs.

The following sections will present five different male street workers who, in various ways, do not fit the dominant narrative of straight-forwardly 'exploited youth' (or other narratives that have been identified), and explore three themes that have been under-examined by the majority of social scientific literature on male prostitution: space and the material underpinning of street life; street relations and emotional instrumentality; and violence and the self-management of identity. The intention is first to reveal some of the tremendous diversity that exists among male street workers, and then to situate their lives within common social conditions, which are often ignored.

This material is based upon nearly nine months of ethnographic field-work in a US West Coast city conducted in intensive but intermittent periods from mid-1999 to mid-2001. Most of this time was spent working with a small harm reduction agency that served male street prostitutes and emphasized a harm reduction approach.[3] Two additional weeks were spent living in a tenement hotel near the primary hustling scene. It also includes the liberal use of three academic works that examine the non-sexual aspects of male street workers' lives: *This Idle Trade* by Visano (1987), *The Times Square Hustler* by McNamara (1994), and *Mean Streets* by Hagan and McCarthy (1998). After presenting this work, I will return briefly to the question of the political foundations that lie beneath representations of male street prostitution, and suggest some possible alternative directions, which might be fruitfully explored in the future.

Five lives, five experiences

Stephen[4] began working in a male Asian massage parlor in New York City immediately after leaving home at age eighteen. Now thirty-one, he describes his childhood as 'difficult, but not terribly abusive.' His gay identity became a major point of contention with his parents during his teen years, and he left home ready for the freedom to explore gay sex. He found a new 'family' (his term) organized around gay sex work: a group of approximately 20 boys and men, mostly white and aged sixteen to twenty-five, who lived together, did drugs together, and hung out with each other on the street while working and playing (the distinction between these two activities being not entirely absolute). Trusting no one over twenty-one unless they were in the group, Stephen found among his friends community, support, affection, and affirmation of his gayness. Stephen did not work on the street as he was able to earn more in the massage parlor ($35 to $40 per trick), but even the off-street work was difficult, and he says sometimes he felt like he was working 'in a sweatshop.'

Unlike other street workers, Stephen did not maintain a strictly 'professional' attitude toward his work. Desperate for affection and gay affirmation, he looked to his clients for these things, even following a few that he liked to their homes as an uninvited guest. At the other end of the spectrum, he sometimes rifled through the wallets of his clients, a fact that caused him to be beaten up a few times. He continued to steal, however, and learned to enlist the support of the house management by talking back to angry victims ('This guy's trying to pull something!'). Stephen says that he experienced 'a lot' of scary situations, nearly getting raped once, but that his attitude (and the attitude of his friends) was overwhelmingly dismissive: 'I was more worried about not being able to work with all the cuts and bruises on my face than anything else. We almost expected to get raped. It was no big deal.' The group would offer support to each other in such situations, 'not by processing and stuff, but just by being there. We'd take them to the hospital where they treated us like shit because we didn't have any money.' Stephen notes that at a certain point the police began to arrest everyone on the street, forcing everyone into the bars. 'Only those folks who couldn't get in kept the stronghold out on the street, but most found a way in despite the difficulty' (either sneaking in or via fake IDs).

Stephen says his entire life revolved around prostitution during these years. He did, however, manage to put himself through college, though the experience was 'entirely alien' for him, divorced as it was from the rest of his life. His upper-middle-class parents gave him money for school, which enabled him to use his earned money only for recreational commodities, particularly drugs. He readily shared his money with his street family, most of whom had significantly less access to cash. The overall lack of income in the network forced the group to live in 'a lousy neighborhood' and in extremely crowded conditions. (Six people each lived in four different flats, 'but people would bring friends if they needed to crash, so there were usually more like ten to fifteen people at a time.') Stephen emphasizes that he was not economically forced to do sex work, and that despite the difficulties he encountered, he found affection and affirmation of his gay identity.

At present, Stephen continues to do sex work, though now he does elite-level outcall, advertising solely through word of mouth. He earns $350 per hour, and uses the money to support his graduate studies at an upper-tier university. He says that he takes a very different attitude toward his work today, keeping it distinct and largely separate from his personal life. He stays in touch with many of his former friends, but infrequent phone calls have replaced the intense bonds that once existed.

Jeremy, a somewhat rundown-looking 33-year-old, speaks at a mile a minute, and seems to be on speed most of the time. He has a difficult time tracking a single topic, and our conversation wanders in and out of coherence. He's very pleasant, but is clearly prone to excitability and anger when talking about any emotional topic. During these flashes, he often stands up quickly and paces for a few seconds before sitting back down. He does not seem directly threatening, but woven within his rambling tales are stories of domestic abuse with prior boyfriends. Jeremy cannot understand why one of his young lovers cried and cried after he hit him several times. He falls deeply in love with boyfriends and does not understand why things never work out, or why some people take 'an attitude' toward him. Nor can he understand why some people victimize each other on the street, though he is together enough to avoid those who do (except for those he loves). At times he nearly cries when relating his story, particularly in relation to boyfriends who have left him, but his emotions change quickly and flash by before any detailed self-exploration occurs.

Jeremy gets a little bit of money from his family, but he generally has little contact with them because they wish to (once again) place him in a mental institution. He also receives a monthly SSI (Supplemental Security Income) check for his disability, but the total amount he receives pays only for his basic expenses, so he works as a prostitute to pay for drugs and other incidentals. Given his age and appearance than many others, he is less able to attract clients than many others; however, he finds enough men who are willing to pay to survive financially, even with (or perhaps because of?) his erratic interpersonal mannerisms. He works most frequently in bars, but he sometimes works on the streets as well. Occasionally, he attempts to work in cruising zones that are not understood to be for prostitution, and expresses frustration at the 'negative attitude' he receives when he asks people for money.

When I see Jeremy at a health clinic several months after our initial interview, he is accepting help from a conservative Christian group of some sort, and is accompanied by a woman in her early twenties. Several of his friends have expressed displeasure at his association with the group, but he doesn't care who helps him, as long as he gets some help. He says that he has been off speed for three days and is still waiting to come down. He decided to quit because the paranoia was becoming too intense: he recalls standing on a street corner for a very long time, afraid to leave. I suggest he stay away from Polk Street if he wants to stay off drugs. He agrees: 'There'd always be people trying to drag me back into it.' Jeremy still jumps from topic to topic during our conversation, but he seems somewhat calmer and more coherent than before.

Kevin is a sixteen-year-old runaway who works on Polk Street in San Francisco. He left home at age fourteen to escape the physical abuse of his father, and speaks with anger about the way social service agencies only allow him to stay for three days before reporting his whereabouts to his family. He knows exactly what he can get from each agency and what their rules are regarding parental notification, information that is shared amongst his peers on the street. He uses speed regularly, and his face is covered with sores that have resulted from compulsive, speed-induced sessions of picking at his skin. He used to be homeless, a situation that exposed him to theft and violence from other homeless youth. More generally, however, other youth acted as sources of friendship and information regarding where to sleep, where to get food, and other details pertinent to survival on the street. One of the reasons Kevin chooses speed over other drugs (the selection of *some* drug seems predetermined) is because 'We have all these great conversations about life and philosophy and stuff. When you're on heroin, all you do is sleep and wake up and then you need to get money. That's your whole life. I don't have to pay to sleep!' Like most other youth, Kevin tends to hang out with others who do the same drug, mostly due to the incompatible paces of life produced by the various substances.

At first, running away for brief periods and getting high on the street offered Kevin a sense of adventurous fun. Drawn further into street life, however, he turned to prostitution after he had left home for a longer period and became desperate for money. Kevin was deeply affected by his experience doing sex work: 'I don't see how anyone with a brain can be bought and sold like a piece of meat and still think of themselves as a whole person,' he offered. 'It took me a long time to get over that, though I'm not through it yet. It will be there forever.' While he used to be certain he was straight, Kevin is no longer so sure: 'I didn't put myself in a crutch to maintain my sexuality as much as I would like ... Every time I saw some guy I felt like I was letting myself down, like I was telling myself I wasn't heterosexual any more ... 'cuz I started to like it sometimes.'

Kevin now spends time hanging out with his friends, especially a 31-year-old named Paul who Kevin calls his sugar daddy. 'He helps me turn tricks,' comments Kevin offhandedly. Though it was not entirely clear to me if Kevin and Paul have ever had sex, I find out later that Paul has a reputation for getting young kids like Kevin high and then having sex with them without a condom, despite the fact that he is HIV positive. Whatever the case, Kevin clearly likes Paul. 'He is not a forceful person. He used to give me stuff all the time, almost like an infatuation I've had with girls before … I would miss hanging out with him if I ever left.' Whatever adversity Kevin faces, however, he wants to make it clear that he is not the victim service agencies make him out to be. 'I've lived my life out here, and I've lived a lot more than most people. I've had a lot of good times too.'

Timothy is hard to hear over the blaring house music he has playing in his room. It's 2:00 a.m., and he is in a heavy sweat from working out and practicing martial arts. Timothy is living in the same tenement hotel as I am, but his room, unlike most of the others, is very clean and well-ordered. His bed is much nicer than the others too – it is clearly not from the hotel – and his stereo seems expensive. And powerful. Knowing how paper-thin the walls are, I wonder how his neighbors can tolerate the noise, but no one seems to be coming by to complain.

When I tell Timothy about my project and ask if he might be interested in doing an interview sometime, he immediately informs me that he can't: 'No way man. I'm planning to write a book about hustling myself,' he says, 'so I don't want to give you all my secrets. I will tell you this, though. Psychologists don't know shit about hustling. They're reading about it in books. That's like trying to learn about swimming by reading.' Having said that he won't disclose anything, Tim nevertheless proves talkative.[5] He tells me he is twenty years old. He was originally from New York City, but he left there three years ago because he's fleeing probation. 'You have to know how to work the police. Like if they stop me and say "Where are you staying?" I tell them, "At the Holiday Inn, motherfucker. D'ya want to see my key?" See, they aren't used to being talked back to, so that takes them off guard.' The whole point seems to be to appear tough and street-savvy. He continues, 'See, that's a hustler. A hustler works the street. There's a difference between hustlers and prostitutes. A hustler will, like, play a straight guy. It's like, some guy comes up and wants to do something, you have to be, "Oh, I don't know. I'm straight. I don't do that." "Well, how about for some extra money?" See, a hustler works the street. A prostitute will be on his belly getting fucked in all of three months, all strung out on crack.'

Timothy jumps around from topic to topic, but the common thread underlying each story seems to be self-promotion. 'See this guy,' he says, quickly flashing me a name in a computerized address book, 'This guy is into some serious shit. Mafia stuff. I saw this guy in Chicago. Me and him are real tight. I could have someone killed if I needed to.'

Timothy says he's been working the streets for 'a long time' now. His current plan is to obtain a fake ID (cost: $300) and obtain a job at a local gay strip club in which the workers also regularly turn tricks. 'I'm young, and I want to do all this before I get to be some old, crusty shit.' Despite his forceful presentation of self, Timothy alludes to difficulties entailed by his choice of life: 'It's great to ride fast, but still, when you crash you wish you were going fifty-five.'

Ernest, age forty-one, is one of the oldest street hustlers I have met. Ernest has been working the streets for years, and Ernest insists he can still obtain tricks. The point is clearly a source of pride for him, and it seems apparent that his identity as a street hustler is tied in with his sense of attractiveness and self-esteem. Nevertheless his body looks somewhat ragged, both from a life on the street and regular speed use.

Not surprisingly, Ernest is a somewhat marginal figure within the network of street workers. Though he knows most of the people in the scene, it appears he never spends much time with them beyond passing conversations on the street. Ernest seems somewhat bitter about his isolation from the social scene, telling me flatly, 'You have to buy your friends out here, either with money or drugs. That's pretty much what people want.' Ernest's one stable contact is his lover, a partner of several years with whom he lives in a nearby hotel. His lover is currently on disability, and the state pays Ernest a small sum to act as his caretaker. The amount is not enough to live on, however, so he supplements the sum by writing fraudulent checks. (I was never sure if these were stolen or forged.) He writes the checks, buys an item of significant value, and then returns it for cash before the store has an opportunity to find out that the check did not clear. Taking care of his lover and check fraud are Ernest's primary sources of income these days, but he remains committed to occasional prostitution, identifying himself more in relation to his work on the street than anything else.

Some of the above five individuals fit fairly well into the three representational strategies identified by West and de Villiers, while some do not. Even individuals who more or less fit, however, exhibit divergent traits which are not part of the standard narratives. Kevin, for example, exemplifies the image of the desperate runaway in many ways, yet his emphatic rejection of a victim identity poses a difficulty for service agency narratives, as does his insistence on the mutuality of the relationship with his sugar daddy/pimp. Stephen, likewise, closely approximates the image of the gay-identified youth who has chosen prostitution as a means of forging gay community and gaining sexual experience with men, yet the various difficulties he encountered with clients (ranging from unrequited desires for a relationship to confrontations over theft) are notably absent from most portrayals of the gay prostitute. And while Timothy presents himself in a manner congruent with the 'dangerous delinquent,' his open homosexuality would seem to give him a problematic relationship with the role of aggressive street tough. Seeing Timothy during one of his self-described 'crashes' also might render him a more vulnerable and less threatening figure.

Yet if the three dominant narratives ignore certain elements of the lives of those who come close to fitting, they render invisible those whose lives are less useful politically. Jeremy, for example, is not only older than most sex workers, but more mentally unstable. Through prostitution he finds a way to live outside of the psychiatric institutions his parents placed him in, as well as the means to participate in a lifestyle of casual sex and drug use which he generally found enjoyable (though his opinion regarding this shifted over time). Meanwhile, Ernest's desire to embody the sexually desirable image of the 'prostitute' extends somewhat beyond his social reach. While all three of these 'outliers' share certain traits – they are all gay-identified and find in prostitution something of a lifestyle or an identity they enjoy – they also have important differences, both in the manner in which they fit into the larger milieu of street hustlers, and in terms of their experiences with clients.

Yet while emphasizing the individuality of each street worker can act as a necessary corrective to the somewhat homogenized portrayals created in the past, an unmitigated focus upon individual experience carries its own dangers. Liberal gestures toward the uniqueness of each person are inadequate if they fail simultaneously to identify structural characteristics within the larger social scene, problems and dynamics with which each individual must contend. Liberal notions of 'uniqueness' also fail to identify patterns in the ways varying groups of individuals tend to come to terms with these structures. In the following section, I therefore examine three structural features of street life that are seldom discussed in the literature on male prostitution. These issues are particularly important given their near invisibility within the hegemonic narrative of the 'exploited teen.' In some ways, what follows may seem to veer into a study of the social dynamics of male street life rather than a study of male street prostitution, but part of my point is precisely that the non-sexual aspects of male street prostitution have been ignored. In order to correct this imbalance, the literature on male prostitution must be augmented by the literature on male street life (and vice versa).

Space and the material underpinning of street life

For those living on the street without many resources, daily activity often revolves around attempting to find what is needed for survival: food, shelter, clothing, bathrooms, and, for many, drugs. The desperation of this search is reflected in the innovation individuals often display in finding spaces, and the rapidity with which opportunities are seized upon. Many shelters and food banks, for example, find themselves having to police the activities that occur in their bathrooms, lest someone begin engaging in behavior whose illegality could threaten the standing of the agency. Similarly, public locales that have been abandoned by their owners have the potential to be quickly taken over and converted into unofficial 'squats' for living or regular 'shooting galleries' where homeless drug users can inject. As homeless people do their best creatively to appropriate their physical environment, utilizing it to meet basic needs, they often find themselves in conflict with shopowners, police, and other stewards of the local territory.

Conflict over bathrooms is an example. Bathrooms serve multiple purposes for many on the street, offering one of the few private spaces that homeless people are able to find. A bathroom can become a site not only for relieving oneself, but also for cleaning up, turning tricks, sleeping, reorganizing one's possessions (especially hidden items such as cash, weapons, or narcotics), and injecting drugs. Conflict over these spaces is pervasive in areas where homeless people congregate. More than one of the restaurants and bars in the local area have installed buzzer systems which prevent all non-authorized access to their bathrooms, hoping, by such a measure, to take away any incentive homeless people might have to enter their premises. Most of the local merchants have opposed the installation of a public toilet in the area, arguing that the facilities will predominantly be used to shoot up and to turn tricks, and that it will draw still more homeless people to the area. As a result, many homeless people urinate in alleyways, and the sight of human faeces on the street is fairly common.

In the course of his work with street hustlers, the director of the agency I worked for, Terry, found that sometimes the guys would use the agency bathroom in order to inject drugs. Terry ended up telling all of the people using his services that the toilet was broken and keeping the door locked. Volunteers and board members were allowed to use the bathroom when no street workers were present, but they were advised not to speak of the subterfuge. Although Terry followed a policy of harm reduction, and was not ideologically opposed to the provision of spaces for 'safer shooting,' he was concerned that the illegal nature of the practice would be discovered by the police, thereby threatening the agency. Terry was also concerned about the possibility of an overdose, a scenario which, though less likely with him present, could be used to shut down the program. Terry chose to lie about the actual status of the bathroom because it was apparent that the clients would beg and plead if they knew of its functionality, and would feel hurt if he denied them access. He made a few exceptions to the rule based on the trust he had established with one or two individuals, but in general he did not allow even non-drug-using clients to use the bathroom. None of the volunteers, including myself, offered any criticism of Terry's policy; instead, we actively collaborated with the manoeuver by not asking for the keys when clients were around.

The lack of basic amenities clearly does not affect all male street workers equally. For example, Kevin only prostituted sporadically, finding it too distasteful to engage in on a more regular basis. Like many other runaway youth, Kevin confronted a seemingly endless series of desperate situations as he struggled to survive. However, while most of the young men who prostitute do so only when desperate (Hagan & McCarthy, 1998; West & de Villiers, 1993), Kevin's experience does not reflect the smaller number of individuals who involve themselves in the work on a more fulltime basis. Indeed, for this smaller group, sex work can provide a means through which they are able to support themselves in much greater comfort than many of those around them. Timothy, for example, had never been homeless in his entire street career, at least according to his version of events. 'This is the lowest I've been,' he said during our discussion, gesturing to the unblemished hotel room surrounding him, 'and this ain't so bad.' For those who are able to prostitute successfully on a fulltime basis, the work can provide a relatively stable source of income. Stephen's earnings from the massage parlor, which he pooled with his friends who worked on the streets, enabled him to live in a shared apartment. While the amount of money varied, and might seem low in relation to middle-class standards, it is a great deal more than is available through most other options on the street. Even by seeing only one to three clients a day, most sex workers are able to lead lives that are considerably easier than the lives of those who do not engage in prostitution. As an adolescent male street prostitute in Hagan and McCarthy's (1998) study explained:

> I'm a young urban professional ... like I go out, I make some money ... I mean I don't sit there and panhandle and get all of maybe twenty bucks a day. I get all of twenty bucks a half-hour ... So, uhm, I'm a 'yuppie' street person in a sense ... I can afford to live, and they're literally surviving. We are all really just surviving, because none of us know how to live. All we know how to do is survive, except we [those of us in the sex trade] survive a bit easier. (ellipses in original; p. 89)

Like Timothy and Stephen, this youth's experience on the street is made radically different from Kevin's early ordeals simply by virtue of his access to cash.

Furthermore, street youth who engage in prostitution sometimes obtain access to other resources, which are unavailable to their non-prostitute peers. For example, they may receive invitations from older men – often known as 'sugar daddies' – who seek longer-term relationships (West & de Villiers, 1993). Many young men on the street actively desire such relationships as they offer substantial material benefits over street prostitution. As Weisberg (1985) comments, 'It maximizes personal safety and financial security, and it lessens the psychological and physical demands of numerous anonymous sex partners' (p. 161). While some workers view such relationships as a threat to their independence, in general having a sugar daddy is seen as a prestigious accomplishment: 'It is proof of one's lovability, approval, acceptance, desirability, and smart operating' (Caukins & Coombs, 1976, as cited in Weisberg, 1985, p. 161). Frequently, those with sugar daddies will continue to supplement their income through ongoing street prostitution; however, some who form more stable relationships with their benefactors use the association as a means to leave street life altogether.

For a variety of reasons, not every individual on the streets has equal ability to engage in prostitution. As noted above, the majority of young men on the street, like Kevin, find the idea of having sex with another man personally degrading, resorting to it only during times of extreme need. Others who are more favorably inclined toward prostitution can face other types of barriers. Ernest's participation, for example, was severely limited by his age and relatively low 'bodily capital,'[6] facts which required him to rely primarily upon other activities in order to support himself. Similarly, Jeremy's age and mental difficulties restricted his access to clients. Like Ernest, Jeremy depended upon an outside source of income (his family and monthly disability check) to pay for basic necessities, and he used his prostitution earnings in order to purchase drugs and other incidentals.

There are also differences based on race and class background that shape one's ability to prostitute, particularly for those who seek sugar daddies (who are overwhelmingly white and middle-class themselves). One sugar daddy I spoke with, while sitting in a café on Polk Street, pointed to a noticeably well-groomed young man with middle-class Gap-style clothing who was standing outside and appeared to be hustling. 'That kid is new,' he said. 'He's been well taken care of. He'll be picked up by someone real quick. He's cute, not like some of the other guys out here … Most of the guys [who act as sugar daddies] are looking for someone they can take care of, someone who can be their son.' Another sugar daddy I spoke with wanted to find 'someone who won't bring too much drama into my life,' and reported terminating relationships with youth who stole from him. Terry similarly noted that many of the older men 'pick a kid up and take them home for as long as they can stand them,' kicking out the youth when the 'chaos factor' becomes too great. This preference for stability enables those youth who are most accustomed to middle-class ways of being, and whose habitus is least affected by street life and drugs, to find older men who will sponsor them, while leaving behind others who are more reliant upon the street.[7]

The conditions under which an individual engages in prostitution play a significant role in shaping his experience of sex work. While those who are relatively well off are able to pick and choose their clientele, those who are materially desperate find themselves pressed to accept any opportunity which comes their way. Desperation exacerbates the risk these individuals feel they must take, making them significantly more likely to be arrested, to find themselves with a dangerous client, to accept extra cash for unsafe sex, or simply to have sex with someone they find exceptionally unappealing. The task of formulating these situational or 'class' differences within street life has not been sufficiently explicated in prior work, which tends to treat 'male street prostitutes' or 'street youth' as somewhat homogeneous categories.[8]

Street families and emotional instrumentality

With few economic options available, male street-based sex workers are often pressed to scrutinize one another for their survival needs. Even those who are living like 'street yuppies' need to obtain resources on a daily and sometimes immediate basis, leading many to take an instrumental approach toward other people, which frequently sanctions taking advantage of others. The 'hustler' prototypically embodies this relational orientation, seeking to 'work the streets' by manipulating others and turning every possible situation to his benefit. Those who fail to operate this way run the risk of becoming victims, of becoming mere 'prostitutes,' as Timothy put it.

For those who are new to the street environment, the instrumentality of social life on the street can come as a shock. Unfamiliar with the rules of the street, and unconnected with the street networks that might offer protection, newcomers can become relatively easy targets for muggers and con men (Bresnahan, 1995). 'You can barely trust anyone out here,' Kevin told me. 'Most of the people on the street are just out for themselves. They'll stab you in the back. Ninety percent of them are like that. I found that out the hard way.' (For similar comments, see Visano, 1987, pp. 140–1.) Older, more experienced sex workers sometimes view those who are entering the street scene for the first time as potential resources. Seeing their vulnerability, some hustlers quickly move to offer assistance in orienting the newcomers to the scene. For experienced hustlers, these relationships provide access to a subordinate who can perform undesirable tasks: running errands, creating distractions while others shoplift, acting as lookouts, and carrying drugs or weapons (Visano, 1987). In referring to his own status as a 'newcomer,' Visano describes the power imbalances that operate within these exchanges:

> They expected immediate deference in exchange for cooperation. They would brook no challenge to their instructions. I was advised 'to keep my mouth shut and just listen' even when they hurled insults at me. It was especially difficult listening to seasoned straight hustlers take great

delight in elaborating sordid details about the violence they inflict on clients and various recalcitrant newcomers. Their casual threats of violence reinforce subordination on the part of all outsiders. (p. 53)

Other hustlers approach newcomers with more kind-hearted intentions and approaches. As one experienced hustler remarked: 'We is all in the same shit. You see yourself in these fish. They're scared … I'm human too. I'm tough too, but a pussy cat when I see a really young boy looking around. No place to go. They's just cruisin' for a bruisin'' (Visano, 1987, pp. 135–6). Nevertheless, in almost all cases of tutelage, it is expected that the newcomer will form a relationship that materially benefits the more experienced partner, not only through the performance of subordinate tasks, but also by paying a cut of his earnings as he learns how to prostitute (Hagan & McCarthy, 1998). These relationships are not entirely one-sided, however. Newcomers gain food and shelter during their critical orientation phase, and also learn the skills which they require in order to become independent (Visano, 1987). After a few weeks of apprenticeship, newcomers typically seek to redefine their relationships and place themselves onto equal footing with their teachers (Visano, 1987).

The early phases of a relationship also can become a time of testing as one individual attempts to see if he can manipulate the other to his benefit. In my own work dispensing syringes, I was repeatedly asked by the young men who visited if I could give them additional syringes, despite the fact that they knew the agency's policy specifying that needles must be traded on a one-for-one basis.[9] Terry likewise advised me not to dispense any cash as 'It would change your relationship with the kids forever. You'd be just another resource and nothing else.' Terry also warned me to be on guard against any attempt to obtain anything illicitly from either me or the agency. Although the decided majority of the young men did not attempt to steal anything, the possibility was sufficiently present to necessitate increased policing activity on our part, as well as to produce a heightened guardedness between the sex workers themselves (for similar comments, see McNamara, 1994).

Within this context, the immediacy of the quest for resources gives those with better access increased social power (Visano, 1987). Ernest's comment that 'You have to buy your friends out here, either with money or drugs' speaks to this situation. One of the other street-based workers, Michael (who, at thirty-nine, was one of the older hustlers) suggested an even more cynical reading: 'You don't buy your friends out here, you rent them.' The need to form instrumental relationships places together individuals who would not associate with one another but for material need. Kevin, for example, described one of the people he used to hang out with regularly, Tom, as 'this dorky kid,' adding 'he's a retard.' Nevertheless Kevin spent a great deal of time with Tom because Tom still lived at home and used the street only as a short-term recreation activity (such youth are sometimes called 'weekend warriors' [Sims, 1999]). Kevin did not really like Tom, but he appreciated Tom's access to material items, including the fact that he possessed a car.

This process works in reverse as well, potentially leaving those without access to cash socially isolated. For example, Ernest noted that one of his friends had once received a full year's worth of disability checks which had been wrongly withheld. 'He had a lot of friends for a while, but he spent that $7,000 in one month. Those guys are gone now, and hardly any of them are going to pay him back.'[10] While a great deal of money, $7,000 is not a sufficient amount to alter one's life circumstances; thus, it makes sense to obtain some social benefit from the money by spending it quickly on those with whom one wants to party. This also creates the conditions for reciprocal involvements when others come into cash, even if the majority do not entirely pay back whatever 'loans' they may have received. In the case of Ernest's friend, however, the process may have backfired if those taking advantage of his bounty decided it was likely to be a one-time occurrence, and therefore failed to reciprocate.

For some, the tendency toward relational instrumentality completely disrupts all possibility for strong social ties. As one young man remarked: 'I don't have friends. I have associates. People who I socialize with. You know, because there's people who say they want to be your friend and they turn around and stab you in the back' (Clatts et al., 1999). Among many adolescent prostitutes, however, the proclivity to view others primarily in terms of their immediate usefulness is mitigated by the formation of close-knit social networks. Hagan and McCarthy (1998) found that 54 percent of homeless youth form close social networks of several individuals which they refer to through familial terms (such as 'brother'), and further suggest that many of the remaining youth form close networks which utilize a more general terminology of friendship. For such individuals, street families play an essential role in making day-to-day survival on the street possible. As one homeless adolescent in Hagan and McCarthy's study described it:

The way poverty on the street works, twenty bucks can go a long way. Like you can feed four people on twenty bucks, or you can feed one. It's just a kinda thing where you have to work together and pool your resources. Like if I find a big bag of buns in the dumpster, it's better to distribute those and not just myself eat buns all week. Somebody else'll find tomatoes, and then we have tomato sandwiches. The food doesn't go bad, and you can just eat it really quick. (p. 162)

Beyond meeting material needs, street families serve important psychological functions, providing companionship and support. Stephen, for example, spoke of having 'one hundred percent confidence' in his friends from the street, arguing that the intensity of street life brought them close together:

When you go through some of the things that we went through, it's like going through a war together or something. You start to feel intensely about everyone in the group. You'd just do anything for them ... We would always be looking out for each other. Like if someone needed food or something, then we'd give it to him. Or one time I starting getting too involved with drugs, and they were there for me. They confronted me, but not in a mean way, but in a way that felt good, that showed me that they cared about me.

According to Kruks (1991), director of youth services at a gay and lesbian service center in Los Angeles, 'Many of these youths feel so bonded to their street family that they may have little desire to leave street life' (p. 517).

While some youth manage to establish genuinely reciprocal relations with each other, others find themselves in dependent relationships of various sorts, particularly with sugar daddies or, as noted above, with more experienced hustlers. Kevin complained about the first sugar daddy he had: he had ultimately chosen the streets rather than live under the conditions that were gradually imposed:

When I first moved in with him, I didn't even realize it was for the sex. It's like, just suddenly someone is being nice to you, and you don't know why. But if you get something, you give something, I learned that for sure. So then it was OK, but like, he wanted me to stop hanging out on the street and go back to school and stuff, and I was like, 'See ya later.'

Yet, based upon my interviews with men who act as sugar daddies, it seems that most relationships do not become all-encompassing. According to one middle-aged patron, one of the young men he sees shows up only about once every three or four weeks, relying upon him to provide a 'landing pad' where he can recover whenever he bottoms out from extensive periods of drug use and whoring. Another patron, who himself lived in a tenement hotel, had relationships with a number of sex workers, typically seeing them briefly (a day or two at most) whenever they dropped by his room.

Kevin's involvement with his sugar daddy provides an exceptional case, in that Paul, the older man, was not Kevin's patron as much as his pimp, actively helping Kevin turn tricks and living off the proceeds. A second youth, a seventeen-year-old runaway named Nic, also reported that his 29-year-old lover, Ronald, helped him to work and shared the resulting money. These cases are notable in that the literature typically reports that pimping is not an activity which occurs with great frequency, or at all, among men (Allen, 1980; James, 1982; Weisberg, 1985; West & de Villiers, 1993). The dynamics involved in these two relationships, however, were quite different than what is described in the literature regarding men who pimp women. Both of these 'pimps' (a term not utilized by the youths, nor, as far as I know, by the older men themselves) formed exclusive working relationships with the boys, and involved themselves closely in the work, helping Kevin and Nic find places to solicit and looking out for them with their clients. While Kevin described Paul both as his sugar daddy and as his friend, Nic thought of Ronald as his lover. Furthermore, both Paul and Ronald were active participants in the social network of hustlers; indeed, Ronald turned tricks on his own. Both Paul and Ronald were clearly older and more experienced than their younger partners. However, in some sense, both of the older men were peers to the boys, a situation unlike the fixed-status arrangements that prototypically characterize pimp–prostitute relations between men and women. Nevertheless, Paul and Nic did exercise some degree of control over the teens: Kevin looked to Paul for permission when I asked for an interview, and I only learned of Nic's relationship after a scene of domestic violence in which Ronald had hit Nic on the side of his head and left him bleeding. (Nic left the relationship as a result of this incident.)

The distinction between reciprocal and instrumental relations may not always be easily discernible, especially as the social fiction of reciprocity is often needed to maintain instrumentality. It is unlikely, for example, that the 'dorky kid' tolerated by Kevin would have known of Kevin's genuine feelings toward him. Many hustlers similarly attempt to downplay the material basis of their interactions with clients in order not to insult them and to encourage repeat business. Older patrons may be described somewhat instrumentally as 'sugar daddies' or amatively as 'lovers,' but both terms may conceal mercenary impulses. Older patrons may act more or less instrumentally toward hustlers as well, discarding one young man after a time in favor of a newer, younger body (West & de Villiers, 1993), or forming a long-term relationship which helps enable the young man to come into a gay identity and obtain work off the streets (Visano, 1987).

The discrepancy between street scenes that facilitate the formation of strongly knit street families and others that foster a greater degree of instrumentality in social relations has a great deal to do with the level of desperation on the street. Within New York, for example, McNamara (1994) notes that those who are more desperate for money – particularly those who utilize crack regularly – are less able to form strong social bonds of reciprocal aid. While it was the older workers in my study who expressed the most cynicism regarding the possibilities for friendship on the streets – an opinion which, perhaps, related most to their marginality within the hustler networks – it seemed to me that their access to alternate sources of income allowed them to be less instrumentally focused than those who lived under conditions of near-constant desperation. It is notable, however, that even among street families that are more amatively based, the demands of the environment lead to the frequent dissolution of social ties (Hagan & McCarthy, 1998; Visano, 1987).

Violence and the self-management of identity

Given that male prostitutes tend to be young and have access to cash, it is not surprising that hustlers sometimes find themselves targeted by more physically dominating individuals who seek to take their earnings by force (Weisberg, 1985; West & de Villiers, 1993). Indeed, assaults against street-based sex workers are more common than assaults against other street youth, precisely because others recognize that prostitutes have access to cash (Hagan & McCarthy, 1998). The criminal status of prostitution makes it less possible for hustlers to rely upon the police, as does – when this is a relevant issue – their runaway status (Weisberg, 1985). Prostitutes also have to deal with potential violence from their clients, including the possibility of rape (West & de Villiers, 1993).

For those who are isolated on the streets, the fear of being assaulted results in considerable energy being expended to avoid vulnerable situations. Jeremy, for example, told me of how he had been accosted by four young men who demanded that he pay a 'toll' each time he walked by. Jeremy addressed the situation by simply 'laying low' and approaching the area only during the daytime, a solution he found much safer than risking a confrontation. Ernest dealt with danger by relying upon magical beliefs, once showing me the amulet he kept 'for protection,' a tactic which may or may not actually help to ward off would-be attackers, but which at least instils a degree of confidence in the situation.[11] Concern for one's safety can permeate a street worker's lived experience. As Ernest put it, 'You have to watch your back out here. You never know who's going to be coming up on you. They watch you and watch you and wait until you're alone.' Kevin also feared violence from others, telling me that he sometimes used speed as a way to stay awake, preferring not to make himself vulnerable by sleeping in the open at night, 'so you're not just laying out there in your bag, waiting to get popped.' In a study conducted by Clatts and Associates (1999), a young man similarly reported that he would flee to the relative safety of prison rather than sleep on the streets: 'Sometimes I would go and hop a [subway] and purposely get arrested, just so I can sit in jail and have a place to stay' (p. 147).

For youth within street cliques, the struggle to protect oneself becomes somewhat easier. Hagan and McCarthy (1998) note that concern regarding safety is the most frequently mentioned reason why street youth join families, easily outranking the desire to be socially connected to others or the desire to obtain food and other material goods. Given the concern members of street families have for safety, it is not surprising that individuals who are more vulnerable tend to join more readily than those who feel more secure. Hagan and McCarthy (1998) report, for example, that female street youth are more likely to join street families than their male counterparts. Nevertheless, the longer a young male is without housing, the more likely he is to join a street family. Given that young men constitute between 63 percent and 80 percent of the street youth population,[12] the overall number of adolescent males involved in street families exceeds the number of adolescent females.

One of the most important demands made in exchange for community participation is that members back each other up in a fight, essentially without hesitation and no matter the cause (McNamara,

1994). Without this arrangement, community members would rapidly lose their ability to protect themselves. In addition to offering protection, the group establishes other community norms. Many of these rules are the same as those that are generally abided by on the street: sharing any drugs or money one has, paying back loans, and not giving information to the police (Visano, 1987). Beyond this, however, the core members of the hustler community enforce, or attempt to enforce, occupational norms upon other workers who are either new or simply less well integrated into the group. These rules militate against underpricing; specify that a worker is not to approach a potential client when another hustler is already talking with him, and prevent workers from beating up 'good clients' and thereby scaring them away (Allen, 1980; McNamara, 1994; West & de Villiers, 1993).[13]

The enforcement of community norms is not an automatic process, often being achieved through violence and threats of violence against those who transgress (see, for example, McNamara, 1994: 67). More than taking action as individuals, street-based sex workers will often attempt to mobilize others in order to render retaliatory punishment. The manner by which a sex worker will attempt to mobilize others has a great deal to do with the implicit power hierarchies that exist within the group. The following vignette shows how these dynamics can implicate even the service agencies involved in the area.

Don started throwing punches right in the dining area. The abruptness of the attack took Jeremy by surprise, even though he and Don had been getting into it verbally for about fifteen minutes. People didn't usually attack one another in the middle of the agency – they need to be able to go back, for one thing. Whatever the case, Don's sudden ferocity had Jeremy on the ground, and his wild swings were making sure he stayed down. Terry, who ran the hustler-focused service agency, was quick to intervene. Terry grabbed Don and forcefully pulled him back. The other three kids in the room moved in quickly as well, physically separating the two. Don angrily struggled to free himself from Terry's grasp. 'CALM DOWN, DON!' commanded Terry, but he soon lost his grip, and Don turned around and hit him. Don pulled the punch a little bit, uncertain at hitting this man who provided for him in so many ways, but the blow still landed with some force, squarely on the side of Terry's face.

A silence fell upon the room, just for a moment – clearly a line had been crossed. 'Get out, Don!' commanded Terry. 'I'm sorry, Terry,' said Don. 'Get out of here,' Terry repeated. 'Now!' Don took off, fast. Running down the stairs, he shouted back 'Fuck you, Terry!' 'We'll talk about this later!' offered Terry, but Don was already beyond his reach. Grabbing the door, Don slammed it shut as he left, shattering the glass and, as it turned out, breaking the lock as well. Terry encouraged the young men who had witnessed the altercation to leave Don alone, but also announced that Don was no longer welcome at the agency. 'He's 86'd,' he said simply, 'at least for a while.'

Don began to vent his rage by going on a mini-rampage through the neighborhood. The day after breaking the door, he saw Terry in a local café, went inside and started yelling obscenities before throwing hot coffee on Terry's shirt. Later he broke another window at a neighboring store, and was kicked out of at least one bar for causing problems. Terry decided to let the other street workers know who had broken the window, and about the coffee. They let Terry know they would give Don an 'ear beating' and tell him to knock it off. Bringing group pressure to bear wasn't necessarily going to work, however, for the simple reason that it might not amount to much. Michael, one of the older and more experienced hustlers, thought about intervening with Don himself, but decided against doing anything. 'He's probably too crazy to understand anyway. Even if you beat him up, it wouldn't do anything.' Noting that Michael obviously feared Don's 'street heat,' I figured that Michael was finding a convenient rationalization to do nothing. However, I couldn't blame him either. I certainly had no desire to face Don, should he return.

Terry was in a bit of a jam. If he went to the police, he would lose the trust and respect of the guys on the street. The entire premise of Terry's work was that he was unlike the other service agencies – he would not police the guys or tell them to quit doing drugs or engaging in prostitution. If he called in the cops, he'd be seen both as weak and as something of a traitor. He asked some of the guys to hang out in the office for a few days during dinner in case Don showed up. A few agreed, but with some grumbling. Privately, Michael told me that he didn't mind helping, 'but I don't want to babysit.'

Knowing that he could not get guys to watch his back indefinitely, Terry figured he had one trump card he could play. 'If Don makes it impossible to work, I'll just shut down for a few days, and I'll let people know why.' Without food or a place to get out of the rain, Terry figured that the guys would make it clear to Don that he had to back off.

Thinking about the implications of this, I realized just how crucial Terry's agency was to the guys' survival. Yet without police protection, he was subject to the same logic of street violence as anyone else – a fact that tied Terry to the scene much more closely than most service agencies. The fact that so many people relied upon Terry gave him more power and leverage than most, but ultimately he had to make the same calculations of force as everyone else on the street.

In the above situation, Terry first attempted to utilize his prestige within the community in order to protect himself. When this appeared as though it might not work, he was forced to consider employing his own positional leverage – vis-à-vis a temporary interruption of services – in order to convince others to respond to his need.

In a separate instance, Ernest threatened to spread a false rumor that another street worker was a snitch in order to take revenge for some stolen drugs. Ernest seemed to feel confident in this plan, saying, 'That prick has screwed over so many people that the shit is bound to come back on him. All I have to do is set it in motion.' In yet another example, a sugar daddy I spoke with commented that when one of the guys stole something from him, he would usually be able to get it back by spreading word on the street as to what had happened. His social standing within the group as a 'good client' was such that the workers were often willing to apply pressure to the person who had taken the object to return it. These interactions highlight the implicit hierarchies within the group, revealing ways in which one's high standing can offer a degree of protection from harm, while being held in comparatively low regard can make one vulnerable to false accusations.

Given that street-based sex workers are responding to a pervasive threat of violence both from casual onlookers and from within the community itself, it is not surprising that they put a great deal of energy into managing their reputation within the community. The need to maintain one's street reputation has been discussed extensively in the context of inner-city life by Anderson (1999). He describes the techniques an individual must enact in order to maintain his or her street reputation: 'A person's public bearing must send the unmistakable, if sometimes subtle, message that one is capable of violence, and possibly mayhem, when the situation requires it, that one can take care of oneself' (p. 72). These patterns were clearly demonstrated within my own fieldwork. Not only did the question of Don's alleged 'craziness' arise in the encounter with Terry, but others clearly worked to create the appearance of an intimidating presence. Beyond telling me about his mafia contacts, Timothy, for example, told me that he had sparred with martial arts film star Steven Segal, and showed me a rather nasty-looking throwing knife. Threatening activities have an occupational benefit as well, for while hustlers take action to prevent paying tricks from being beaten up, being thought of as having the *potential* for violence encourages clients to pay (Visano, 1987). Fostering an image of potential violence also helps in attracting those clients who seek dangerous-looking 'real men' (Kaye, 2003).[14]

The need to create a powerful representation of self extends to the discussions that workers have with each other and the ways in which they discuss life on the street. Street hustlers often portray their lives on the street as being full of adventure, excitement, and fast action (Visano, 1987). Street life is depicted within these narratives as a place for 'survivors' where individuals live by their wits and enjoy their freedom, particularly their independence from parental and school authorities (Visano, 1987). Hustlers' accounts do not necessarily ignore or underplay the difficult aspects of street life, but rather glorify the difficulties involved as foils against which they can prove themselves. One street-based sex worker, for example, argues that:

> [E]ven when I froze my ass, it was fun. It's a high out here. I guess, I'm like a fucking rebel. Christ, the more I last out here, the tougher I feel. That's pretty neat. All the action. (Visano, 1987, p. 115)

Even tales of childhood abuse become grist for the creation of an aggressive identity. Visano (1987) noted a tendency for hustlers to speak with him at great lengths about their abusive pasts, and queried a worker about it:

> What else have they got? They were hurt bad. Now they're smart. What it says is, 'Listen Jack, I didn't take this from my old lady, so I ain't going to take it from anybody else.' It makes them feel tougher. That's why. It gets them ready for anything. They'll dish it out to their tricks, even to other kids. Don't think they just talk about it to you, no way. They rap about it to their buddies, all the time. (p. 109)[15]

Notably absent from these stories are instances of being humiliated, or of being forced to do something in order to survive which makes them appear weak and vulnerable. Narratives that expose an individual as anything other than in control must, in fact, be countered at once. For example, after one adolescent sex worker teased another about seeing him sift through the garbage, the second youth very loudly proclaimed 'I was not digging through the garbage!' This need to conceal vulnerability and maintain the appearance of power can affect one's daily strategies for survival. Another adolescent hustler told me that he refused to go to the shelter because, he emphatically said, 'I am not homeless.' Similarly, one of the sex workers in McNamara's (1994) study refused to complete his community service for a prostitution charge because he did not wish to be seen cleaning the subways, a tactic which, while preserving his status, placed him at greater risk of future imprisonment. These decisions follow a similar logic that Bourgois (1996) noted in his observations of young men who eschew the legitimate labor market in favor of dealing crack, a job which at least affords them a degree of 'respect' in relation to their peers.

Also absent from the street hustlers' boastful narratives are accounts of the wide variety of innovative tactics they employ to defuse or otherwise circumvent conflict. The most obvious of these is the attempt simply to avoid others who might be dangerous, as Jeremy did when threatened by the group who demanded a 'toll.' Others who are unable to avoid threatening people might attempt placating strategies. For example, I witnessed one youth make a direct appeal to another (much more menacing) hustler with whom he had a conflict: 'I know we don't always get along, but I want you to know that I still pray for you.' Whether self-interested or not, this comment served to allay the tension which had been rising between the two. When measures such as these are unworkable, some take the option of moving to another city. Many street kids, in fact, move along a circuit from city to city, staying in one area until either they become bored or 'the heat,' whether from police or from others in the scene, is too great. Still others decide that the violence on the street is too prevalent, and leave altogether. Jeremy, for example, decided to quit working when his fear of others – prompted by his run-ins with a neighborhood gang and heightened by excessive speed use – mushroomed into a debilitating paranoia. Even the effort to appear intimidating and ready for violence – the tactic those who are more powerful rely upon to ward off conflict – can be seen in this light as an paradoxical manoeuver: while the approach involves the suppression of any public display of vulnerability, it exists as a tactic only in relation to an implicit recognition of possible victimization.

Conclusions

A number of insights arise from the above observations. Perhaps, most important, this work underscores the importance of poverty in shaping the social lives of most street-based male prostitutes, including their need to prostitute and their ability to negotiate the terms of paid sex. Although considerable diversity exists within the population, most of the participants become involved in this work because of basic economic needs. (Social factors such as a given individual's desire for gay sex or community also shape the choice of prostitution over other options.) While this observation regarding economic necessity is unsurprising, the way the exigencies of poverty both heighten the importance of peer relations and shape the contours of these relations is less discussed. This study also suggests that some older men are able to participate in limited ways within the social networks of street youth as 'sugar daddies,' and that these men constitute an important (if problematic) locus of resources for some young men.

Another issue highlighted by this study involves the manner in which class and classlike elements shape the lives of street youth. Class privilege extends from one's ability to take advantage of youth services to one's ability to form successful relationships with sugar daddies, and potentially shapes one's ability to meet casual clients as well. The ability to present a 'tough' and aggressive image of self is a crucial survival skill that also is class-inflected. Middle-class norms of masculinity do not generally favor demeanors that are mild; thus, the need to deploy threats and violence can work against one's ability to receive aid from social service agencies and sugar daddies. As Bourgois (1996) documents in relation to street-level drug dealers, this process can militate against one's ability to leave the street scene. Most generally, class is a primary factor in shaping the social response male street prostitution receives from the state and other mainstream institutions, determining the broad outlines of policy response from the general society.

A third critical area of inquiry concerns the role of social service institutions within street life. While some research has been conducted regarding the role of welfare within recipients' lives (for example, Edin & Lein, 1997), very little has been written about the experiences of street youth with the agencies that serve them (though see Bresnahan, 1995; Hecht, 1998; Snell, 1995). Among the youth I witnessed, it was clear that service agencies constituted a much-needed, yet sometimes frustrating, source of resources. Like Kevin, many of the young men expressed great anger at the way agencies refused to offer more extensive services without controlling intimate aspects of their lives (fostering familial unification, demanding an end to drug use or sex work, rigidly enforced curfews, etc.). It was also clear that taking advantage of services through any necessary means – including the creation of sympathetic 'victim' selves – constituted another important strategy for daily survival.

This final comment, again, calls attention to the context in which representations of male street prostitution are made. With notable exceptions, the academic study of prostitution has often focused narrowly upon sex, as if once individuals transgress the sexual norm, the only matter of any import is the origin, significance, and (sexual) consequences of that transgression. Representations by social service agencies often extend this by focusing exclusively upon the sexual degradation of 'innocent youth,' thus rendering certain populations invisible, downplaying questions of prostitute's agency, and ironically reinforcing their sexualization. Both academic and social service approaches tend to marginalize questions pertaining to daily life on the street, particularly the ways in which prostitute identity and the activities of prostitution intersect with other elements of street life. Meanwhile, traditional analyses of 'street life' *per se* ignore figures such as the male prostitute as he fails to epitomize the macho image of the street tough. Beyond asking how male prostitutes do (and do not) differ from other men on the street, these difficulties point toward the need to devote greater attention to the gendered ideologies that inform ethnographic representation. If the politics of representation have left us with two problematic figures – the (feminized) victim runaway and the (hyper-masculinized) street thug – it seems necessary to do more than simply mix these literatures into a socially incomprehensible image of the 'sexually victimized street tough.' A more nuanced examination should detail previously unexamined issues, such as the way street youth sometimes present an image of powerlessness in order to exert power vis-à-vis the social service agencies, while creating an image of toughness in order partially to address their real vulnerabilities on the street. Such an approach begins to create images that document suffering without equating it with absolute powerlessness, and which examine male street youths' propensity toward violence and 'toughness' without ignoring sites of dependency and 'weakness.'

NOTES

1   This chapter is a revision of a chapter from my MA thesis in Anthropology at San Francisco State University, 'Boy Prostitutes and Street Hustlers: Depicting Male Street Prostitution' (Kaye, 2001).

2   Bourgois (1996) partially escapes this trend by discussing barrio men's experiences of subordination within the legitimate labor market, but even these are treated as paradigmatic instances in which barrio men hold to street definitions of masculine 'respect' over and against the possibility of participating in the service economy. The macho identity of the primary subjects is thus reaffirmed, while the compromised identities of men who choose to engage in the gendered performances associated with service work are not carefully explored.

3   This harm reduction approach involved street outreach, running a needle exchange, preparing and serving food, distributing clothes, condoms, etc. Through this work, I developed some manner of contact with approximately eighty to one hundred individuals who worked on the street. Because of constraints placed upon my research (which I write about in some detail in my thesis [Kaye, 2001]), I was able to conduct only a limited number of in-depth interviews, including five with current street workers, three with others who had formerly worked as hustlers on the streets, three with 'sugar daddies,' and four with social workers who were directly involved with local street youth. Additional information comes from numerous informal conversations I had with the director of the harm reduction agency.

4   All names are pseudonyms.

5   To be clear, I obtained consent to utilize this material on a second occasion when Timothy did not seem high.

6   I derive the phrase 'bodily capital' from Loic Wacquant (1995, 2003), who argues that individuals without access to symbolic capital (such as education) instead invest their energies toward the development of their body's potentialities. While Wacquant developed his analysis in relation to boxers, here I use the term to mark the way in which one's perceived attractiveness provides one with greater or lesser saleability in the sexual market. (Wacquant [2003] briefly notes this sense of the term as well.)

7   Ironically, service agencies and sugar daddies thus often compete for the same youth, leaving others behind.

8   In relation to street youth, some exceptions to this general trend can be found in Kipke et al. (1997), Raymond et al. (1999), and Sims (1999). See also Glauser (1997) for an excellent example related to street youth in the Third World. Passaro (1996) begins such an analysis in relation to gender differences among adult homeless individuals.

9   This policy was based on the precarious legalities of the needle exchange program. While this program is technically illegal, police have indicated a willingness to tolerate these operations if they do not 'facilitate' drug abuse by introducing more needles onto the streets. Those seeking more needles,

meanwhile, may have wanted them for themselves, or they may have sought extras in order to sell. At the time of my research, needles had a street value of $5 each.

10 The social rationality of economically irrational behaviors – spending $7,000 in one month, for example – was explicated by Whyte (1943) in his study of an Italian ghetto community.

11 Ernest hoped his amulet would help ward off police as well as attackers.

12 Janus et al. (1987, as cited in Hagan & McCarthy, 1998) found that 63 percent of street youth in Toronto were male; Raymond et al. (1999) found a higher figure of 76 percent in San Francisco, and Clatts et al. (1999) report an even higher figure of 80 percent for New York City. These statistics reflect the different uses of space in which male and female runaways engage. While females and males are equally likely to have experience with running away from home, females are more likely to use shelters than males (Research Triangle Institute, 1994). For an analysis of a similar phenomenon among adults who are homeless see Passaro (1996).

13 While male street workers (particularly those with dependencies on drugs which require larger amounts of cash) occasionally threaten and steal from their clients (McNamara, 1994), there is a general recognition that this is bad for business. Therefore, only those clients who refuse to pay are typically subject to violence at the hands of the workers (see McNamara, 1994; Visano, 1987; West & de Villiers, 1993).

14 I thank an anonymous reviewer for reminding me of this point.

15 In other contexts, stories of abuse are on occasion deployed to different effect, as when street youth sometimes utilize them as a means of making themselves appear to social service agencies to be more deserving (Snell, 1995; Visano, 1987). In either instance, the stories themselves might (nor might not) be factually true, yet the meaning given to the events is altered in such a way as to create a different identity for the narrator as either a street tough or as a victim.

enforced ab/normalcy: the sex worker *hijras* and the
    (re)appropriation of s/he identity

Mashrur Shahid Hossain

Let's start with fix(a)tion

Robin is a fifteen-year-old boy living at Shakhari Bazaar, Old Dhaka,
Bangladesh. His mother is a homemaker and his father a small shop-
keeper. Apart from his study, Robin loves going to the cinemas and
reading books. But what he likes most is getting up early in the
morning, only to stare in absorbed fascination at a neighbor, the main
goalkeeper of a local football team – how he flexes his biceps, how he
curves his back for stretching – during physical exercise on the roof of
the house opposite theirs. Robin likes it because he feels it like thunder
throughout his body and it leaves him hard. But he likes not that he likes
it; he does not understand why he a boy will feel attracted towards boys.
He has heard of gays and managed to swallow a handful of gay-based
films, but he dared not talk to anyone to clarify what 'gay' actually
stands for and – *Hai'allah!* – if he belongs to this group! He is further
dispirited, ashamed and irritated by his own assumption that he lacks
the macho in him and that he is 'effeminate' – probably a *hijra*? So his
feeling for the boys? The fact is: he has always been like this; when he
was a kid he would stealthily watch his father rubbing soaps during
bathing; at school recess or during *adda*, he gladly offers to massage his
friends' shoulders; the posters he collects, by saving from tiffin money,
are mostly of hunks, of topless hunks, from *Hollywoody* Chris Evans to
Bollywoody Hrithik Roshan. His mother must have smelt, but been
ignoring, something unusual, something 'diabolic,' in Robin, but now
she feels threatened. It was reported that Robin recently told one of his
friends that he's not going to marry. The mother decides to stop
anything 'shameful' to happen and makes arrangement to marry Robin
to one of his cousins within a couple of weeks with a conviction that
marriage will re-channel Robin's sexual drive. Robin is perplexed; he

cannot announce that he is a '———', but he is confident that he cannot cheat his would-be wife; well, why would he cheat himself? Robin leaves home and takes shelter at the place of a *hijra* he met earlier. It is during his stay with that *hijra*, whose actual profession, Robin soon gets confirmed, is sex work, that Robin discovers that he is – *Hai'allah!* – a *koti* (a gay in masquerade)! Under the *hijra's* guidance, Robin starts changing her/his attire and attitude: mostly s/he is wearing a female outfit and is adopting 'feminine' demeanors. Though s/he decides to keep her/his cock intact, as this would discourage her/his easy identification with the traditional *hijra*, s/he will now live as a *hijra* doing sex work at night. Her/his parents will never accept her/him as s/he is, and will not compromise with her/his sexuality. So this is a way open for her/him to '**** boys hard' without being Robin. By assuming the masquerade of a woman (Robin → Ravina), s/he may have managed to escape the pressure of normative sexuality, but not without a sense of being forlorn, being thrown away.

This is a real story with some details modified to protect the identity of the person concerned and to cover a number of issues. This story should give us an idea of four major problems that a Bangladeshi *hijra* confronts: ignorance, secrecy, otherness, and oppression. Let me mention here that the *hijras* who this chapter chiefly deals with are the woman-performing[1] intersexuals living in Dhaka, Bangladesh.

The Western conception of and English taxonomy for gender and sexual orientation may not fully express what *hijra* signifies. Traditionally, a *hijra* is a 'hermaphrodite' or a 'eunuch' or an 'intersexual.' In recent days, *hijra* has become a much more blanket term incorporating – culturally invariably – hermaphrodites, intersexuals, transsexuals, *kotis*, and MSM (men who have sex with men). So, even 'transgender' does not accommodate this plurality of gender identity. I, however, prefer 'transgender,' acknowledging its exclusionary nature but tapping its connotation of transcending gendering, to designate the *hijra* because traditionally a *hijra* is a person with 'equivocal malformation' (Solaiman, 2009). To summarize: *hijra* is a 'transgender,' minority[2] community in Bangladesh, India, and Pakistan. These people are born with certain biological characteristics that problematize sexual identity, leaving them swinging between male and female sexes. In Bangladesh, a *hijra* is a fe/male person who is biologically male (and, in some cases, sexless) but who thinks and asserts herself as a woman, and, accordingly, performs 'femininity' and is sexually driven towards men. To a great extent, the *maiggya*, the bottom-performing 'men' are *hijras*.[3] Culturally, they are identified as 'naturally' abnormal, freaks, deviant, hence a constant target of derision, abomination, oppression. While *hijra* has traditionally been a sexually naïve (in some cases, sex/less or eunuch) community, a majority of present-day *hijras* are sexually mobilized and assume sex work as a profession, or pastime fun.

This chapter is an outcome of my venture in making a short film on the *hijras*. While I was collecting background information for finalizing the screenplay, I found that only a couple of books were available on the local market, most of which were published in India. As for the non-*hijra* people, most of them either are not interested in or are ill informed about the *hijras*. The internet provides only sketchy information. I then, along with Jewel, my student, visited Badhan Hijra Sangha, to my knowledge, the only *hijra* organization in Dhaka: we watched *hijras* rehearse for an upcoming stage performance, and later talked to them, especially to Joya, general secretary of Badhan, and Konok, a young sex worker *hijra*. I found that sex is an all-time favorite with these so-called sexless people: their talks and reminiscences are like smoky spirals, vibrant and intertwined, betraying passion and indifference, anger and frustration, charged with funky frankness and aggressive sensuality, expressed with a vengeance; I was then thinking of the phrase 'with a vengeance' … soon I replaced it with 'with a *jouissance*': wasn't there a feeling of celebration? Wasn't there a sort of desperate attempt to come to terms with the exclusionary praxis of normative sexuality? An assertion of normalcy that people outside have denied to them? It dawned on me that sex work cannot simply be a means of earning for the *hijras*, not simply a have-to-do; it has every potential to be a means to transcend, a means to celebrate, a means to make sense of meaning/less life. What I tried then was to understand this very paradox of the combination of sex and sexlessness through a theoretical framework.

This chapter relies on talks with a couple of *hijras* and on review of a small handful of literature. It concentrates on the process of making and unmaking of the *hijras* in society as well as the role that *sex work* can play in the remaking of them. First, the chapter traces how cultures designate the *hijras* as 'abnormal'; second, it records the predicaments of the *hijras* placed in a heterosexist society; then there is a psychoanalytic analysis, after the Lacanian/Davisian mode, of the desire and fear related to the enforced ab/normalcy; and finally, this chapter views sex work as a site of assertion and liberation for the *hijras*. It argues that sex work has potential, even if it is unrecognized, to operate as an enabling mechanism for the *hijras* to re/appropriate an/other identity interpellated by the 'normal' society, a mechanism through which a carnivalesque *jouissance* may be released, which not only de-reifies identity but, more important, celebrates diversity.

Conditioning of an/other

Who is a hijra?; Hijra is a hermaphrodite; Why is a hijra hijra?; Compulsory binarity fetish

'Is it a boy or a girl?' This is invariably the first question that people ask when a child is born. Also invariably do people expect, conforming to the phallogocentric codes the world abides by, that the answer should be an excited shout: 'BOY!' If it's a girl, well, people do not always mind, at least they do not when there is no question of property inheritance or lineage maintenance. Imagine then what happens when a newborn's sex cannot be identified! 'OH NO!!!'

In most cases, this baby whose sexual identity is dubious will later become hijra.

It is suggested by all the Indian and Bangladeshi authors[4] writing about the hijras that hijras are 'made' instead of being 'born.' What these writers explored and critiqued are the socio-cultural factors that are ultra active in stigmatizing the hijra community. OK. But it is sheer sentimentality to assert that one is *not* born as a hijra. Apart from the *kotis* and the MSMs whom I'd call the 'hidden-hijras,' an (intersexed) hijra is born as a hijra. But being a physico-genetic disorientation, it usually surfaces at adolescence. So there is no hijra kid, so there is rarely easy/ early identification. Unlike gay or lesbian experiences, being hijra is not primarily a matter of sexual orientation, cultural constructs, or choice of partner. Being hijra – originally – is neither a mental disease nor exclusively a social product. It relates to what one is born 'with.'

Hijra is a conglomeration of alternative gender identities[5] ranging from hermaphrodite to eunuch. *Hermaphrodites* are people of indefinite biological sex. In most cases, hermaphrodites are *intersexed*, possessing 'both masculine and feminine traits' (Hossain, 2006). *Transsexuality*, popularly known as 'gender dysphoria,' is a somatic condition in which the person feels s/he is trapped in a body of the opposite sex. *Transvestites* are 'cross-dressers': they wear dress, which is traditionally made for people of the opposite sex. While transvestism is chiefly a sexual fetish in which people on their choice *perform* a pose, a masquerade, transsexuals suffer

120

from the dichotomy of two sexes and are desperate to fit by surgery into any *one* category socially accepted. A *eunuch*, on the other hand, is a castrated man: a person whose testicles have been removed, or whose penis is cut off, or whose penis and testicles have been removed. Acknowledging the plurality (for example, transsexual and eunuch) and inflections (for example, *koti*) of *hijra* identity, we may see *hijra* as Butler sees woman: as 'a term in process, a becoming, a constructing that cannot rightfully be said to originate or to end' (Butler, 1999 [1990], p. 43). This chapter, however, chiefly addresses the male-to-female intersexuals and transsexuals living in Dhaka and on sex work.

Etymologically, the word 'hijra' was arguably derived from Urdu. In Urdu, the word *hich* designates 'something without a proper place' (Majumder, 2005, p. 3); *hich-gah* then refers to being 'nowhere.' In Nepalese language, the word *hij* suggests lack of masculinity, or in a derogatory sense, 'a kept man.' These references carry the sense of belonging to nowhere or suggest a site that is obscured. In this sense, a *hijra* is situated on what Bhabha (1994) calls 'liminality' for not fitting into any of the sex/gender binary opposites the heterosexist society approves of or conceives as 'normal.' That this normalizing practice is both somatic and semantic is evident in the sexist languages such as English in which you have to use the pronouns 'she' or 'he' to refer to a person; even the nonsexist 's/he' or 'she or he' fails to transcend heterosexism. Should then we go for a pronoun like 'hir' suggested by Leslie Feinberg, an American transgender writer, in *Transgender Warriors* (Bristow, 2007, p. 227)? Or the one like 's/he' referring derogatorily but 'effectively' to their being 1/2? Well, no fun is intended!

The process of abnormalizing/othering the *hijras* starts with their birth, with the *dai-maas* (old ladies who substitute for doctors in helping women give birth in Bangladeshi villages) or the doctors. What happens when a baby is born − *Hai'allah!* − with an XXY or X chromosome?[6] These intersexed babies could be Merms or Herms or Ferms.[7] The *dai-maas* or the doctors either fail to identify the sexlessness/dubious-sexuality of the baby born, or, if they determine it on the basis of what the genitals look like, they just leave it unacknowledged and assign 'one' gender to the baby; usually they identify the baby as a boy to minimize future complexities. There is little evidence that sexual surgery (or castration or circumcision) takes place in Bangladesh to fit the baby to one sexual identity.

Parents thus may or may not be aware of their *son's* sexuality, but in both cases they keep it secret from the boy himself, making him develop ultra-masculine demeanors so as to counter potential femininity; in cases in which the boy knows of his hijraness, the parents instruct the boy never to disclose it to anyone. At the base, there is one primal fear: deviation. Be it through surgery or through silence, the heterosexist mechanisms attempt to transform the intersexed hijras into 'normal' beings. The formula remains simple, hence essentialist: what is not common is not-normal. What is not XX or XY, is freak, is 'XXX'!!!

When the intersexed hijras are growing up, they are tutored to perform as per the gender-specific modalities: if s/he is 'designated' as a 'boy,' s/he will live and look like a boy. This is what we may call, by re-structuring Lacan's term, a 'matured mirror-phase': the 'unified, inde-pendent self' (Brooker, 1999, p. 138) that the hijra-boy sees in the mirror (the mirror of society and other's eyes) is far different from her/his actual self; it is far more alienating (see below). To a hijra, the mirror image then represents not a 'desired unity,' rather an antagonistic image that the child wishes to escape. The boy is caught 'in a dynamic of 'insufficiency' and 'anticipation,' in Lacan's term, moving between 'the image of a fragmented body to ... the orthopaedic vision of the totality' (Brooker, 1999, p. 138; emphasis mine). The 'boy' is torn between the discrepancies between her/his anatomical body, gender identity, and gender performance, three 'corporealities' that Butler identifies in her discussion of 'drag' (Butler, 1999 [1990], p. 175). Mismanagement of these discrepancies soon starts surfacing as signs of ab/normalcy: the hijra cannot help but talking and walking and dressing like a girl. Already s/he has earned the derisive label 'maiggya'; in the near future, s/he will be psychologically assaulted, even physically abused, by the boys. S/he is not welcome in, nor does s/he enjoy much, the boys' ad/ventures. S/he is not welcome in, though s/he has a knack with, girls' secret privacies. Sensitive adults are sympathetic towards her/him; the conservative are indifferent; the mischievous are aggressive. S/he is made to understand s/he is not like others: s/he is abnormal, alienated, unheimlich, other.

The ab/normalcy and alterity are strengthened when a hijra reaches puberty. Her/his physical and sexual development appears problematic, incomplete, and s/he feels attracted towards boys, which as s/he is indoctrinated are sin and taboo for her/him. S/he starts understanding that s/he is not suitable for conventional marriage; in some cases, especially in the poor, uneducated and less advanced communities, the man comes to know only after marriage that s/he is a hijra: either he is impotent or is not aroused by women. While lust for men seems to stay insatiable, producing psycho-sexual trauma, an equally strong repulsion for girls is developing: a girl is what s/he intends to be but cannot; girls are those who are desired by men and can have sex with the boys but s/he cannot. 'If I were born a girl!'

There are a number of hijras in Bangladesh who live closeted. These people mostly hail from rich or aristocratic families and are not willing to risk family status and personal dignity, because hijras in Bangladesh are considered abominable, freakish, abnormal. Even those who accommodate themselves as hijra usually maintain dual identities: relatives may know someone as 'Ahmed,' for example, but s/he is 'Diana' when she wears female getup and sells sex. Even hijra activists like Joya have to maintain masks!

It is important to note here, however, that the hijras in India, and to a limited extent in Bangladesh, enjoy greater privilege and recognition than the intersexed do in the USA or Europe. The reasons may include some historical and religious associations. For example, a number of hadiths, such as Bukhari LXII, 25 (cited in Malik 1999) show patience with the khusra and mukhannath, the Arabic synonyms of hijra. The Hindu hijras have deities to worship: Siva (also known as Ardhanariswara, 'androgynous') and Baal Tripura Bahuchhara Mata. The hijras were reported to assume certain high positions, even political ones, during and after the Mughal Empire. Perhaps because of hijras' 'androgynous' traits, they were considered to be transcendental, spiritually powered to bless and curse people. Adnan Hossain lists three points at which the social status of the hijras in India, and to a limited extent in Bangladesh too, is different from that of intersex people in Europe:

- they are thought to be spiritual, so the domestic ritual of blessing a newborn baby by the hijras still prevails;
- they are easily visible, mainly when they are collecting tola (money collected as a form of donation) from different shops and bazaars;
- they are tolerated, to such an extent that a hijra named 'Shabnam [Mausi] has been elected a parliamentarian in India' (Hossain, 2006).

All this, however, does not suggest that hijras are accepted as 'normal'; they remain freakish, abnormal, abject: 'You should not despise them, but … well, never talk to them; just ignore them; they are dangerous, you know!' For example, a poem in a blog called 'Bangladeshi Women' describes hijras as 'queer creatures' who are raunchy, aggressive, and violent (Khanam, 2008).

Curiously, this outrageously prejudiced poem appeared in a blog called 'Bangladeshi Women,' the sex/gender identity the *hijras* aspire to and loathe, in a demonstration of Freudian ambivalence.

The *hijras* elicit ambivalence because of the discrepancies between gender identity and gender performance. Semiotically, signs have meanings not only by their reference to real objects, but also by their difference from other signs, their binary opposites. Binary opposition 'is the most extreme form of difference possible' (Ashcroft et al., 2000, p. 23): birth/death, man/woman, white/black, good/evil. These binary constructs are the major factors in constructing social reality. This splitting is supremely political, and in many cases repressive. Binarism usually privileges the first term – birth, man, white, good – as definitive, thereby reducing the second term to its inferior. The second aspect of any binary system is that it cannot appreciate anything in-between. It suppresses

> ambiguous or interstitial spaces between the opposed categories, so that any overlapping region that may appear, say, between the categories man/woman, child/adult or friend/alien, becomes impossible according to binary logic, and a region of taboo in social experience. (Ashcroft et al., 2000, p. 24)

Our society takes certain physical aspects such as color, facial features, and sexual organs as signifiers of individuals' subjectivity. These fetish-like aspects subjectivize an individual in a given 'discursive regime' founded on binarism. More than that, these fetishes exclude anything and anyone that does not fit into this binarism; therefore, those that do not fit court transgression. I would like to call this discursive practice 'compulsory binary fetishism.' Since the construction of *hijra* does not fit into the binary opposites and, more important, secures the seed of subverting heteropatriarchal authority, the compulsory binary fetishism of normal(ized) society has repressed the *hijras* as scandalous.

If woman is 'other' and the colonized subject is 'other,' *hijras* are less-than-other. If men are the 'I' and women the 'other,' *hijras* are 'in-between-I-&-other' … Well, the '&'? … The question is: are they less than a man and more than a woman? Islamic *sharia'h*, to some extent, authenticates the *hijra*: the *khatib* (the chief 'priest') of Baitul Mukar'ram Mosque, the national mosque of Bangladesh, opined: 'Islam has nothing against the *hijra*. They can attend the *jama'at* at mosques. When in *jama'at*, the *hijras* will stand *after the men and before the women*' (quoted in Husain, 2005, p. 13; emphasis mine). Society, however, takes them as not-man and not-woman or less-than-woman. But – *Hai'allah!* – couldn't *hijras* be more than either 'men' or 'women,' because they are sex-transcendent, something like angels? Isn't that the reason why *hijras* have been considered to be 'good' for young children?

> They say I am transgressive
> But I say I am transcendent
> I am the god incarnate
> An anonymous hermaphrodite
> (quoted in Hossain, 2006)

Conditions of an/other

'Hijra' is a slang; Psychological dominance; Religious trauma; Few human and political rights; Career problems; Marriage is a nightmare; Sexual problems

Society has decreed that *hijras* are less-and-double: they are double because they share biological/behavioral aspects of both man and woman; they are less because they do not belong to any category. Society has little – should we say, nil – to offer to them. Rather the media have been ultra active in generating and popularizing reductive images of *hijra* as deviant, lack, clown. Since the majority of the population are not exposed to the nature and lifestyle of the *hijras*, they take what the ideological state apparatuses (ISAs)[8] present as granted, and act accordingly! The life of a *hijra* is invariably a chronicle of shame and oppression.[9]

INTERPELLATION 1: HIJRA IS HIJRA!
Despite religious tolerance, historical background, and the continuing ritual called *chheley nachano* (initiation of babies) in which *hijras* play vital roles, being *hijra* is a 'curse'! The word is now an offensive slang in Bangla: if a boy is called *hijra*, the boy is designated as 'effeminate,' and being effeminate is – *'oops! it's a universally (?) ac/claimed disgrace!'* The very utterance of *hijra* propagates an inevitable sense of abomination and deprecation: they are impotent; they are sexual deviants; they are nasty; they are abject!

Because of having sexual ambiguities, *hijras* always remain stressed. Instead of offering mental and moral succor which could have helped them overcome numerous psychological complexes, society appears as Duo Raani (Evil Queen, the stereotype first wife of the king in Bangla folk tales), constantly hammering upon their 'deviations,' reminding them of their 'abnormalcy.' These interpellations rob hijras of a comfortable growing up, leaving them incessantly belittled and irritated, causing severe psychological distress and regressive behavioral development which ultimately consolidates the 'hijra myth':[10] they *are* offensive, aggressive, easily inflamed, often sadistically coarse and cruel. Having suffered from an inferiority complex, their personality remains ill-developed and their confidence level hardly surfaces.

INTERPELLATION 2: YOU ARE SINFUL!
Almost invariably, hijras suffer from guilt consciousness resulting in neurosis. It is commonly believed that 'their "state of mind" was self induced and [so] a dangerous sin' (Leyla's Chayhane, a website dealing mainly with issues of transgender from Islamic perspectives, 2008).

Interestingly enough, religions do not explicitly designate transgendered people as abominable or sinful. In the *Mahabharata*, for example, Arjuna the hero once assumes the guise of Brihon'nola, presumably a hijra (Majumdar & Basu, 1999, p. 5); the biblical God showers blessings on eunuchs (Husain, 2005, p. 10); the prophet Mohammad (s.a.s.) was reported to accept a *mukhannath* 'as a fellow praying Muslim' (Leyla's Chayhane, 2008). Speaking through common sense, since the intersex 'body' is not chosen, being hijra cannot be sin.

INTERPELLATION 3: YOU ARE SUB-HUMAN!
So a hijra should not be vocal enough for her/his human and political rights. Being literally head-to-foot subalterns, they lack the agency. The binary-b(i)ased bureaucracy could recognize only two sexes, men and women. Since the hijras do not strictly belong to either of the two, some serious socio-cultural problems arise.

- Hijras do not usually resort to court unless they have to; they have a strong conviction — 'well, not conviction, it's the fact' — that traditional law never entertains their interests; rather, as a hijra responded with a shout: 'What the ****** could do is to exploit and manipulate us!' For most cases, they resort to their own *shaalish* (informal court for law and punishment) system usually led by the *Gurumaas*, the hijra mentor-mothers.
- Hijras have no security — they are frequently harassed by ordinary people and police officers alike — and there is no one to complain to. Husain reports how two hijras in the Khulna district were assaulted by a local police officer after a brawl at the officer's newborn son's *chheley*

nachano programme: the officer tore down their dresses, beat them, cut their hair, and left them gravely injured on the street (Husain, 2005, p. 28). The condition of the sex worker *hijras* is worse: often are they raped, and robbed of their earnings. Joya reported how on a winter morning after a nightlong 'gangbang' some young men forced her[11] to stand naked in a marsh for a long time (Husain, 2005, p. 50).

- *Hijras* are mostly illiterate. Husain reports that 47 percent of the *hijras* he interviewed had never been to school and only 4 percent had passed the school certificate exam. He found only one person, Pahari Hijra, who is a graduate. The reasons for illiteracy include poverty and social pressure: 'The schoolboys would taunt me as *hijra*, so one day I stopped going to school,' said Purnima (Husain, 2005, p. 67).
- *Hijras* have no health rights. Doctors either don't care or are 'afraid' of their 'outrageous' activities (Husain, 2005, p. 19). Sociologically, the outcome is disastrous: *hijras*, being mostly sex workers in conditions in which condoms are difficult to secure and carry and use, suffer from various sexually transmitted infections, including HIV/AIDS, without access to treatment.

The synonym of the derisive '*hijra*,' which many a writer including Nihar Majumder finds useful, is *obo-manob*, meaning 'subhuman.' As long as they are deprived of basic human rights, Majumder ironically opines, they should be called *obo-manob*.

INTERPELLATION 4: YOU HAVE NO SEX: NOT MALE, NOT FEMALE! The most traditional job that the *hijras* are associated with is *chheley nachano*. The *chheley nachano* is a traditional ritual taking place just after the birth of a baby; the word *chheley* is a sexist term like *man*, meaning 'boy' but here referring to 'baby,' and *nachano* means 'making other dance.' The ritual involves the *hijras* coming in a group to sing and dance; they play with the newborn baby and pray for her/him, in return of which they are given a handsome amount of money by the parents or households of the child. This, however, no longer generates enough earnings. Because of family planning, the birth rate has decreased, and the fewer the births, the less the *hijras*' earnings. The second major job is collecting *tola*: this too generates less income than previously and at the same time can be dangerous, even fatal, when shopkeepers get aggressive and assault *hijras*. Husain lists 17 different professions that the Bangladeshi *hijras* do take: *chheley nachano*; collecting *tola*; performing at cultural programs or dancing as 'extras' in commercial Bangladeshi films; acting extras; peon; maidservant; worker at *bidi* (a kind of cheap local cigarette) factories; worker in the health programs of different non-governmental organizations (NGOs); field worker for selling condoms; working at hairdressers; *baburchi* (cook); working at *bathans*; laborer; smuggling; sex work; dancing at brothels; and *Gurumaa* (Husain, 2005, pp. 23–4).

The hijras cannot get a job at offices or established companies *as hijras*; if they present themselves as males, they may. But only 'may' because most hijras are illiterate.

Hijras cannot cast votes *as hijra*; if they want to, they have to be enlisted as male voters and have to stand at male queues during voting.

Hijras cannot open accounts in banks *as hijra*. Purnima has a bank account, but she has to present herself as a 'man' to open it and run it (Husain, 2005, p. 68).

There is no separate prison cell for the hijras. They are usually held in 'male cells' and have often been sexually assaulted.

The hijras cannot die *as hijras*. The Muslim funeral system arguably offers no established ritual for anyone belonging neither to the male nor to the female sex. So the family are expected to present the deceased hijra as a 'man' (or a 'woman' maybe); only then can the imam carry on with the funeral ritual (Husain, 2005, p. 32). *'I'm sure that we've our place in God who will not ask if I am a man or woman because God created us, didn't HE?'* I don't know if the creator is 'he' or 'she' or 'androgynous' or 'sexless,' but what I found out is that hijra is a performativity, or more accurately, a transgressive performativity, a point I'll come to soon.

INTERPELLATION 5: YOU ARE IMPOTENT! YOU CAN'T MARRY!

Hijras are traditionally considered to be impotent, but many of them have sexual drives! Some may even ejaculate. Hijras, especially *kotis* and the transvestites, do marry, but these are customized, unofficial marriages. Mostly, they live together with their *parikhs*, the lovers. However, hijras' relations with their 'hubbies' or *parikhs* rarely last long: marrying a hijra is still not socially and legally accepted, and a hijra cannot – *'how could they?'* – give birth to children. The hijras, however, are very serious about their sexual partners … unfortunately, it is often one-sided. Moreover, the main concern of many of the so-called 'lovers' is to 'use their body for some time' and to steal their earnings whenever there is an opportunity. 'You cannot trust guys,' said Diana (Husain, 2005, p. 39).

INTERPELLATION 6: YOU ARE SEXUALLY DEVIANT. YOU ARE A FAG!
Hijras are considered sexual freaks, or more accurately, perverted homosexuals, and homosexuality is still an extremely grievous taboo in Bangladesh. This association of the *hijras* with homosexuality is long established: 'Leyla's Cheyhane' reports that the British *raj* during the colonization period 'passed a law in which the *hijras* were described as "sodomites" and people who did "homosexual offenses."' Queerly and erroneously, the 'sodomy' is confused with 'homosexuality' or 'gayness,' which is not the case: gayness does not necessarily include anal penetration. More erroneously, gay men are popularly associated with 'effeminacy' and are sometimes confused with *hijras*. One reason for this may be the increasing visibility and availability of the *kotis* who pass both as gay and *hijra*. Bangladeshi gays are, however, antipathetic towards the *hijras*, a curious topic, which is beyond the scope of this chapter.

INTERPELLATION 7: YOU ARE A PROSTITUTE!
Sex work is the major profession of the *hijras* living in urban areas. And sex work, termed as 'prostitution,' *veshyagiri*, is hated. *Veshyas*[12] are outcasts. And a *hijra veshya* is doubly outcast: s/he is repulsive, s/he is dirty, s/he is sinful. Doubly estranged, s/he is really a *hich-gah*!

Gazing at an/other

Mechanism of the gaze; fragmented body; castration complex; hijras as transgressive

The predicament of a woman or a gay or a *hijra* in this phallogopathic world is the same: they are other, either because they have no cock or because they are not heterosexual. This normative sexuality is based on the textual and sexual politics of body. 'Body' is a potential site for construction of identity and hegemony. It assumed great significance in the eighteenth century with the development of eugenics and statistics, which differentiates the normal (so, ideal and beautiful) physicality from the not-normal (hence ugly and abnormal) one. In the nineteenth century, the body was explicitly politicized with the reification of racism: the Manichean allegory of white/black, master/slave, ruler/ruled has been widely used to legitimize colonization. Along with that came Darwin with his theory of the descent of man. The oldest of the body politics relies, however, on sex difference: the hairy, fleshy configuration between legs determines if one is privileged (in case of the man/other binary) and normal (in case of the male–female/other binary).

'Normalcy', as Davis puts it in his seminal 1995 book Enforcing Normalcy, is 'a location of bio-power'[13] in which the 'normal' person 'has a network of traditional ableist assumptions and social supports that empowers the gaze and interaction' (Davis, 2001, p. 2402). Normalcy is a dangerously relative term: it is constructed by gaze and maintained by socio-cultural panopticon. Cultures neatly 'split' the body into good and bad categories: there are good and bad body parts (face, lips, eyes versus penis, vagina, underarms); there are good and bad body structures (tall versus short); there are good and bad body complexions (fair versus dark). Davis asks, 'why it is imperative for society at large to engage in Spaltung?'[14] He himself gives the answer, famously: because it recognizes that 'wholeness is in fact a hallucination' (Davis, 2001, p. 2403).

The mechanism of gaze is informed by desire and fear. Davis observes how the critics and audiences alike have been obsessed with the beauty of the Venus de Milo, the armless, severely damaged statue of Aphrodite. Despite its mutilation, she is called 'Notre-Dame de la Beauté' (in Heinrich Heine's words), 'Our Lady of Beauty.' How does it happen? To Davis, the observers here tend to ignore the lack, rather imagines and 'mentally reforms the outline of the Venus,' thus creating a presence that is absent: it is an act of 'sanitizing of the disruption of perception' (Davis, 2001, p. 2407). This renegotiation is necessary, for a limited or disabled body exemplifies the fear of incompleteness of moi and castration complex.

The disabled/limited body reminds the observers that 'the "real" body, the "normal body," the observer's body, is in fact always already a "fragmented body"' (Davis, 2001, p. 2411). According to Lacan, the infant never perceives its body as a totality; it rather sees body as an assemblage of imagos:[15] separate parts or pieces such as hands, legs, heads. When the self is being developed, these fragments are forced to assume totality leading to the formation of an image of a whole body. At the 'mirror-phase,' the child sees a perfect whole body in the mirror and associates its fragmented body (corps morcelé) with that unified self. From now on starts its donning or pursuing an identity, the illusory wholeness, which is not her/his. In this sense, coming in contact with a disabled/ limited person is the reincarnation of the suppressed imagos; the object of desire, the hallucinatory wholeness, is replaced by the object of fear, the fragmentation. This specular moment 'between the armored, unified self and its repressed double – the fragmented body – is characterized by a kind of death-work, repetition compulsion in which the unified self continuously sees itself undone' (Davis, 2001, p. 2410).

To the physically 'normal' observers, I argue, *hijras* mirror the incompleteness of being. This inverted mirroring leaves the observer anxious to re-armor itself with newer codes and associations: in order to separate itself from the resurrected incompleteness, it designates the *hijras*, in Freudian terms, *unheimlich*, uncanny, unfamiliar, so abnormal.

Disability, with its association with mutilation and fragmentation, is also an unwanted reminder of the castration complex. According to Freud, the threat of castration from the father helps the infant overcome its primal Oedipal complex. The infant girl accepts her 'absolute inferiority' because she *lacks* the penis; the infant boy admits his 'relative inferiority' because he does not want to *lose* his penis (Andermahr et al., p. 24). The confusion of these two competing drives is settled with the infant's entry into the patriarchal order, and the acceptance and absorption of the values and codes it propagates. In this sense, coming in contact with a disabled/limited person such as a lame person or a hermaphrodite is a real/is/ation of the symbolic, the visualization of mutilation and castration: the object of fear is back!

In the case of *hijra*, castration is both symbolic and literal – 'here is a man who is no-man' – leaving the observers internally and intrinsically jolted. The settled self confronts what Davis calls 'repetition compulsion' in which it 'sees itself undone – castrated, mutilated, perforated, made partial' (Davis, 2001, p. 2410). With a similar fear and move, the observer then tries to dispel the illusion of threat by alienating and marginalizing the object as 'abject.'

The politics of this forced splitting – *Spaltung* – has some sadistic-affirmation strategies too. The alienating of the *hijras* as physically uncanny re-gratifies the observer's illusion of being complete. The alienating of the *hijras* as impotent/eunuch reasserts the observer's potential of regeneration. It reassures the observer that castration is not done!

Hijras thus appear as transgressive beings, subversive of normative sexualcy. They also work as a foil against which heterosexism relishes its sexuality and potency.

This interpellation, however, ironically betrays the inconstancy of patriarchal heterosexism and the performativity of gender. Eve Kosofsky Sedgwick and Jonathan Dollimore show, in their separate studies of sexual dissidence, 'how heterosexuality is already internally unstable or incoherent and … is shadowed by its "other", … as a necessary, desired and feared, aspect of itself' (Brooker, 1999, p. 93). In *Gender Trouble*, Butler (1999 [1990]) proclaims that gender is not a noun, a *being*; gender is a verb, is 'always a doing' (p. 33). Now, if gender is 'enactment,' not given, then it can be enacted in unexpected, subversive ways. *Hijras* demonstrates that it can be.

Chheley nachano: performing an/other

Sex worker hijras; sex work as liberating alternative

Most present-day urban *hijras* ranging from the intersexuals to the *kotis* are sex workers. In fact, *hijras* historically have been sex workers. 'Leyla's Chayhane' tells us that the prophet Mohammad (s.a.s.) was reported to give a *mukhannathun* a place in society 'so that they didn't need to earn their money with (sic) erotical entertainment' (Leyla's Chayhane, 2008). Majumder reports that *hijras*' sex profession was in vogue during the Mughal Empire; during the reigns of the Muslim *rajahs*, *hijras* were appointed as *darwans* (doorkeepers) and shared kings' beds (Majumder, 2005, p. 44). Though many *hijras* were reported to assume different honorable and high positions during the Mughal period and the British Raj, there is, however, no denying the fact that sex work was always a major and lucrative occupation for the *hijras*.

This should not lead us to conclude that *hijras* invariably are/were sex workers. Sex work is not a job necessarily to be revered by the *hijras*, nor is this the only job they feel they are suited for. Traditionally, prostitution is strictly forbidden among the *hijras*; the *Gurumaas* usually sanction against and slander sex work, and distance themselves from the *hijras* who do sex work. The jobs considered to be dignified for a *hijra* are *chheley nachano*, collecting *tola*, and providing entertainment. This tradition is still maintained by the *hijras* living in rural areas. The (sub)urban *hijras*, having been exposed to sex clients, have had the scope to live by sex work which the *hijras* of rural areas don't have. Most sex worker *hijras* in Bangladesh live in the cities, chiefly in Dhaka, and more than 60 percent of the *hijras* in Dhaka are sex workers (Husain, 2005, p. 26).

Even among sex workers, the *hijras* are at the periphery. Majumdar and Basu's study of the male sex workers in India presents four kinds of MSM or Dhurani: (a) *Khandan Dhurani*, (b) *Lahari Dhurani*, (c) *Adat Dhurani*, and (d) *Aqua Dhurani*.[16] This division is based upon socio-economic status and cultural conditions. Significantly enough, the *Aqua Dhuranis*, that is the *hijras*, are marginalized by the gay male sex workers and placed both socio-culturally and economically at the bottom:

KHANDAN DHURANI

⬇

LAHARI DHURANI

⬇

ADAT DHURANI

⬇

AQUA DHURANI (*Hijra*)

Figure 6.1 The socio-economic status of the Dhuranis
(Source: Majumdar & Basu, 1999, p. 57)

Hijras are sex workers – mainly, but never only – because of the lack of other professional opportunities. Their traditional jobs are no longer sufficient for their living, and they have always been ostracized from socially accepted jobs. Remarginalized by economic and social forces, *hijras cash in on the body to survive*. This is becoming their main profession, and they are thriving.

At this point, it is important to note that *hijras'* viewpoints about the job are curiously enriching:

- They are aware of the stigma associated with the sex profession and they may leave the profession if they are offered any 'decent' job.
- They enjoy the profession as this is a way of satiating their sexual drives and asserting their status as 'girls'; Kanak said that if s/he gets a 'decent' job, s/he will leave sex work as a *pesha* (profession) but maintain it as a *nesha* (pastime/hobby).

The second point I found worth noting, and it sparked the idea for this chapter: while it's true that sex work is a 'job' that *hijras* take mostly out of necessity, sex work is still a desired site where they can assert their be/ing. Sex work, despite its conventional universalist association with shame and disgrace, is an act of emancipation, of wild justice, of self-assertion.

133

'Sex work as liberating altarnative'

In response to being designated as transgressive, sex work is counter-transgression in action. It is an act of going beyond the periphery set by the patriarchal society, a carnivalizing of socially indoctrinated mandates regarding normalcy and decency. As Sedgwick suggests in *Epistemology of the Closet*, 'transgendered and transsexual identities present models of gender liminality, since they suggest a transitive movement that escalates any fixed boundary between male and female, masculinity and femininity' (cited in Bristow, 2007, p. 208).

- Sex work is an engagement, involvement, and dialog with the very society that ostracizes the *hijras*.

- It is an act of emancipation, of coming out of culturally constructed cocoon.

- It is liberation from the suffocating feeling of belonging to *hich-gah*, nowhere. Even ironically or illusively, it 'attests' to the *hijra's* identity as fe/male, a non-male.

- It is, even if unintentionally so, an act of mimicry, thus parodying, the set categories of normative sexuality. Instead of maintaining the 'hijraness' as masquerade, in the sense Joan Riviere used it in her influential article 'Womanliness as a Masquerade' (1929), the sex workers appropriate the masquerade 'in the spirit of mimicry and parody,' in the line of Judith Butler who sees in masquerade a potential for affirmative subversion (Brooker, 1999, p. 131). An 'instance of performativity, masquerade serves to emphasize how all identities are constructed and open to play and transformation'; thus, instead of confirming or conforming to hijra's stereotypical fixed roles, sex work is a masquerade that can critique and destabilize the 'essentialist assumptions of sexual identity' (Brooker, 1999, p. 131). The very performativity thus betrays the fluidity and inconstancy of sexual identity maintained by the heterosexist, hermophobic society.

- It offers a gratification of — *Hai'allah!* — sexual drives which society so often ignores or denies. It is a celebration of Ginsbergian 'juvenescent savagery, primitive abandon' (Raskin, 2004, p. 68).

- It is a potential space which offers the *hijras* release from what we may call 'cunt envy,' the 'penis envy' subverted. The *hijras* are invariably antagonistic towards women: they *lack* vulvas that render woman so attractive to the men; they *lack* ovaries which enable women to give birth to children and so lead men to marry them. Sex work is a stage on which they *perform* woman.

- It is a counter-discursive ছেলে নাচানো : in Bangla, *chheley* means both young boy and man; *nachano* means both 'to make one dance' and 'to flirt.' So while *chheley nachano* means making fun with the newborn baby, it could also mean flirting with guys. By making love with the *hijras*, the men who disregard the existence of *hijra* as a 'normal' being work as instruments in legitimizing and establishing the existence of the *hijras* not simply as entities, but as sexual beings.

- It is an expression of *jouissance*: 'an extreme, unsettling experience of enjoyment, delight, or jubilation' (Brooker, 1999, p. 124). The term is much more forceful in French, denoting a sense of 'ownership as in "enjoying a right," of playfulness, and is associated with sexual orgasm' (Brooker, 1999, p. 125). Psychoanalytic theories perceive it as contrasted with the experience of 'lack.' A pre-Oedipal drive, *jouissance* in the infant boy is thwarted by the threat of castration and later finds its release in the site of woman. In the case of *hijras*' male–male relation, *jouissance* is redirected towards men, the representation of the chastizing father: it then could be read as an unconscious act of revenge and refilling, compensation for the lack of phallic power.

- It is an appropriation of the grotesque, of abnormality, by manifesting the subversive power of the carnival. To Bakhtin, 'grotesque' is associated with the subaltern, the common people. During the medieval carnivals, the lower order commoners assumed a special power: they enjoyed the pleasures of body by eating, drinking, and promiscuity as well as the license to 'lampoon the authorities of church and state' (Brooker, 1999, p. 23). This 'act of subversive nose-thumbing' suggests a space in which the oppressed can symbolically dethrone, profane, parody, and dismantle their oppressors. Sex work offers *hijras*, the 'grotesque' community, this carnivalesque site: the so-called 'asexual,' 'sexless,' 'subaltern,' 'freaks' assert their 'ability' to enjoy being 'fucked in the ass'[17] at the very premise of the homophobic society.

- It may operate as an escape mechanism for many a gay man who falsely assumes the identity of *hijras* and lives accordingly only to meet sexual demands. This occurs primarily among lower-class gays who, mostly illiterate, are in most cases not acquainted with gayness. While gay subculture is flourishing in Bangladesh, semi-clandestine hooking ups and parties have become a way of life; but these gays are mostly educated, urban-oriented, and from the middle and upper classes. The lower-class gays often live a rather suffocating straight-acting life. Though there are MSMs and male sex workers, it is difficult for boys to retain their socially accepted identity and live 'gay.' So they enter a *hijra* community and adopt a new name and getup (but these hidden-*hijras* seldom acknowledge their gayness). Some of them retain triple identity: 'normal' boy in family life, playing 'hijra' at night, and actually 'gay.' This adaptation helps them to lead a manageably satisfying sexual life without being decried and boxed in by the society as 'faggot'.

- It is an act of self-sufficiency and economic independence. *Hijras* have their own community. The head of the community is an elder *hijra*, the *Gurumaa*. Whatever a *hijra* earns, s/he is supposed to give the *Gurumaa* half. But earnings through sex work are not to be shared, because sex work is not an acceptable job. This gives a sex worker *hijra* authority over what s/he earns.

- It overtly values the body. The body, for which *hijras* are ostracized and stigmatized, has assumed, using Marxist terms with a different and affirmative connotation, both 'use-value' and 'exchange-value.' The sex worker *hijras* are used here as commodities, no doubt; but being a commodity may not be seen as devaluing of self and dignity. This could rather be seen as irony, a reversal of the un-usability or worthlessness of a *hijra* body, an assertion that 'hijra-sex matters.' More than that, unlike the alienation of the laborers in capitalist societies, *hijras* are alienated neither from the product of their labor nor from its value. The enjoyment and the earnings are all her/his.

- It is writing body ahead! The very physicality of the body has long been used as 'a text for deviant embodiment' (Brooker, 1999, p. 183), inscribing and establishing hegemony. If so, this same site could effectively be manipulated to attest resistance and reinstate subjectivity. The *hijra*'s body, which is the cause of shame and violence, now becomes the locus of resumption of power and identity.

Hijras (are supposed to) perform: s/he is a soft, loving 'lady' while playing with newborn babies, or an aggressive, shouting 'macho' while collecting *tola*. Sex work provides her/him with a different kind of performance: here she performs an/other, wearing the persona of a woman, who is in love and making love with a man. Being fucked, s/he gender-fucks![18]

Being hermaphroditus

The word 'hermaphrodite' is derived from the name of Hermaphroditus. This beautiful, handsome boy was the son of Hermes and Aphrodite (Hermes+Aphrodite=Hermaphroditus). Once Salmacis, a *naiad*, bathing in a pool, felt attracted towards the boy but was rejected instantly. After a while, Hermaphroditus dived into the pool thinking that the *naiad* had left; Salmacis was excited seeing the boy undressing; she dived too and embraced the boy. When Hermaphroditus was struggling to free himself, she prayed to the gods not to separate them. The gods listened to her, and Salmacis merged with Hermaphroditus. What appeared was a person who was neither Hermaphroditus the boy nor Salmacis the *naiad*, neither a man nor a woman. Hermaphroditus became both. Unfortunately, this mythical reference with its sense of affirmative plurality and potential of performativity is rarely given serious attention.

'*Hai'allah! Why then has this romantic association been ignored? Why are the hijras seen as freaks, not as angels who are also sexless/sex-neutral? Isn't God itself sex-neutral?*'

The plurality and ambivalence of sexual identities need to be renegotiated, to be queered. If sexual and gendered identities are performative, they are always in the process of becoming and are always subject to reconfiguration. The normative/normal(ized) sex/gender system is nothing more than conventional: cultural, not natural. After the emergence of queer studies and queer culture, gender can no more be limited within binaries. We could even expect, what the early gay liberation movement aimed to attain: 'an *androgynous world* ... within which gender would no longer be relevant' (Andy Metcalfe & Martin Humphries, quoted in Brooker, 1999, p. 8; emphasis mine).

One should, however, be alert to the fact that recognizing the sexual identity of *hijras* as 'another sex' should not lead us to conclude that the *hijras* are the 'twilight zone.' While acceptance of this may sound progressive, it is still political. Taking twilight as transition suggests lack, incompleteness, to-be-finishedness. *Hijra*, like every sign, is in-process, but hijras need not be thought as in transition; they are what they are; they are *they*; they *are* hijras. Their bodies may look male or female; they may feel like men or women. It is the privilege of having an indeterminate and intermediate identity that permits a person to move between different sexes, a quality that the mainstream sexes lack.

Sex work renegotiates the identity of a hijra. It seems that, like the Camusian Sisyphus, the hijras transform social imposition – sex work as a means of survival, as shame – into an act of jubilation – sex work as enjoyment, as affirmation. Again her/his identity is identified with her/his bodies, but here is a curious appropriation: no more does the body play the definitive part; it is the hijra who determines the use of the body.

NOTES

1 In this chapter, the italicized words *perform* or *performance* refers to Judith Butler's conception of gender as performativity.
2 I refrained from designating them as 'subaltern' because of their increasing access to human rights and political participation. Most of the hijras are, however, crucially marginalized and stigmatized.
3 These three are the common features that manageably put the varieties of hijras within one term: *maiggya* is a Bangla word meaning 'effeminate man'; 'bottom' is a person who adopts the receptive and/or submissive role in a sexual act (I, however, prefer using 'bottom-performing'); 'men' is put in quotation marks as most of the hijras, including many of the *kotis*, like imagining and seeing themselves as 'woman.'
4 It is important to note here that there is not much documented information about hijra community – biological and sociological facts – available in Bangladesh. The community has only recently received attention and scholarly works on them are rare.
5 The word 'alternative' is used to mark differences between what is considered to be 'mainstream' sexuality – man and woman – and non-mainstream sexuality. I, however, deny using the hierarchical, heteropatriarchal word 'third sex' despite its usefulness.
6 Females are born with XX chromosomes and males with XY.
7 'Herm is a hermaphrodite with one teste and one ovary and external sex organs that are somewhere in between male and female. A Merm has testes but ambiguously-shaped genitalia. A Ferm has ovaries but ambiguously shaped genitalia.' (Scott, 1999)
8 ISA, or Ideological State Apparatus, is conceptualized by the Marxist theorist Louis Althusser. ISA includes the media, education and the church, etc., through which hegemony is solidified.
9 The conditions of the hijras that the next pages elaborate have started to improve to a limited extent as Badhan Hijra Sangha started to attend the

problems organizationally and a number of NGOs and other organizations, for example the internet group Gay Bangla, are working for/about hijras.

10   'Myth' in the Barthesian sense.

11   Most of the hijras in Bangladesh prefer considering themselves as women and have female names. Joya wants people to call her 'Apoo,' a Bangla form of address to one's sister.

12   The Bangla word *veshya* invariably refers to female pros.

13   In Michel Foucault, bio-power is 'a political technology for manipulating the body' (editor's note in Davis 2001, p. 2402).

14   *Spaltung*, is a Freudian term, later elaborated by Melanie Klein, meaning 'splitting'. It refers to a mechanism through which an infant is led to divide (split) 'whole' things into *good* and *bad* 'part-things'; for example, 'good' body parts (e.g. eye. lips) and 'bad' body parts (e.g. armpit).

15   From Lacan's 'Mirror Stage': 'Among these *imagos* are some that represent the elective vectors of aggressive intentions, which they provide with an efficacy that might be called magical. These are the images of castration, mutilation, dismemberment, dislocation, evisceration, devouring, bursting open of the body, in short, the *imagos* that I have grouped together under the apparently structural term of *imagos of the fragmented body.*' (quoted in Davis, 2001, p. 2410).

16   *Khandan Dhurani* includes gay and transsexuals coming from rich families; *Lahari Dhuranis* are transsexuals from the middle class; *Adat Dhuranis* (also called '7:45 Dhurani' because they are available at parks etc. from 7:45 p.m.) are from low/nil-income brackets; and *Aqua Dhuranis* are what we call hijras (Majumdar & Basu, 1997, pp. 50–55).

17   From Alan Ginsberg's *Howl*, l. 29: 'who let themselves be fucked in the ass by the saintly motorcyclists, and screamed with joy.'

18   'Gender fuck,' a noun, is used to signify the disruption of the heterosexist bipolar gender system.

C   Money and Sex

7   Let's Talk About Money

Alys Willman

It is safe to say that most sex workers are not in the industry for the sex. Specifically, it is *fast money* that pulls people into the industry and often keeps them there even when there are other alternatives. Around the world, sex work offers much more money in fewer hours than other jobs to which the people engaged in sex work have access (Moffatt & Peters, 2004; Levitt & Venkatesh, 2007; Willman, 2008). For women, the majority of sex workers, the sex industry is one of the few labor markets in which they consistently earn more than men of their same skill level (Pickering & Wilkins, 1993; Edlund & Korn, 2002).

But despite its clear economic foundations, economists have traditionally had little to say about the sex industry. There are two key reasons for this. The first is a certain moral bias about what constitutes rational behavior, which pervaded the discipline until very recently. Standard economics is the study of rational behavior by individuals, which often inadvertently leaves out groups or individuals who engage in activities considered irrational. Many criminal activities have fallen into this category, as things no one in her right mind would do. In the post-*Freakonomics* world, however, things are different. Economists are now beginning to apply their analytical tools to study illicit networks, treating supposedly irrational actors as if they had legitimate reasons for doing what they do. It turns out, perhaps not surprisingly, that actors in illicit markets respond to incentives in much the same way that actors in formal sectors do.[1] This recognition has led economists into new territory, from organized crime to suicide bombing, and many things in between, including sex work.

The second reason for the dearth of economic literature on sex work is much more practical. Economists generally work with numbers, and it is extremely difficult to get reliable data on commercial sex. Because most transactions happen off the books, information about them rarely makes its way into any formal accounting. Where prostitution is criminalized, economists can use police data, but this of course only gives information on a small segment of the sex worker and client population, and only limited information at that.

Recently, economists have overcome these limitations by collecting their own data, giving rise to some exciting new analyses of commercial sex markets. Their work has followed two main areas of inquiry. The first is the simple question of why sex work is so much more lucrative than other lines of work, especially for women. The first formal economic model to be published in an academic journal, 'A Theory of Prostitution' argues that sex workers' wages are higher than other women's in order to make up for lost position in the marriage market (Edlund & Korn, 2002). That is, women (male sex workers are not considered) enter sex work for a lack of marriage options – and women can only be either wives or sex workers, not both – and then demand higher pay to compensate. While the practical flaws of this conceptualization will be obvious, it did make an important contribution in factoring in the issue of stigma to understanding earnings in sex work.

More recent work has placed stigma at the center of the model. Using data from the US, Della Giusta et al. (2006, 2008) look at how clients and sex workers weigh the potential loss in reputation associated with taking part in commercial sex, and how this determines the price they will pay or accept. The degree of stigma, and with it the risk to reputation, will vary with context, and to some extent with gender as well. In their study, the authors also predict the impact that different policies will have on supply and demand of commercial sex.

The second area of interest has centered on the role of economic incentives in driving risky behavior of both sex workers and clients – specifically the effect of condom use on the price of sex. Using formal surveys of sex workers, Rao et al. (2003) and Gertler et al. (2005) examined the prices for protected and unprotected sex in Calcutta and Mexico, respectively. Rao estimated that sex workers who regularly use condoms earn 79 percent less than those who don't. Gertler's study of Mexican sex workers estimated that sex workers could charge 24 percent more if they agreed not to use a condom, and up to 47 percent more if they were considered attractive (a measure of bargaining power). Both studies have been instrumental in influencing the debate over HIV/AIDS policy toward the commercial sex sector, by framing the issues as one of economic incentives to risk, rather than a real lack of information on the part of sex workers and clients about those risks.

My own work (Willman 2008, 2009, forthcoming) adds further nuance to this analysis, by looking at the ways different risks interact (for example, the risk of disease and the risk of violence) and the importance of working conditions in influencing risky behavior. Using the experience of sex workers in Managua, Nicaragua, this work shows that while sex workers negotiate more money for sex without a condom, they charge much more to take risks of assault, for example by going with clients to places they do not know well, or going with multiple clients at once. In addition, the type of workplace conditions matter immensely to the degree of autonomy a sex worker has to deal with risk and negotiate appropriate compensation. These findings help place the policy emphasis on working conditions and how they might be improved, rather than on changing the behavior of individuals – whether sex workers, managers, or clients.

All of this work has been helpful in illuminating the decisions of individuals in sex work. We know much less, however, about the overall organization of commercial sex markets and how they integrate into the local, national and even global economy. For example, how is the market structured in different contexts? Who are the actors involved and what are their roles? The International Labor Office (ILO, see Lim, 1998) conducted a groundbreaking study of the sex industries in Thailand, Indonesia, the Philippines, and Malaysia. From this, the term 'sex sector' was coined to refer to an integrated economic sector centered on commercial sex that is connected to economic and social life and that contributes, directly or indirectly, to economic growth, employment and national income. Unfortunately, the ILO study remains the only project to date to have attempted to map the dimensions of the sex sector on a national or regional scale.

Ethnographers have stepped in to offer several rich descriptions of the organization of the sex sector in specific contexts, and some of these have considered its economic dimensions. Teela Sanders (2004a, 2005b) offers a rich description of the indoor commercial sex market in Birmingham, UK, including a discussion of the role of economic incentives in decisions about risk in sex work. In her earlier work, Laura Agustín (2005d) reviews the structure of the sex industry in Spain from an economic and cultural perspective, elucidating the ways in which commercial sex is entangled with other business sectors and social institutions.

So, yes, we have begun to talk about money, but we are only just starting. Notably absent from the conversation have been the voices of sex workers themselves. The next two chapters, with two contributions by sex workers, are important steps toward a greater inclusion in the dialog and a better understanding of what money really means to sex workers. Drawing on both personal experience and interviews with other sex workers, the two chapters that follow delve into the ways in which money – especially fast money – draws workers to the sex industry and keeps them there. They show how sex workers deal with the same financial issues as people in other lines of work, and in so doing they illuminate the ways in which sex work is like other forms of labor. Economists would do well to pay closer attention.

NOTE

1   Particularly influential has been a 1998 study of the financing activities of a drug-selling gang, showing how gang members respond to incentives (higher wages, prestige) and disincentives (risk of imprisonment or death) in very rational ways under the constraints present in their neighborhoods (Levitt & Venkatesh, 2000).

8   Show Me the Money: A Sex Worker Reflects on Research into the Sex Industry

Jo Weldon

> I've been getting a bit introspective about my work in the sex industry for the past several weeks. I just had a memory of some guy passing out thousands and thousands to the dancers one night (he had just gotten a fat cash bonus on a deal), and he had a pretty good vibe about him. He half-jokingly said, 'I really resent that you ladies are just after my money,' and I half-jokingly said, 'Dude, I don't want this chump change, I want your fucking job.'

The above quote is from me, speaking in my blog on 4 October 2006 (see http://gstringgirl.livejournal.com). The story, which is true, is illustrative of precisely why we dancers were there that night – for money.

As it happens, I'm terrible with money. Because I'm often in speculative conversations about strippers, their place in our culture, and their motivations for stripping, I frequently hear how terrible all of us are with money. Over the years I've considered this: I started stripping less than a year after graduating from high school, and have stripped the majority of my adult life. Almost all the men I saw were successful and responsible (as far as I knew) and they were throwing away large amounts of cash on something they didn't need. Where would I have learned to be good with money? (Note: this was written before the economic crisis we are currently enjoying.)

How does anyone learn to handle money? Marian Friestad, PhD, professor of marketing at the Lundquist College of Business at the University of Oregon and past president and fellow of the Society for Consumer Psychology, says, 'In the United States, talking about money is harder than talking about sex' (Getlen, 2005). As a sex worker who is frequently interviewed for research and theses, I believe Friestad is right. While every interviewer asks me whether I was sexually abused as a child, none of them have ever asked me a single question about the financial mindset, or even the financial motivation, involved in my decisions to work in the sex industry. No one – including the casual interviewer who is not doing research but is curious about my job – has ever asked me if my parents argued about money in front of me, if I got an allowance, if I had a job in high school, if I was raised to value money as a form of status or simply as a means to an end, and so on. This makes me question the socially acceptable assumption that leads researchers to believe that the questions they are asking are worth asking. The implied attitude seems so widespread that I wonder if it doesn't enter into many other areas.

I'm going to touch briefly on a few areas where I've noticed that the discussion of money tends to be taboo when sex work is discussed in academic and legislative environments. Of course there are more pressing issues – HIV/AIDS, child prostitution, trafficking. I am certainly not suggesting that these issues take a back seat to the issue of money. But if you want to know why sex workers get into sex work and want to understand their psychology, wouldn't you ask how they think about money and work?

When research is conducted as to how and why sex workers enter the industry, the questions 'How were you raised to think about money? Did both your parents work? Did your mother stop working after she had you? Did your parents fight about money? Did you have an allowance?' are rarely, if ever, asked. The questions that are asked often presuppose the conclusions the researcher has reached before outlining their research. The question 'Were you ever sexually abused as a child?' certainly expresses an attitude toward sex work. That attitude, and the reasons that the question is considered appropriate to ask, should not be ignored.

I believe that the reason questions about money are so rarely asked is that people continue to think only about the sex involved, and not about the labor. I suppose that if you did ask, you'd be supporting the idea that sex work is partially about money. This seems to be the elephant in the room whenever prostitution is discussed in academic and/or legislative environments. We can understand why second-wave feminists never ask. But I am not even talking about them, honestly. I understand that they cannot afford to concede any points sex worker advocates make because they would lose their funding if they did (speaking of money issues which are rarely discussed when sex work is the subject). But I digress.

Much of the current psychological literature about sex work refers to either deviance or post-traumatic stress disorder resulting from sexual abuse. I believe that these are vital issues and should not necessarily take second place to the psychology of earning and handling money. However, it seems to me that if the financial element does not enter the picture in any form, the results of these studies can provide only a fragmented view of the psychology of sex workers, and certainly not a view complete enough to be applied to developing legislation, whether that legislation is designed to address the needs of sex workers, or − if sex work is considered an ill of society − how to prevent it from happening.

I reviewed many lists of names of papers and studies about sex work, looking for research on the needs of labor − sex workers at work − rather than research related to or supporting suggested governmental controls. Papers that addressed the financial concerns of sex workers were so rare that at first I thought there were none at all. Since money is generally the source of food, shelter, status, health care, community, child care, and more, it seems odd that all these issues are addressed primarily as they are affected by the sexual standards and behavior of the interviewees, and rarely as they are affected by their understanding of and feelings about money. I am simply puzzled that financial psychology seems to be viewed as almost entirely irrelevant.

My own experiences in both casual conversations and interviews by journalists or researchers are telling. People who find out I have worked in adult entertainment, and sometimes even my sex work clients, have so frequently asked me certain questions that it seems to me that the assumptions they reflect must permeate our society's consciousness. Because researchers are a part of our society, I assume that they are not immune to the common perceptions of sex workers as desperate, abused, amoral, predatory, lazy women. I believe that the research questions that they ask must be examined on this basis, and the reasons for those questions explained.

In a recent conversation on a message board at stripperforum.com, a person relatively new to the group asked if it was really all about money. Every respondent to her post said that yes, they began dancing for the money. In another recent conversation on the same message board, a person posted that she was doing research about dancers and wanted to ask them about their childhoods. She posted, 'I am looking to examine the psychology of women in the adult trade and need to have conversations with various women, of any legal age, regarding their upbringing, childhood, young adulthood and current life status' (Stripper Web, 2009).

The respondents to this all objected vehemently to the poster, saying things like, 'I am a little bit sick of people wanting to question our childhoods and upbringing to see if it somehow relates to us choosing to strip for a living.' 'Who's to say that we have any type of special "psychology"?' 'Are we not normal human beings just like everyone else?' When the message poster reprimanded them for jumping to conclusions and said she was surprised by their reactions, one said, 'I'm actually very open a lot of the time to talking about dancing, answering questions and whatever people want to relate to it at the time for free. I just get a bit tired of the whole childhood issue being brought up time and time again that's all …'

The one thing the workers talk about most, the one thing they show up for day after day, is very rarely discussed in research. How they feel about money is rarely, if ever, compared to the way other workers feel about money. Instead, their sexual deviance is questioned at every turn. Yet few workers ever say, 'I got into it because I needed the sex.' In *Taking It Off, Putting It On*, Chris Bruckert (2002) observes of the studies she has read that 'Perhaps the most telling finding was how few comments were made by interviewees about sexuality; it appeared to be largely incidental' (Bruckert, 2002, p. 89).

An article by SWEAT says, 'People enter the profession for various reasons, the most common being unemployment or a desire to improve their income' (Health 24, 2007). Bruckert also documents the ways sex workers seek to make more money, writing, 'Workers [strip joint dancers] may see themselves as entrepreneurs, and put a great deal of effort into maximizing their income through grooming and other skills' (Bruckert, 2002, p. 148).

Often researchers approach the concept of whether or not sex workers make a lot of money. It is not so much the amount of money they make, but the immediacy of access to money that motivates them. I am compelled to state what I believe is a fact: prostitutes, as well as legal or semi-legal workers such as strippers or dominatrices, can apply for a job in one day, work the night of that same day, and make enough to pay a bill the next day. There is no substitute for this in our society. Until we acknowledge the unique economic need sex work fulfills, and acknowledge money as a primary motivation for working in the sex industry, there can be no useful approach to solving any of the problems in and around the sex industry.

Yet, as I stated at the beginning, this money comes at a unique cost. It separates the women who would do such a thing for money from the women who would never do such a thing for money. The constant search for a single unified field theory of why sex workers are doing what they do cannot be solved by addressing only the sex side of the equation when a worker claims to be doing it for the money. That some researchers claim these workers are in denial shows that the researchers themselves must also be in denial. They are in denial about their inability to accept that their theories are not comprehensive enough to address the many issues that occur in sex work.

The work side must be addressed. Prostitutes aren't just having sex; they are having sex for money. They have a different relationship with an agent who takes 20 percent of their money than with a trafficker who takes 100 percent of their money. The flow of money in the sex industry is the most likely indicator of the motivations of those involved in the transactions. And yet the questions are never asked; financial desperation is examined, but never financial motivation. Beliefs about sex and morality are examined, but rarely beliefs about money and the work ethic. The simple exchange every other laborer makes – doing something relatively undesirable for compensation – is treated as deviant, when in fact that element is the most normal thing about the decision to enter the industry. The financial experience the women are having is often assumed to be completely irrelevant compared to the sexual experience the men are having; the experience of the men is taken to define the exchange, in a way that to me doesn't seem very feminist.

In *Money, A Memoir*, author Liz Perle (2006) notes that 'when it comes to money, women everywhere have so many fears and fantasies in common.' The word 'prostitution' is not in the index of her book, but it's safe to say that many women often default to the idea of prostitution when they are broke. Many women who would never actually have sex for money have told me they wished they 'could,' or have suggested that they might as well have. Of course my saying this is anecdotal, but I'm fairly certain that thorough research among women who are not from rich families would prove that at least half of them would say that when they were broke, the thought had crossed their minds – not, perhaps, very seriously, but in the sense that it's something they might do. I have no idea if this question has ever been asked of women outside the sex industry, but wouldn't it be useful information in the debate about whether or not sex work is work to know how often women who are having financial trouble consider prostitution, even just as a pure fantasy? And to know how often that fantasy is not about sexual expression, but about easy money?

When I read about stripping, certain sentences leap out at me, such as this one from Alison Fensterstock, a former commercial stripper who is one of the founders of the burlesque convention Tease-O-Rama: 'You make money … You watch your income come in physically bill by bill … This is the most immediate way of making money' (Fensterstock, 2005, p. 74). This is a psychological experience that as a former stripper I can easily identify with; it is one of the conditions of sex work that influenced the way I handle money. I believe similar conditions influence most workers who handle cash and that they contribute to creating a significantly different understanding of finance than the understanding of the more commonly recognized population of workers who receive checks twice a month. When comparisons to other jobs are made, this aspect is rarely if ever mentioned, as if, without the stripping, all other things about the jobs are equal to other jobs. But the ability to acquire a job entirely without a resumé and to leave your first working shift with cash makes more of a difference to most of the women who decide to do it than the social and sexual aspects.

Another point of interest to me is that I constantly hear people say to women in the sex industry, 'You'd better be saving up that money.' I find this to be presumptuous. First, most sex workers aren't making as much money people think they are. Furthermore, most younger workers may be making a living for the first time and there's no reason whatsoever to think that they would be any better with money than most young people. And on top of that, they make their livelihood watching men who are usually old enough to be authority figures spending money most unwisely. And to put it all in context, 'The Commerce Department reports that the average US household didn't save so much as a penny last year, as Americans either accumulated more debt or dug into the savings they had to pay bills and buy goods' (Money News, 2006). So the odds are very much in favor of the person saying this to the worker having no savings themselves.

Furthermore, our society still encourages a 'white knight' fantasy for women. Some have commented that the movie Pretty Woman implies that prostitution is a great arena in which to find a white knight (which, given our society's general attitude about how sex workers 'end up,' is unlikely to have much impact on a young woman's expectations of the work). In studies, most sex workers aren't even asked if they expect to meet a white knight, although it's well known that many women, the majority of whom are not in the sex industry, dream of marrying a rich man. In A Girl Needs Cash, author Joan Perry (1999) says that when she began to be concerned about her financial future, 'I began to ask my female colleagues in the brokerage world and elsewhere what they were doing about their financial futures [and] I found an epidemic of the White Knight Syndrome, and a weird repetition of my own circumstances ... debt, and virtually no investments.' When people assume that sex workers are particularly prone to bad financial decisions, they are displaying a prejudice against sex workers that is completely irrational. But this prejudice is widespread: just ask around. The belief that sex workers are somehow set apart from the rest of the human race extends to this assumption that they are not only different about money, but they are also worse with money than other people.

In *Women and Work* (Dubeck & Borman, 1997), the segment on prostitution states, 'Research consistently shows that the majority of prostitutes enter the field for economic gain.' Is this news to anybody? So why don't researchers more frequently discuss how a limited job market can be a powerful motivator toward prostitution? Why do they call the economic constraints that motivate all of us to spend more hours than we want doing things we could care less about 'coercion' only when it comes to prostitution? Why do they claim that it's all about sex, when it's so clearly so very much about money? And doesn't ignoring these very important facts lead to proposed 'solutions' for 'problems' that have no practical basis for success?

In the literature that I've encountered, several important issues related to money and sex work are not explored in any depth. Interestingly, while the significance of the financial psychology of sex workers has been minimized, the financial decisions of the clientele represent an area that has been even less explored.

I would like to suggest some starting points for looking to solutions to this telling – and, I suspect, crippling – gap in the studies regularly being conducted. First, researchers must be willing to suspend political polarization on the subject of sex work. That is, they must regard it as a form of work that is uniquely distinguishable from all other work by its sexual element, and uniquely distinguishable from all other sex by its financial element. That is not to say that it is isolated from the sexual and gender issues in other forms of work, but simply that its relationships are uniquely structured. Second, research that is in opposition to – or at least not in support of – government goals such as rehabilitation or abolition of sex work must be supported. No objective research can be conducted if the only research that can get substantial funding (there I go, talking about money again) supports only abolitionist agendas. And, hird, some research must be conducted that does not ask the workers if they were sexually abused as children. The asking of this personal question presupposes not just the right of the interviewer to be intrusive, but also presupposes the answer to that question, and is an indicator of extreme bias.

Finally, studies of coercion must be considered part of a body of studies about sex work, rather than the whole. Alongside such studies there need to be studies of more 'privileged' workers if we are to gain any kind of 'larger picture' that can usefully inform policy decisions. It makes no sense to try to apply the same solutions on the one hand to women who are bound, beaten, and deprived of any of their earnings, and on the other to women who are making a choice, even if the choice is an unhappy one. These two groups, which are not the only two groups in sex work, are not in the same position, and must not be assumed to be operating in the same structures. Demonizing clients is a dead end. It can only 'clean up the streets' while doing nothing to improve the lives of women in the sex industry. Every person in the sex industry who is not physically forced to work in the sex industry wants those clients. If they cannot have them in safety, they will seek them out under dangerous conditions.

9 Selling Sex: Women's Participation in the Sex Industry

Melissa Petro

In the past decade feminist theory has endeavored to posit sex work as 'work,' an income-generating activity that, like any other, may be taken up agreeably or disagreeably and under economic necessity. The very term 'sex worker' identifies those engaged in various aspects of the industry as 'workers,' implying a likeness between sex work and other forms of labor – everything from manual labor to professional work (Kempadoo & Doezema, 1998). What distinguishes sex work from other forms of employment, however, is the way the industry has historically, contemporarily and cross-culturally been criminalized by the state and stigmatized by popular society (Overall, 1992). The notion of sex worker as 'victim' has prevailed since the early to late 1980s (Barry, 1984; Dworkin, 1981; MacKinnon, 1989) and continues to dominate the dialog on sex work in the form of disproportionate attention paid to the issue of 'trafficking in women.' In sociological research, sex work has been studied as a 'deviant' occupation (Cannon et al., 1998; Wood, 2000), associated with drug use (Green et al. 2000), violence (Barnard, 1993), mental illness (Chudakov et al., 2002; Roxburgh et al., 2006) and sexually transmitted disease (Scrambler & Scrambler, 1997). Only recently has sex work been likened to other mainstream traditionally female occupations (Wood, 2000), considered a service industry (Brewis & Linstead, 2000a; Sanders, 2005a) and a form of 'emotional labor' (Chapkis, 1997; Sanders, 2002). Given the political climate, women who choose sex work do so under significantly more stress than individuals choosing other occupations.

The following is a presentation of data from a 2002 ethnographic study exploring the relationship between female sex workers and their chosen professions. Specifically, this chapter considers the ways and circumstances in which women feel compelled to enter the industry, as well as the reasons why, having once begun, women decidedly continue to sell sex.[1] This study found that while most women purportedly enter the profession for economic gain, money is not the only reason women choose sex work and nor is it the only reason why most remain in the industry. Once women have entered into sex work, the industry operates in a way that manufactures consent for continued participation, as the sex worker comes to understand sex work as 'work' and as she reconciles her identity with the identity imposed upon her by her profession. Working from a feminist assumption that all women are constrained by social, political, and economic inequality between the sexes, this study is consistent with other studies on sex work that dispute the belief – as anti-sex-industry feminists would contend – that women who work in the sex industry are inherently more oppressed as sex workers (Wood, 2000; Murphy, 2003; Sanders 2005a). 'Rather than understanding power as a monolithic social force oppressing women,' states Wood, 'power is understood to be a contested, negotiated social resource that is constantly being enacted during interpersonal encounters' (Wood, 2000, p. 7).

The methodology for this study included extensive participant-observational research conducted in The Hague, Amsterdam, Berlin, Krakow, Warsaw, London, and New York City, including sixteen formal interviews with women from various aspects of the industry. An important aspect of the methodology was the presupposition that choices being made by any individual sex worker are principally informed not only by that individual's gender but also by her geopolitical location – her race, ethnicity, nationality, and immigration status – as well as by her socioeconomic background. Told largely in women's own words, this chapter contributes an international perspective to the growing body of feminist research on the sex industry, highlighting contrasts between women's experiences in light of their variant personal and political locations.

'I did it ...'

> I stood outside of Flashdancers and looked at the marquee. And I said to myself, man, if I step in there ... it's gonna be a whirlwind. It definitely would be. I knew I wasn't gonna be able to come out of it for a while. I stood there and thought, what's the path to take? Am I gonna slowly crawl? Because prior to that I was just barely getting by. I thought, am I gonna continue to, like, struggle, or am I gonna pull myself up financially, right now? And I decided to go in. And do it. (Lauren)

As for most workers, women who enter into sex work do so most commonly for economic gain (Roberts, 1992). Of the women I interviewed, all participants named 'money' as a reason for entering into sex work. It was often the case that the loss of a job, a broken relationship, or some other type of dramatic life change precipitated a woman's decision to become a sex worker, as was the case for Theresa, an American woman working as an exotic dancer in New York City, whose reasons for becoming a stripper were as follows:

> The first time I did it I was stuck in Florida and I needed money to get back. I was with my cousin, and we had my godson with me and went to go visit her brother and we got in a fight with him and we had spent all our money. We had no way to get home. And it was like 'what are we gonna do?' So, I was like, all right, fuck it, let me see, I'll go dance, you know? I'll give it shot, you know, just to make the money to get home.

But while money was a recurrent motivation in becoming employed in the sex industry, it was rarely a woman's only reason for choosing sex work, and nor can economic necessity be claimed as most women's sole reason for remaining in the industry. Prior to becoming sex workers, a number of women reported feeling 'fascinated' with or 'curious' about the industry, some women were first attracted to the sex industry because they reportedly perceived sex work as 'exciting' or 'interesting,' and a number of women described experiences of choosing sex work over or in addition to other occupations. Such was the case for Anna, a Dutch woman in Berlin who worked part-time as a music teacher before taking a second job as a prostitute. As a music teacher, said Anna, 'everyone was so polite, so – educated. It was too much. I had the feeling like I had more energies. It was not enough for my life. I wanted to do something which is dangerous, exciting.'

Like Theresa, Tamara explained how she felt financially compelled into sex work. After migrating from Russia to New York City, Tamara worked in a shoe store while living with a boyfriend. 'When I broke up with my boyfriend,' she reported, 'I have to pay for my own apartment, which is I don't have enough money to pay for it, so I start working – that's why, that's what's bring me thinking to work in strip clubs.' Tamara worked as a go-go dancer in New Jersey for less than three months before finding a job as a waitress. 'When I start[ed] working in a restaurant,' Tamara explained, 'I wanted more to come back to dancing.' She continued, 'It was so much fun – to show your body, you know, to see how the guys likes you – it [was] a good feeling.'

Whereas all the participants included in this presentation of data described scenarios wherein ultimately – for economic and other reasons as well – they willingly agreed to sex work, no one reported having made such a choice without some measure of difficulty. Not surprisingly, the sex workers I interviewed were cognizant of the stigma attached to women's participation in sex work, many themselves having internalized preconceptions of what the industry was like, including stereotypes of the 'kind of women' who would do this 'kind of work.'

Chantelle, a Dutch woman working in the red light district of Amsterdam, spoke explicitly of those preconceptions:

> Let's just say I had a nasty way of looking at girls who did this. But a lot of people have that. They think oh, uh, dirty and stuff like that. But then she told me that she did this and, uh, I went with her a few times, to see how it was and, uh, yeah, I liked it. I kind of liked it.

Similarly, Holly, an American woman working as an exotic dancer in New York City, described her experience of being introduced to the industry by a friend:

> I went out one day with my friend and I'm like 'where've you been, what have you been doing?' And she told me [she had begun working as a dancer]. I tried on the shoes and she showed me all this money, all this cash, and I'm like 'are you kidding me?!' I had my own perspective on dancers, prior to working. I had never been to a strip club so I was always thinking, you know, [dancers were] sluts or whores or things like that – any negative image that you could probably think of. When my friend did it, I was like wow, if she can do it, I can do it too.

'Of course you never think, oh, someday I am going to be a prostitute,' said Valencia, an Indonesian woman working as a prostitute in The Hague. 'But,' she continued, 'you learn. You see what goes on. Then you try it, and it's interesting enough, and you like it.'

Given their initial reservation, it is interesting to consider the processes that changed these women's minds so much that they not only entered initially but continued to participate in the sex industry.

The manufacturing of identity

Studying the labor processes of factory workers at a piece-rate machine shop in the US Midwest, economist Michael Burawoy theorized that in order for an oppressive institution such as capitalism to exist, workers must, in some way, give consent to their own oppression (Burawoy, 1982). 'Conflict and consent are not primordial conditions,' said Burawoy, '... but products of the particular organization of work' (Burawoy, 1982, p. 12). Consent, according to Burawoy, is '"manufactured" at the point of production' – in the environment within which a worker sells his or her labor. In recent years, researchers such as Brewis and Linstead (2000a) have considered the work of Burawoy in relation to the labor processes of sex workers. Research on sex work (Wood, 2000; Murphy, 2003; Sanders, 2005a) has also considering the earlier, pivotal work of dramaturgist Erving Goffman, who theoretically understood the individual as an assemblage of reactions and adjustments to his or her social situations (1959) and whose ethnographic research explored the effect of the institution on the individual (1961). Whether studying mental patients confined to asylums or housewives adjusting to the institution of marriage, Goffman believed that 'any group of persons – prisoners, primitives, pilots, or patients – develop[ed] a life of their own that becomes meaningful, reasonable and normal once you get close to it' (Goffman, 1961, pp. ix–x).

In the spirit of Burawoy, this study considers how women's consent to participate in the sex industry is 'manufactured on the (sex) work floor' – the literal and figurative environment within which a sex worker works, including the physical space (for example, the club, brothel or window), the people that occupy that space (including co-workers, customers and management), and the general rules and attitudes, both public and private, that exist within and in relation to that space. By asking sex workers to describe their working environments, and by considering their narratives in relation to the theories of Goffman – who surmises that 'the world view of any group functions to sustain its members and expectedly provides them with a self-justifying definition of their own situation' (Goffman, 1961, p. x) – we may further understand the meaning sex workers make of themselves and their jobs.

The sex work floor

'When you first get hired they sit you down and tell you the rules,' explained Holly. 'It's a – business. They try to keep it clean; they try to keep it consistent. The rules and regulations keep the place the way it is.'

As with any workplace, the environment within which a sex worker works – what I call 'the sex work floor' – is mediated by both public and private transcripts. Public transcripts, described here by Holly, are the rules of conduct defined and proliferated by the management in accordance to the law, including what services may or may not be offered, how the worker gets paid, how much she should charge, and what percentage or 'house fee' the management will collect. Equally, if not even more influential, are the private transcripts, the largely unspoken, implicit rules of the environment that work in relation to (and often in spite of) the explicit rules. Private transcripts are 'the way things *really* are, the hidden organizational practices including 'the tricks of the trade' sex workers learn on the job, picked up through what Murphy calls 'informal socialization methods' (Murphy, 2003, p. 314), including friendships, mentoring relationships, and watching one's co-workers. Together, public and private transcripts function, in part, to create the sex work floor, a predictable working environment in which the worker consents to sell her labor.

'I was so nervous!' Chantelle said of her first time. 'I called my friend – she also worked – and I hanged on the phone all the time with her, 'oh, what should I do?' But when I have my first customer, then the nerves were gone.' '[You learn] by seeing,' Tamara confirmed. 'The first night was kind of a screwup. I make fifteen dollars the first night. But there, after a while, day after day you start getting more experience, you start being a – I got good.' 'I wasn't very good at dancing when I started,' Theresa recalled with a laugh. 'I wasn't very used being nice to people if I don't want to. I'm not used to serving people. I'm not used to smiling. Now I can do it – no problem.' 'Over the duration of time, [customers] are repeating themselves in a sense and so you just learn,' said Holly. Anna similarly commented that prostitution, after time, becomes 'routine.'

On the sex work floor, sex work becomes work – to quote Chantelle, 'just another job' – as sex work becomes routine, sex workers become skilled at their jobs, and the ways in which sex work is similar and dissimilar to other occupations become apparent. In her interview, Amanda quipped about how her psychology and marketing degree was oftentimes useful as a sex worker. Likewise, Holly – a marketing major – said that working as an exotic dancer involves marketing oneself. Anna compared her job to that of being a teacher in that both professions required 'pleasing' people. Chantelle said that her job as a prostitute, compared to a former job working at a bar, were 'exactly the same –

except you have no sex at the bar.' In both scenarios, Chantelle said, 'you're serving people.'

In comparing sex work to other occupations, participants reported enjoying a sense of 'freedom' not typically afforded by other professions. Anna, for example, said that as a prostitute 'you are your own boss. You are independent.' Lauren, an American woman working as an exotic dancer in New York City, also used the expression 'you are your own boss' to describe the job of an exotic dancer. An advertising agent prior to working in clubs, Lauren compared the two environments: 'I can't even think of going back to the corporate world,' she said. 'You work really hard in a corporation and you're not getting compensated. You can't see the end result. [As an exotic dancer] if I work really hard all night long, at the end of the night, I cash out and say "Wow, there's my reward."' Like Lauren, multiple participants, in comparing their jobs to wage or salaried positions, reported feeling relatively more in control of the amount of money that they made each night. 'I [make] good money' said Holly, 'because I don't give up. I just keep going and going. You're there for a full eight hours, you might as well make as much as you can.'

Theresa and Lauren both worked as waitresses in strip clubs before transitioning to work as dancers. Comparing the two professions, Theresa said:

> Waitressing is very hard work. Well, I mean dancing is very hard work [also]. But, in one sense, [as a dancer] you're not getting treated the same [as a waitress]. If you're a dancer and you want to sit and relax and have a drink, you can. You can basically do what you want on your own time. As a waitress, you're constantly being boxed at, you're on your toes the whole time. You just don't have the same freedom – as you have as a dancer.

Similarly, Lauren said:

> Waitressing and dancing are worlds apart ... [As a waitress] the management is all over you. Like, you have tabs and you're running around trying to get drink orders because [for every one] drink order you make one or two dollars. And [management is] constantly telling you [what to do]. They're always watching you; they're on your butt. Whereas, as a dancer, once you pay your house fee, it's up to you. You can sit all night, you can work all night; no one's bothering you.

Above all, sex workers claimed to feel a sense of 'freedom' at work, felt free to negotiate interpersonal encounters and episodically decide what they would and would not do for money. Negotiation with customers was described as being principally constructed around four variables: what the customer wanted, what the woman was willing to do, the amount of money the customer was willing to pay, and the rules of the club.

In her interview Chantelle briefly described a negotiating experience she had with a customer. 'Yesterday,' she said, 'there came a guy and he wanted, he asked me if I could put a dildo in his – butt. I said, "Well, yeah I can do that." Why not, if he wants to? But then he asked me if I could open the curtains. I said no.' Comfortable with anally penetrating a customer, Chantelle was uncomfortable with opening the curtain, partly because the state forbids unlicensed public performances of sex, and partly because, as Chantelle said, 'I can just as well play in a porn movie' – something that Chantelle was apparently uncomfortable in doing.

Theresa described an experience negotiating with a customer when she first took a job as a dominatrix. 'I worked in a dungeon,' she said, 'and it was perfect for me because it was no nudity and [at that time] I didn't feel comfortable taking my clothes off.' She continued:

> There are guys that are into eating shit and getting pissed on, which at first I had a problem with because it entails – well, to pee on someone you have to take your pants down. You get more money for that but at first I couldn't do it. I said to the first guy that I see that, I was like, 'Would you mind if I go in the bathroom and pee in a cup?' and he was like 'OK, no problem!'

Chantelle and Theresa, like all sex workers I met, had 'rules' – what they would and would not do for money – including what Sanders calls 'bodily exclusion zones' (Sanders, 2005a, p. 326). Chantelle, for example, reported that for no amount of money would she have anal sex with a customer, nor would she allow oral sex to be performed on her. Likewise, Valencia said, 'I never kiss, and he cannot lick my pussy [because] that's personal.' Lisa and Kirstie, two German table dancers at a club in Berlin, allowed all customers to touch their arms and legs but gave only certain customers – customers that they 'liked' – permission to touch their breasts, and only then for an extra fee.

The construction of boundaries is a well-documented technique sex workers employ to separate the private from the public, and to categorize the sexual encounter as professional (Brewis & Linstead, 2000a; Sanders 2002, 2004a).[2] However constructed, boundaries serve to manifest within a sex worker a sense of agency, as workers are allowed by their working environment to define for themselves what they will and will not consent to.

Following one's own rules, in addition to house rules, contributes to the routinization of sex work, a finding consistent with Sanders (2004a), who further theorized that one function of the routinization of sex work is to achieve compliance. 'We decide what happens and not the men,' Lisa asserted. 'We say, "okay, you can or you cannot and that's all and when you don't respect it then you can go. I'm sorry but you're not respecting."' Similarly, Kirstie said, 'Why do [guests] think they can touch me? Some men think, "I'm the guest, I can touch the girl" but [for each girl] it's different. They must ask.' By developing practices, sex workers assert control over the male client and take command over the sexual transaction.

Chantelle and Valencia both commented on how their right to refuse customers functioned to keep them feeling safe. When asked what made her feel safe at work, Valencia said, 'I'm really careful and I select my people. I talk with people, if somebody's looking for trouble I don't take them in.' As a general rule, Chantelle reported that she refused to service certain customers – anyone who 'who look[ed] dirty', 'smell[ed]', or appeared intoxicated. Chantelle also reported that the building where she worked had cameras in the halls and alarms connected directly to the police 'so that no one ever [got] beaten up or taken up the ass or anything.'[3] Similarly, Valencia described how legislative policy in The Hague gave her a sense of security. 'Here, they can control everything,' Valencia said. 'Everything you see is controlled. Our names are registered. They keep the names of all the prostitutes so if somebody's killed they'll know who it is. It's a safe feeling here in Holland.'

Separate and unequal

Only two respondents could name no reason besides money for entering and remaining in the sex industry. Veronica and Alex, interviewed together, both migrated from Russia to Poland with the intention of working as nude dancers. In their joint interview, they explained how a lack of economic opportunities in their home country motivated their migration. Educated to become a history teacher, Alex reported, 'It is not very possible to find a job [in Russia].' Likewise, Veronica explained:

It is not that I prefer [sex work], but if I work at my profession in Russia, I will have only thirty dollars a month so you understand … I finished medical school, I don't have a job. I never work [as a pharmacist after graduation] because it's not very good money … [Working as a dancer] I have in one day money which my parents have in one year, I have in one day. So it's very good business.

The term 'transnational sex work' refers to women working in sex industries outside their country of origin. For many, migration is perceived as an opportunity to improve one's socio-economic condition, and sex work is one of limited options available to women looking to migrate – one that women purport to prefer to, for example, working as a domestic, working in a restaurant, or entering into a paper marriage (Kempadoo & Doezema, 1998; Altink, 2000; Buchowska, 2000).

According to Alex and Veronica, all but two of their co-workers were migrant women, most coming from Russia and Ukraine. When asked why they didn't work in a club with Polish women, Veronica said it was because 'Polish women hate [migrant workers].' While Alex expressed the belief that they were working at one of the best clubs for migrant women in Poland, Veronica reported feeling very unsatisfied with working conditions, including what she considered to be unreasonable hours. '[We] have to work seven days a week,' she said. 'I can take one day off in two weeks.' The two went on to describe how working conditions differed for Russian women in Poland because of racism expressed by both management and customers. '[The management] hates Russians,' said Veronica. 'It was the same in a club where we work before,' said Alex. 'Polish people are horrible to us,' Veronica continued. 'You know for example I was with some Polish guy and he said "Oh, you fucking Russian go back to Russia. We will not pay for you. We can pay for Polish girl, not for a Russian."' 'In Poland,' said Alex, 'it is better to be prostitute than be Russian.'

Multiple informants confirmed the segregation of white women working in their home country from immigrant women/women of color, as well as a discrepancy in earnings and working conditions. Jackie reported that German women typically worked in Berlin's higher-priced clubs, Eastern European women worked in typically lesser-quality clubs and Thai women worked in still-lesser-quality clubs. When asked if migrant women ever worked in higher-priced clubs, Anna replied, 'Not so much, no. They must be very pretty and they must speak German.' Lisa and Kirstie reported that at their club there were no women of color and only one Russian woman, who spoke fluent German. When asked what kind of relationship German prostitutes had with migrant women, Anna said, 'German women don't like migrant women. There are too many women already. They only drive the prices down.'

'... for the money'

In listening to sex workers' understandings of themselves and their work, it is interesting to consider Goffman's idea of 'defensive practices,' strategies and tactics employed by individuals to protect their world-view and manage the impressions of others (Goffman, 1959). We can assume the women I interviewed, much like the rest of us, desire to think and project an image of themselves as decent, respectable, free thinking individuals competent to make decisions. To do so, they must somehow overcome the damning assumption that remains unsaid: the pervasive myth that all sex workers are either dirty, cheap, and willing to do anything or else desperate, naïve, and coerced (or somehow all these things at once). By describing the rules they created for themselves, as well the 'freedom' their job enabled them to experience, the women I interviewed were implicitly refuting the notion of the sex worker as a victim, not in control of her actions or circumstances.

With this theory in mind we should consider the difference between sex workers' purported sense of safety and the actual measures taken to protect workers from physical harm. Although in The Hague Valencia worked in what she perceived as a safe environment, she and her co-workers – mostly migrant women or women of color – worked in a building without the alarms, cameras, or security guards reported by other women such as Chantelle, a Dutch national. And while she reported that being able to turn down customers gave her a sense of control, in her interview she admitted to having 'never' turned down a customer. When asked if there were ever instances of violence she had heard of, Valencia replied, 'Just last week someone's cut up in here.' She motioned to her breasts. 'They find her legs thrown under the bed.' Her words aptly describe what Brewis and Linstead found in their own research, on which they remarked how 'it is emphasized by advocates of the sex workers' perspective that all prostitutes seek ... freedom within their labor process, even those who seem to work in the most dangerous and unpredictable of situations' (2000a, p. 86).

Describing their time in the industry as a temporary means to an end was another defensive practice common to all but one interviewee's narrative. Only Valencia, a full-time prostitute for twenty-three years, described sex work as 'normal.' For most women, like Theresa, sex work was perceived as a 'job to get you to where you want to go.' Similarly, Lauren described sex work is 'goal-oriented' and believed that most women entered into sex work to 'work towards something' such as purchasing a car or paying college tuition. This was the case for Holly, who initially took a year off school to work as a dancer as a way of paying off college and credit card debt only to delay returning to study indefinitely in favor of sex work. Holly said:

> I was so set on finishing school, as quickly as possible. But now I think school will always be there ... I guess maybe you tell yourself things. I tell myself that [stripping] is good for me – for right now. I tell myself that this is something that I'm doing just to put myself through school.

'I am young – of course I want to do something in normal culture,' said Veronica. 'I want to have a good education, but now I must work for it.' Similarly, Tamara said, 'I wanna quit. I wanna get some education, I wanna go to school, but right now I don't have the money for it. I have to wait, until I start making good money. Because [stripping] might pay the costs.'

While sex work may be similar to other forms of work, sex workers' narratives spoke both implicitly and explicitly of how sex work was not a 'normal' job. 'I've got a normal job,' Kirstie said. 'I work in a kindergarten in the week, and I work here on the weekend [as a table dancer]. When people say, "what is your job?" I say "I dance, okay, but my normal job is at kindergarten."'

'I guess [exotic dancing] is not "normal"', Holly said, 'because of – respect. Sometimes, or a lot of times – the majority of the time – you don't have respect if you tell somebody your job.' Holly was reconciled to the stigma she felt as a sex worker by the comfort she gained in knowing her job provided economic security. 'I can make ten dollars an hour and have respect,' said Holly, 'or I can make the money I make and – not care what people think.' Similarly, Anna said, 'The stress of not having enough money is bigger than the stress of being a prostitute.'

When asked in what ways she felt she 'had to' work as a prostitute, Chantelle interrupted. '"Have to" is not in the picture with me,' she said. 'I just – want to. Because I want to – have a good life. If I save the money I make I can have a good life, just like anybody else. Maybe I'll do this job until I'm 21 and then I'll quit. And then I'm still young enough to get another good job.' When asked why, if she liked her job so much, she thought of quitting, Chantelle replied:

> Because of the way people look at this job. They think it's a sinful, minor job, you know? I know one thing. When I leave this job, I won't ever be in guilt. Because I won't ever be in debt. It'll have all been worth it. I'll never have to rely on no one, no man. When something gets broken, I'll have the six or seven hundred guilders I need to fix it. That's why I do this.

Conclusion

While most academics have moved beyond the debate of whether women's participation in sex work is inherently 'coercive' or 'consensual,' popular conceptions of sex work remain monological and sex workers themselves are at odds with the stigmatic identity imposed upon them by their profession. Considering sex workers' narratives in relation to studies of occupational rhetoric helps to understand better sex workers' motivations for choosing sex work. For example, Fine (1996) studied how workers rely on a variety of occupational rhetoric as resources to define their work and their identity. Specifically, Fine studied occupational rhetoric employed by professional chefs, claiming that cooks draw on the alternative rhetoric of profession, art, business and labor to shape how they think of themselves as workers. Similarly, sex workers justify and legitimate their work to themselves and others through analogizing their work to other occupations, and by asserting sex work as taken up under economic necessity. It must be said that women who choose to participate in the sex industry do so because sex work is their most desirable of options, given the options they perceive as available to them. This decision-making process includes a constellation of factors including, but not limited to, economic factors.

The main thesis of this study has been that – having once entered into the sex industry – the sex work floor operates in a way that serves to manufacture a sex worker's continued participation. Through routinization of interaction, as sex workers become skilled at their work, and as the ways sex work is similar and dissimilar to other occupations becomes apparent, the sex worker becomes able to posit sex work as 'work' and define themselves as 'workers.' My findings were not unlike those of Leidner (1996) who studied the effect of interactive service work on the personal identities of insurance salesmen. Leidner concluded that employers, in an effort to maximize employees' effort, reconcile an individual's identity with the identity demanded by work through the standardization of interactions – the imposition of rules, teaching/ encouragement of scripts, and dissemination of affirmative ideologies. Leidner calls what he found to be an important tool for self-motivation the 'making it big' theory, the belief that you earn as much as you are worth.

> [Insurance agents] could live with the knowledge that many people looked down on them, put up with insults, endure futile days of failure and still maintain a sense that their work was compatible with ... social honor, so long as there was a possibility of 'making it big'. (Leidner, 1996, p. 242)

Sex workers' narratives demonstrate a similar sense of responsibility for their own success or failure at work. Likewise, sex workers tolerate the stigma of being a sex worker because of sex work's promised economic rewards. A negotiation between coercion and consent occurs at the point of the sex work floor as aspects of the job workers do not like are quelled by aspects of the job that workers do like (including, but not limited to, the prospect of 'making it big').

Finally, whereas most women reported a sense of 'freedom' and agency in the workplace, it is still true that the female sex worker works in a highly restrictive environment – restricted by house rules, local policy and national and international legislation, but also by stigma which, made obvious in the narratives presented, has a meaningful impact on the choices made and continuing to be made by sex workers. It must also be acknowledged that migrant women, by and large, experience the sex industry differently because of their position as women working in a host country. Migrant women sex workers, as well as women of color, tolerate not only the rigors of sex work, but also those conditions exacerbated by racism/racial 'preference.'

Feminists such as Joan Jacobs Brumberg (1997) acknowledge that, in a sexist society, a woman's greatest capital is her body, which can be manipulated and sold in the form of entertainment. With this in mind, sex work – as researchers and sex workers themselves continually point out – is not as 'deviant' an occupation as often assumed. Because with or without our permission women are still treated as objects, because our bodies are our first – and sometimes our only – commodities, because we are taught from birth how to do so, even as we are taught simultaneously that to do so is not permissible, every women decides what she is willing to sell, and for how much, and to whom. Continual psychological profiling and research with the unintended effect of undermining the physical and mental health of women who choose to sell sex do these and all women a disservice. This study, as well as the studies I have cited, add up to suggest that the isolated and stigmatized nature of sex work may be the greatest contributing factor to sex work being a dangerous profession. This chapter joins a call for decriminalization and destigmatization of the industry, so that women who choose to sell sex can do so with greater protection and less fear, and also so that women who choose to exit the industry can do so with a more hontest, right-sized understanding of themselves and their experiences.

NOTES

1 One study participant's narrative was excluded from this presentation of data, as she had not 'decidedly chosen' to sell sex. Interested in living and wor-king abroad, Anita, a black African woman working as a window prostitute in Amsterdam, was recruited under false pretences by a third party in her home country, Ghana, to migrate to work in the Netherlands. According to Anita, she entered into a binding contractual relationship with this third party without the knowledge that the contract involved sex work.

2 As the work of Brewis and Lindstead (2000a) highlights, sex workers' boundaries are not always easily defined or desired. For example, when asked if she ever enjoyed sex with customers, Chantelle replied, 'No, never. It's just a button, a switch. You know that when you're here, it's your job. If you get into it, and you enjoy it, you're not doing your job.' Later in her interview, however, Chantelle admitted to on occasion 'letting [herself] go' with regulars. When she first became a prostitute, Anna held the 'principle' that 'prostitutes did not get an orgasm.' She said, 'I didn't know much [about working as a prostitute] but that I knew: you don't kiss and you don't have an orgasm.' The longer she worked in the industry, however, the more this changed. 'When I became older,' she said, 'I wanted to enjoy the sex for me.'

3 In October 2000, prostitution in the Netherlands was codified into law. Before this, the industry operated under a 'policy of tolerance' similar to Dutch attitudes towards marijuana and other soft drugs. By making soft drugs legal for sale in a safe, retail environment, the Dutch government believes it prevents users from resorting to the underground, criminal, and potentially dangerous culture of hard drugs. By making prostitution legal, the state hopes to keep legal sex workers like Chantelle employed in drug-free, hygienic environments, safe from physical violence and disease.

D   Sex Work and the State

10 Pimping the Pueblo[1]: State-regulated Commercial Sex in Neoliberal Mexico

Patty Kelly

In the late 1980s, Governor Patrocinio González Garrido took on the great task of modernizing Chiapas, considered by many the most backward and underdeveloped state in all of Mexico. Given it was the era of neoliberalism in Mexico, he used the usual techniques: the privatization of state industries, withdrawal of supports for small-scale farmers in favor of export-oriented agribusiness, a revision of the state penal code that included new and harsher penalties for those found guilty of 'rebellion,' 'civil disorder,' and 'conspiracy.' The governor's vision of modernization though, had some unique elements, including his pet project, the Proyecto Zona Rosa. Through the Project Zona Rosa, González Garrido sought to increase state control over the informal and unregulated prostitution that was becoming increasingly visible in urban Chiapas, as neoliberal policies exacerbated poverty throughout Mexico, resulting in increased rural-to-urban migration and increased service sector employment, including sex work. The project culminated in the 1991 construction of the Zona Galáctica (Galactic Zone), a municipally regulated brothel located in the city of Tuxtla Gutiérrez, capital of Chiapas, where I conducted anthropological fieldwork from 1998 to 1999. In the following pages, I will examine the role of state-regulated prostitution in neoliberal Chiapas, asserting that the relationship between the state and the regulated sex worker is not unlike the pimp–prostitute relationship.

Sex, neoliberalism, and the state

Modernization projects have historically been accompanied by struggles over moral and sexual codes (Suárez Findlay, 1999). The Galactic Zone was created during a time of shift and crisis, a period of rapid economic change, cultural transformation, simmering political hostilities, including the rumblings of rebellion in rural Chiapas, and the militarization of civil society. Unlike the social reformers of revolutionary Mexico, who viewed state-regulated commercial sex as exploitative and decidedly anti-revolutionary, political elites such as Governor González Garrido viewed state-regulated prostitution in neoliberal Chiapas as a path towards the modernization of one of Mexico's poorest states.

Neoliberalism, is, as David Harvey writes, '... a theory of political economic practices that proposes that human well-being can best be advanced by liberating individual freedoms and skills within an institutional framework characterized by strong private property rights, free markets, and free trade' (Harvey, 2005, p. 2). The history of the Galactic Zone may be viewed as a local example of this process of neo-liberal global capitalist expansion and modernization – a process marked by a widening gap between the rich and the poor, the decline of rural life, growing urbanization, exclusionary politics, and, in the case of the Galáctica, increasing state intervention in the sexual and social lives of the Mexico's working classes.

Since the foreign debt crisis of 1982 and the passage of the North American Free Trade Agreement (NAFTA) in 1994, Mexico has wit-nessed rapid economic change and increasing economic integration with the United States and the rest of the world. Yet these changes, touted by neoclassical economists as a cure for Mexico's ills, have benefited few Mexicans. Poverty has increased in both rural and urban Mexico; monthly incomes for self-employed farmers fell by 90 percent between 1991 and 2003 (White et al., 2003, p. iii). The monthly income of men working in cities dropped more than 16 percent between 1990 and 2000 (White et al., 2003, p. 20). Many scholars have documented how poor women and children bear the brunt of the inequalities produced under this new economic order.[2] After the passage of NAFTA, poverty in the poorest, female-headed households increased by 50 percent (White et al., 2003, p. 19). Between 1989 and 1998, public assistance for children living in households receiving govern-ment aid was cut by two thirds (UNICEF, 2005, p. 16). Today about half of all Mexicans live in poverty.

In contemporary neoliberal Mexico, we see an economic moderniza-tion project and a concomitant concern with sex and social order. Through the creation of the Galactic Zone, the government sought, through the strict medical and spatial supervision of sex workers, to confine and con-trol populations deemed 'deviant' while bringing an informal economic activity into the formal, modern, and highly exploitative market.

Becoming a sex worker

The majority of women (some 70 percent) working in Tuxtla's Galactic Zone are the heads of their households. One third of them cannot read or write. The employment options for poor and working-class Mexican women with little education (servant, cook, factory worker) are poorly paid. In her study of *maquiladoras* in Ciudad Juárez, Maria Patricia Fernández-Kelly writes: 'factory work offers wages and benefits that keep women only a step removed from the circumstances that can lead to prostitution' (Fernández-Kelly, 1983, p. 143). Working as a servant, waitress, or cook is generally even less lucrative. Many women who work the streets of Tuxtla as informal, unregulated, and therefore illegal prostitutes do so sporadically in order to supplement income from a poorly paid day job.[3] At the time of this study, the minimum wage in Chiapas was little more than three dollars a day.

Despite their economic need, women's entry into wage labor conflicts with cultural ideals that emphasize a woman's domestic role as wife, mother, and daughter. Women who work outside the home have historically been stigmatized in Mexico. One of the many Spanish words for prostitute, *meretriz*, has its root in the Latin *merere*, meaning one who earns;[4] the link between women who earn money and perceived immorality has deep roots. More recently, the sexual morality of female factory workers has been held up to public scrutiny. As the northern border region began to industrialize in the 1960s, some Mexican women began to enter factory work in the export-oriented and foreign-owned *maquiladoras*. With the passage of NAFTA and the country's turn towards neoliberalism, the whole of Mexico became a free trade zone with even more women entering into factory work. Women, who account for some 60 percent of all *maquiladora* workers, were hired because they were presumed to be submissive, highly exploitable, and less expensive than their male counterparts.[5] Perceived as a threat to a social order marked by gender inequality and female economic reliance upon men, female workers are often associated with promiscuity, immorality, and even prostitution. As one factory worker told anthropologist María Patricia Fernández-Kelly:

> Many people, especially men, treat you differently as soon as they know you have a job at a *maquiladora*. They think that if you have to work for money, there is also a good chance that you're a whore. But I assure you that my friends and I are decent women. (Fernández-Kelly, 1983, p. 135)

While Mexico's industrialized northern border may seem a world away from Chiapas and its Galactic Zone, I suggest they are both part of a similar process of capitalist expansion and exploitation that generates similarly gendered inequalities. The commodification of sexuality and sexual labor is just another part of the service economy that is rapidly expanding under advanced capitalism, along with manufacturing. If the morality of a woman who simply works outside the home may be suspect, one can imagine the suspicion that is directed towards a woman who works outside the home selling sex.

The issue of male financial support figures prominently in women's entry into prostitution. The unemployment, low wages, and other structural socioeconomic circumstances imposed by neoliberalism that propel women into poverty also make it increasingly difficult for men to fulfil their culturally prescribed responsibilities within the household; women must take on increasing economic responsibility, despite cultural attitudes that continue to stigmatize them for working outside the home (Gledhill, 1995; Safa, 1995).

Obligadas, mantenidos, and independientes

In the Galactic Zone, as we shall see, a woman is identified and judged by the relationship between her money and her lover. While the majority of the approximately 140 women who work in the *Galáctica* do so independently, nearly a dozen women are *obligadas*, women obligated or coerced into prostitution by one of two pimps active in the zone. Women in the zone generally became *obligadas* through deception and/ or physical and verbal abuse by men they presumed to be their boyfriends or by women who promise them employment. The *padrote* or *madrote* often takes the woman away from her home and familiar surroundings to a place where she has no social relationships or support, thereby increasing her vulnerability and their control. The *obligadas* in the *Galáctica* generally arrive at the zone by way of the state of Puebla, and for this reason are sometimes referred to as *Poblanas* (residents of Puebla), a word which in the zone has become synonymous with pimped. Ramona, originally from a family of small-scale farmers in rural Chiapas, was working in a small restaurant in Tuxtla when she met a man who became her boyfriend. The two moved to Puebla together and then the beatings began. Ramona found herself working as a prostitute, first in the streets of Puebla and later in the

Galactic Zone for the man who was once her boyfriend and was now her pimp. Sara, another zone worker, denied that the man she called her boyfriend was also her *padrote*, though other zone workers repeatedly insisted that he was.

In contrast to *obligadas*, who are forced into prostitution by men (and sometimes women) who retain control of their earnings, the *independiente* (independent worker) works for herself and may use her earnings to support children or extended family. Leticia, who left school at age eight to become a servant, found sex work offered her the means to leave an abusive husband while also enabling her to support her two children. Mónica became a sex worker a few years after her husband, a police officer, shot and killed himself. Her in-laws had tried to find Mónica work in law enforcement, but could not because she only had a second-grade education. Lorena became a sex worker following a period of conflict with her girlfriend who already worked in the Galactic Zone. During this time, Lorena was staying home taking care of the couple's children, while her girlfriend, earned money through prostitution. The situation, says Lorena, made her feel like 'a little pimp,' so her girlfriend returned to work in the home raising the children while Lorena worked selling sex in the zone. Located between these two types of workers are women who have entered the *ambiente* on their own or due to the persuasion of a partner who is then totally or partially financially maintained by his girlfriend and does not give her a *quincena* (the bimonthly pay check, a term that also refers to the payment a man gives his girlfriend or wife). Such a man is called a *mantenido*, a somewhat disparaging term that refers to a man who, in defiance of cultural expectations, is supported by his female partner.

These categories, though, are blurred, subject to change and contestation, and not mutually exclusive. Ramona was an *obligada* who by the time I met her had become an independent agent.[6] Furthermore, the distinction between a man who is a pimp and a man who simply accepts money from his partner is sometimes unclear. Alicia lives in a small home made of concrete blocks located just off the main highway on the road that leads to the zone. Sometimes, from the taxis on their way to the zone, she or her boyfriend can be seen sitting outside the house. Some workers gossip that her spouse is a *mantenido*, implying both that he is not fulfilling his duties as a man and that she is foolish. One worker says he is a pimp. Alicia herself would likely deny both accusations. Women who do have a pimp, like Sara, nearly always refer to him as their boyfriend or spouse (*esposo*). In addition, most workers, whether they are free agents, pimped, or working to maintain a lover, experience some aspect of exploitation in work; it is often simply a question of degree and nature.

A woman's status as an *obligada* affects the way she both works and socializes in the zone. *Obligadas* tend to engage in less social interaction with independent zone workers and may go to great lengths to protect their *padrote* and his economic wellbeing. They are often seen in one another's company, which allows the women effectively to police one another for the benefit of the *padrote*; when independent workers Leticia and Flor advised one *obligada* to leave her pimp, they were threatened by the other women working for him who said they would inform the *padrote* that they had been 'advising' her.

Generally, women who work as *obligadas* must earn a certain amount each day that they will they give to their *padrote*. Unmet quotas may provoke physical or verbal abuse; in order to avoid these repercussions, an *obligada* may employ a number of strategies: she may work cheaply to attract many clients or, conversely, negotiate the highest price possible with a client; she may work without a condom, which may attract both those clients who refuse to use them and those clients willing to pay more for this service; she may work long hours; and finally she may perform services that other women will not, such as anal and oral sex.

In Mexico, the pimp is generally considered a nefarious character. This characterization is reflected in the Mexican legal system; there is no federal law against prostitution and in Chiapas no state law prohibiting such activity when it is regulated, but the state legal code devotes an entire chapter to the crime of pimping (*lenoncinio*). According to the state penal code, a pimp (*padrote* or *lenon*) is one who 'exploits the body of another in sexual commerce and is maintained or obtains some profit from this commerce, who manages or sustains places destined to exercise prostitution.' Also considered a pimp by state law is someone who facilitates another's entry into prostitution or who opens or manages a brothel, *casa de cita*, or any other place where prostitution occurs. The punishment for pimping is four to eight years in prison and a fine; this punishment is increased by four years if the pimp is working in collaboration with law enforcement personnel. Yet despite this perception of pimping, *padrotes* in the zone and on the street continue to operate freely, while legal prostitutes are regulated and street prostitutes are arrested, reflecting the male domination embedded in both the execution of the law and the practice of culture.

Discourses about the dangers of the *padrote* are common both inside and outside of the zone. Before moving to Tuxtla from the small town of Soyalá, Ana María was warned by her mother not to fall prey to a pimp; she explained to her daughter how they might look and the ways in which they take advantage of young women. Ana María laughs at the irony of her mother's warnings – she now works in the brothel, but as a secretary and says, 'And I have yet to see a pimp!' On a number of occasions, Bárbara repeated a cautionary tale about an *obligada* from El Cocal. The woman was older, tall, and pretty with 'an incredible body.' According to Bárbara, the woman earned a good deal of money for her pimp but,

> ... she got sick with cancer, of the uterus, I think. And do you think he was there to help her? When she died, she was left in her room for three days and there wasn't even money for a coffin. The dogs wanted to eat her! The women [in El Cocal] had to chip in and buy the casket.'

'The *obligadas*,' Bárbara adds, 'are squeezed like oranges and when there is no juice left, they are thrown out.'

Dominant cultural values continue to assert that men are to support women economically, rather than exploiting them for profit. Men who fail to adhere to these norms, even within an economic crisis that makes achieving this difficult, are often considered of questionable moral character. The pimp is someone who not only rejects societal norms, but turns them on their head. Yet the pimp also *embodies* cultural values that assert that female sexuality must be controlled and male sexual 'needs' must be met: by facilitating and controlling the sale of female sexuality while ensuring that other men receive the sexual activity due to them as men, the *padrote* (much like the prostitute), though maligned for the role he plays, also reinforces certain gendered and sexual norms.

While there is some empathy among *independientes* towards those women who work as *obligadas*, many independent workers express disdain towards *padrotes* and others who unfairly benefit from the women's work. Bárbara says if she were able to leave the *ambiente* she would never return to work as a madam or as a zone landlady. Other workers express similar sentiments. One afternoon in Leticia's kitchen, she, Miguel, and I were eating *mixiotes*, a dish of chicken and chillies wrapped in little foil packages. We sat under the watchful eye of Alfonso, a green parrot with glaring orange eyes perched outside the window in the decaying courtyard where residents wash clothes, bathe, and use the common toilet. Leticia and Miguel spoke of the *padrotes*, how they show up with nice, new cars: 'Topaz, Jetta, all the latest models.' They both express disgust as they describe the ways in which the *padrotes* abuse their workers and threaten to tell their families that they are working as prostitutes. Former *obligadas* such as Evita and Ramona express contempt for the men who forced them into prostitution.

The *obligadas* are pitied by other workers and sometimes even scorned for being beholden to a pimp to whom they must give their earnings, and whom they refer to as their lover or partner rather than their pimp. When Liliana left the *Galáctica* to work in an unregulated area in an alley in the state of Morelos, she found she was the only worker there without a *padrote*. Of her pimp, she said to one co-worker, 'You pay a lot to sleep with him!' to which her colleague responded, laughing, 'Shut up, damn China!'[7] Liliana's astute comment reveals the complexity of the *obligada's* relationships: she is both a prostitute and an employee but also, in a sense, a client, giving money to a man in return for intimacy, or the illusion of it.

The *obligadas* often find themselves in the unusual situation of having intercourse with strangers for money in order to have intercourse with their partners, again for money. Of the former *obligada* Evita, Viviana says, 'She is pretty but not very bright,' adding, 'Nobody forced me to do what I am doing.' Mónica refers to the *obligadas* as 'poor things,' and says that she entered the *ambiente* on her own, that 'Nobody put a knife to my throat.' The *obligadas* represent an extreme form of prostitution in which women are directly forced to sell sexual services; it is their presence in the zone that allows independent workers to mask the broader, structural socioeconomic circumstances that brought them into the *ambiente*, replacing them with a discourse of free will.

Conclusion: the state as pimp

The neoliberal state is not unlike a *mantenido* (a man who is supported financially by his female partner or, in this case, the laboring masses). But more accurately, the neoliberal state is a *padrote*, pimping out the pueblo by slashing social services and other state supports, privatizing state industries, promoting 'free' trade and export-led growth, and undermining the sovereignty of the nation, communities, and individuals by ceding to national and international capitalists. As a result of neoliberal economic policies, wealth in Mexico (and throughout Latin America) has become increasingly concentrated in the hands of a few while the majority of the population grows more impoverished. By 1995, the minimum wage in Mexico was lower in real terms than it had been in

1980, when Mexico first began its embrace of neoliberalism (Nash, 2001, p. 8). In Chiapas, only slightly more than one third of the employed population earn an amount equal to or greater than the daily minimum wage (Centro de Informacíon y Análisis de Chiapas, 1997, p. 23). Particularly hard hit are rural populations and those dependent upon small-scale agricultural production. Neoliberal policies have not eased poverty but rather have institutionalized it. For many women living under neoliberalism, entering the sex industry is an alternative to a life of constant economic struggle and material deprivation.

Under Mexican law, facilitating entry into prostitution constitutes pimping and is therefore illegal. To avoid accusations of *lenoncinio*, the municipal government of Tuxtla Gutiérrez, though it built (along with state funds) and administered the Galáctica, did not directly collect room rental fees from sex workers. Rather, the zone operated as something of a public–private partnership. State and city funds were used to build the zone, the city administers daily operations, and private landlords own the *módulos* or barracks-style buildings that house sex workers. As is often the case, sex workers pay exorbitant rents, with owners charging up to thirty pesos a day for a small room containing a twin bed and small table, with a small attached cold-water bathroom.[8]

In addition to its promotion of economic policies that impoverish its people and facilitate entry into the sex-service industry, the relationship is between the state and the sex worker, analogous to the *padrote–* prostitute relationship in other ways. First, both parties would likely deny such a relationship exists. Workers' accounts of their entry into prostitution rarely reflect the broader socioeconomic structures and policies that have left them with few resources, little education, and still less socioeconomic mobility and employment options. Speaking of her entry into sex work, the *independiente* Mónica says, 'Nobody put a knife to me, but always a person is a little bit influenced by bad friendships.' She attributes her entry into sex work primarily to another woman who led her into it, along with what she describes as her own 'insecurity and lack of education.' Alejandra's entry into sex work began when the illness of her mother turned the family's chronic poverty into acute crisis. She remembers the woman who introduced her into the *ambiente* with gratitude and fondness: 'She had a noble heart.' Independent zone workers often express contempt for pimps that exploit *obligadas* in the zone, while expressing little resentment towards the economic policies that have spurred them to work alongside the *obligadas*. Given the politically demobilizing effects of neoliberalism, workers' emphasis upon personal histories (bad relationships, bad [or good] friendships, acute crisis) is not surprising. Yet this approach, one sometimes favored by anti-sex-work feminists, is dangerously apolitical as it fails to examine the larger political, economic, and social contexts within which women enter prostitution.

The state, for its part, views regulated prostitution not as pimping but as a path towards development; in selling the buildings of the Galáctica in which the women work to private landlords, the state has tried to distance itself from accusations of pimping. In Tuxtla, the local government packaged legal and regulated commercial sex as a step forward in the city's economic and social 'modernization.' In addition, like a pimp who takes an *obligada* far from her home community in order better to exploit her vulnerability, neoliberal policies embraced by the Mexican state encourage similar movements of people that engender similar vulnerability to exploitation. For instance, in Chiapas (and throughout Mexico), neoliberal policies that have decreased state supports for small farmers and promoted large-scale export agriculture have further accelerated the decline of rural life and contributed to rural-to-urban migration, uprooting people from their homes as they venture to cities in search of work. At nearly half a million people, Tuxtla is one of Chiapas's fastest-growing cities. There was not one woman who worked in the Galactic Zone who was a native of Tuxtla. All the workers, Mexican or Central American, were from somewhere else.

Like a pimp, the state also abandons sex workers when they are no longer of use. In a recent trip to the zone, years after the period of fieldwork had ended, I sat with Flor in her room, catching up on the latest news. 'Lydia died,' she told me. 'Two weeks ago we buried her.' Lydia had contracted HIV in the zone and upon testing positive '*la corrieron*' (they ran her out of the zone). Authorities in the zone did not seek alternative employment or medical treatment for her, though such treatments are now available in Chiapas. For a time, she worked the streets. She also became deeply religious. Flor begged the zone administrator for a small sum to buy a coffin. The state helped to bury Lydia.

The turn towards prostitution by the women of the Zona Galáctica is a testament to both an ongoing and lengthy history of economic inequality and injustice in Mexico and the tendency of neoliberalism to exacerbate rather than eradicate such inequality. The modernization of Chiapas offers little opportunity to poor Ladinos and still less to indigenous peoples who struggle to enter into an increasingly global society on their own terms. The selling and buying of sexual services in the Galáctica is part of a broader global trend towards increased commoditization and consumption of household activities, sex included. The women of the Galactic Zone are only a small sample of the burgeoning ranks of poorly paid women from the developing world, many of whom are the sole providers for their families, who sell domestic services, such as cooking, child care, cleaning, and sex, throughout the globe, as the neoliberal state, like a pimp, 'squeezes them like oranges and when there is no juice left, throws them out.'

NOTES

1 Pueblo: literally, town; figuratively, civil society, the collective, or most plainly and accurately, 'the people'.
2 For more on the gendered elements of neoliberalism, see Adamache et al., 1993; Nash 1994; Nash & Fernández-Kelly, 1983; Sparr, 1994; White et al., 2003.
3 Women who work in the Galactic Zone are generally full-time sex workers, though they may supplement their income by selling things like clothes, shoes, and make-up on the side.
4 I thank Anne McClintock for this point.
5 For a deeper look at women factory workers in Mexico, see Fernández-Kelly 1983 and Iglesias-Prieto 1997. See Ong 1987 for the Malaysian experience.
6 For a full account of Ramona's story, see Kelly 2003.
7 Because of her Asian features, Liliana is often referred to as 'China' or 'La Chinita', meaning 'Little China girl.'
8 In his work among travesti prostitutes of Brazil, Don Kulick describes the ways in which sex workers' rents are often higher than the market value. In the case of the Galactic Zone, what sex workers paid for the rooms equalled what I paid in rent for a large two-bedroom house in a secure, middle-class neighborhood in central Tuxtla. Because of the high rents, many sex workers who would prefer to live in the city centre and commute to the zone are forced to also live in their tiny, dark, kitchenless rooms.

11 Deviant Girls, Small-scale Entrepreneurs, and the Regulation of German Sex Workers

Anne Dölemeyer, Rebecca Pates, and Daniel Schmidt

Uniquely progressive: a law that failed

The 2002 German prostitution law ('ProstG') is referred to as being 'uniquely progressive' and as representing a 'paradigm shift' with regard to the state regulation of prostitution (Galen, 2004, pp. 2, 195), because the law provides for the inclusion of prostitution among other jobs regulated under the law. This was intended by the Social Democrat/ Green coalition government (1998–2005) to mean that people who register with local trade registration offices as providing sexual services would fall under the usual rights and duties of small business holders or employees of such businesses. Thus registered, sex workers were to be eligible for statutory pension insurance, sick leave, and unemployment insurance. In addition, in consequence of this new status, German work contract law would apply to them, and trade union membership would be an option. At the same time, they would be required to register for sales and income tax, residence law, and work permits, and be subject to building law regulations (concerning, for example, the running of brothels). 'Liberalization' of the prostitution law thus meant falling under administrative regulation. So far, sex workers had been working in a grey zone, sometimes criminalized, sometimes taxed (depending on the municipality), but not subject to the same rights and duties and regulations that other small business holders were subject to. The then Christian Democrat opposition took up the taxation issue and wondered aloud about the state wanting to profit from the earnings of immorality, threatening to abolish the law should they come into government.[1]

Until 2002, the activities surrounding prostitution had been categorized as being in some respects similar to the activities of habitual criminals: for example, prostitutes, as well as 'persons on premises' where it could be assumed that criminal deeds were being prepared, could be asked to identify themselves without further ado by the police (Galen, 2004, pp. 2; 190). The coalition government, arguing that the criminalization of sex workers was based on outdated attitudes towards consensual sexual activities and that the state regulations only served to contribute to the continued marginalization and stigmatization of an already peripheral population, ratified the ProstG law in the hope of contributing to their 'normalization.' This was to be achieved in part by treating sex workers like any other workers, or like any other small-scale entrepreneurs. In part, the normalization was to take place through the use of a new terminology by changing the wording of the law. People engaging in the provision of sexual services were no longer to be classified as having a particular identity ('criminal,' 'prostitute') or engaging in a particular lifestyle (*Lebensweise*), but as engaging in an occupation (Galen, 2004, p. 103; Pates & Schmidt, 2009, pp. 11–46). Similar labels referring to purchasers of sexual services ('punters' or 'johns') have been eliminated in favor of normatively neutral terminology ('customers' or 'clients').

These regulatory and linguistic innovations have had scarcely any impact on the state administrative sector, however, as we will show in this chapter. The juridical causes of failures of the law have been exhaustively analyzed (Fischer et al., 2007). We will here focus on the implementation of regulatory changes and changes to linguistic terms and show the correlation between the two. We argue that how prostitution is governed is not only a matter of law, or, in this case, not a matter of law at all. It is above all a matter of the specific epistemic constructions of the 'nature' of the sex workers by local authorities, the types of problems this 'nature' is deemed to cause, and the range of regulatory options available to the administrators.

Max Weber's point concerning the functioning of the civil service was that:

> The honor of the civil servant is vested in his ability to execute conscientiously the order of the superior authorities, exactly as if the order agreed with his own conviction. This holds even if the order appears wrong to him … without this moral discipline and self-denial, the whole apparatus will fall to pieces. (Weber, 1946, p. 95)

Even if the civil servants who were our respondents met this high standard, their dutifulness would be crimped if the 'order of the superior authorities' was opaque. This is indubitably the case here, as scores of *Land* (state) governments, especially those governed by Christian Democrats, forbade their administrations to implement federal law, actions without precedent in the history of the German Federal Republic (Galen, 2004). The expectation that punitive responses on the part of administrators would be exchanged for regulatory practices – that tax forms would be handed out rather than dispersal orders – was thus not met. But in the series of interviews we conducted over three years with public servants in different German *Länder*, we found that they largely continue their business as usual, though they no longer legitimize their interference through references to legal provisions (which no longer exist), but rather by classifying sex workers' behavior and identities as intrinsically legitimating interference.

We shall concentrate here on two examples of municipal regulations from two different states. For comparative purposes, we have chosen two cities of about the same size (about half a million inhabitants), and similar regulatory practices in some respects *vis-à-vis* sex work. Both Leipzig (in Saxony) and Dortmund (in North Rhine-Westphalia) have defined zones in which sex work is not permitted, so-called 'negative zones' (Matthews, 2005, p. 885), and in both cases local authorities speak exclusively about heterosexual female prostitution when asked to describe their involvement in the governing of prostitution – as if no other type of prostitution existed. The ways in which local authorities regulate prostitution and the subjects involved differ considerably, however, between entrepreneurial and repressive regulation. These differences cannot be explained in Weberian terms. Although the Saxon Ministry of the Interior had prohibited implementation of the new law, the other *Land* (North Rhine-Westphalia) had merely failed to provide for implementation rules. The Dortmund public administrators (and only these) have taken it upon themselves to think through what the legal changes might mean in administrative practice.[2]

In the more liberally governed North Rhine-Westphalia, sex workers are deemed micro-entrepreneurs ignorant of the rules of entrepreneurship and in need of special training so as to file the correct tax returns. In conservatively governed Saxony, the mode of regulation is punitive; sex workers are deemed victims or victimizers. The way sex work is viewed by public authorities and the ways in which it is regulated thus differ substantially between the cities and also (though to a lesser degree) between the different kinds of public authorities. Within these different modes of regulation, the different perceptions of the subjects involved in sex work are reflected in the vocabulary used to describe the sex workers' identities, their work and their habits.[3] Linked to the respective categorizations and ascriptions are conceptions of the legitimacy and grade of 'normalcy' of sex work. Constructions of 'the prostitute,' 'the client,' 'the procurer,' 'the pimp,' and 'the brothel owner' are connected to certain modes of regulation and certain conceptions of the state's tasks concerning prostitution.

As will become clear, there is in fact no such thing as a 'German model' of regulating prostitution. How the subject matter 'prostitution' is perceived, constructed as a topic and formed by administrative measures is a question to be answered in each individual case, that is, for each city or town: the 'girls' are either needy, chaotic, irresponsible (usually in conjunction with drug use), and in need of rescue because they cannot help themselves; or 'deviant' women who enjoy what they do and unthinkingly spread disease, and noise pollution, giving 'innocent' women a bad name, and thus needing to be stopped (or regulated, inspected, and improved) for the public good.[4] Not only are the state employees of different *Länder* bound to the political decisions made by the local ruling party, but, to make things even more complicated, municipal bylaws and local interpretations of federal *and* state legislation provide for a great heterogeneity even from one municipality to the next.

As Lipsky (1980) has shown, Weber's idealization of the civil servant fails on the realities of job. On the one hand, civil servants use their own convictions, epistemologies, and values in order to attempt to organize their environment. And they are of course constrained by overwork, under-definition of their job priorities, and other limitations. Only micro-political analyses (compare Valverde, 2003) of local forms of regulations and of the channels of communication that are responsible for which discourses and practices establish themselves, and in which context (Latour, 2005), can help us to reconstruct the regulation practices in each case at stake, rather than describing a general national or even regional mode of regulation. Further, on a much more practical level, it does not suffice to look at the legal dimension if we are to analyze the regulation type of a country concerning sex work; nor does it make much sense to speak of different national regulation regimes, if these regimes differ locally so strongly. For this case study shows that changing the law alone does not change the position of sex work or the situation of sex workers in a given society.

Reconstructing internal discourses

In our research, we used discourse analysis to dissect the discourses 'internal' to an administration regarding the regulation of prostitution by conducting interviews with local levels of administration. In keeping with these insights into the workings of law, we have recorded the internal administrative discourses using methods more usual to empirical social research. Within a project investigating the regulation of prostitution we recorded over 50 interviews with state and municipal police and internal revenue officers, health care and social workers, employees of non-governmental organizations (NGOs) and represen-tatives of ministries of the interior. These interviews constitute the empirical basis for an analysis that has as its object the logics of local regulation. The interviews focus on the following topics: In what sense is prostitution a problem such that it requires the interventions, and why? How can these problems be solved by the administrators? What are the consequences of these interventions?

In naming the problem, administrators usually classified the sex workers in a variety of ways. For example, a Leipzig municipal police officer whose job was to 'solve' the problem of street prostitution in Leipzig argued that with the shift from the East German to the West German system, the types of women changed correlatively to the types of problem arising for him:

> When this was East Germany, this street [the Nordstraße] was more a place where housewives engaged in street-level prostitution, so totally normal women walked the streets just to improve their income, not because they really needed to. Then in 1990 everything really changed. We now find only girls and women who ply the trade because they have to. And for the most part, they have to because they are drug addicts, at least in our estimation we'd say in about 90 percent of cases, so while they used to engage in housewife prostitution, it's now become drug-related prostitution, you see.

Drug-related prostitution is always compared to 'normal' prostitution, in this case because the former is a problem that is deemed very difficult to combat. The women are deemed to be so much out of control, so hard to reach by punitive measures, that Leipzig municipal police officers started a 'citizens' referendum' in order to initiate a change in the municipal ordinances so that they could fine the clients rather than the streetwalkers. The argument on the referendum included the follow-ing paragraph:

> It has become absolutely necessary to take steps against curb-crawlers who are currently not successfully prevented from making use of women

who are engaged in drug-related prostitution, and who, because of their drug-use, cannot themselves control their behavior.

Discourse analysis usually focuses on the interpretation of public documents – 'programmes,' as Ulrich Bröckling called these – that is, laws, articles, parliamentary debates, reports, and scientific publications (Bröckling et al., 2004; see also Valverde, 2003, p. 3). The underlying hypothesis is that such discourses and their inherent orders or their internal logics or their 'grammars' (to use Foucault's term, see Foucault, 1979), produce knowledge about things, individuals, and the relations between them. Because this knowledge can never ultimately be objective, it (re-)forms reality – most particularly, if the 'knowers' hold positions of power in which they are called upon to classify, rank, and act in accordance with their classifications: The police officer must be able to classify people appropriately into victims and offenders, for example, and treat the two differently. In order to do this, the police officer needs to 'know' the different characteristics of each 'case.' The system of the discourse 'does not open up interpretations of and perspectives on social reality, but introduces rather a reality that comes into being by inscribing itself onto a field of positive knowledge. Thus, knowledge constitutes a social reality of its own. This is what is meant by the productive power of discourses' (Bublitz, 2003, p. 157, our translation). Such analyses of public sources can, potentially, reconstruct particular orders of knowledge; it is possible to deduct from such analyses logics of, for instance, prototypes of governmental forms of regulation and subject classifications.

However, we could argue that the analysis of 'self-generated' texts through interviews with state agents has advantages over the mere analysis of public documents. For while public documents and scientific papers give a good indication of what Mariana Valverde has called 'high-status knowledge,' it is the 'low-status knowledge' that becomes effective within the regulations, that is, the knowledge of the state regulators with whom the ordinary citizen has contact and who together with their activities or administrative operations come to mean 'the state' for everyday purposes (Valverde, 2003, pp. 3; 20; 22). This low-status knowledge is composed of expert knowledge combined with everyday experiences, scientific and mass media discourses, and – above all – professional knowledge, accumulated over the years of experience. This administrative knowledge is the essential basis for understanding the functioning of law as it is symptomatic in (local) regulatory acts.

Framing the debate: public discourses

Aside from the legal changes sketched above that can be expected to frame the discourse, prostitution has been discussed broadly in two ways since the 1990s in the German mass media. First, sex workers are deemed to be in need of social as well as economical rescue, requiring their 'normalization' in the labor market, specifically in the tertiary sector. This discourse is in keeping with the legal changes. The second perspective on prostitution represents it as a problem of public order, crime, and at times also of morality. We find here an alliance of con- servatives (Christian Democrats, Christian Socialists and the churches) with feminists who see prostitution as a cause of trafficking in women, forced prostitution, 'illegal migration,' organized crime, and violence against women. Virtually all forms of prostitution are seen as a result of illegitimate force of a physical, social or emotional nature, and in this discourse trafficking and prostitution become synonymous; the figures most present within this discussion are the faceless traffickers (generally without nationality or with a foreign one) and the female victim, a mostly Eastern European, sometimes Asian, African or Latin American woman (see Berman, 2003; or Doezema, 2006). To prevent these crimes, prostitution must be prohibited (the 'Swedish model').

If we compare the easy causalities in these discourses, where on the one hand, migration from Eastern Europe is immediately seen as linked to trafficking, and on the other hand, indigenous prostitution (so long as it is not 'lowly,' that is, street prostitution) is seen as generally professional and self-directed, we find two roles for the state. On the one hand, the state must stop migration from 'vulnerable' groups, namely Eastern Europeans. On the other, the state must integrate indigenous sex workers into the general labor market. Of course, not all Eastern European women are trafficked – nor are all German women 'free agents' (Pates & Schmidt, 2008).

Two administrative cultures, two different outcomes

Despite the discrepancies, cleavages and discontinuities, the regulatory discourses in Leipzig reflect attitudes suggesting repressive practices combined with a view of prostituting women as deviant (victimizing or victimized subjects), while the discourses prevalent among administrators of Dortmund suggest *regulatory* strategies and view sex workers and brothel owners as more or less 'normal' economic citizens. Thus, while Leipzig administrators attempt to repress prostitution and try to make sex work invisible by displacing it into peripheral spaces, Dortmund administrators take up an empowering approach that aims at social inclusion of sex workers. The differences in these ideologies concerning sex work regulation become clearer if we note that they have implications for the degree of homogeneity of discourses within the administrative services of a town. For the 'responsibilization' discourse is compatible with different administrations, while the 'enforcement' discourse can only be maintained by public order authorities. That is, Leipzig officials have more heterogeneous discourses than their Dortmund colleagues, which is a symptom of the clash between social workers and public-order public servants.

If we divide the public authorities under scrutiny here into social (health care and social workers) and public-order organizations (police, internal revenue and public-order officers), we find that within Leipzig the two types of authorities employ very different regulatory practices. Within Dortmund, on the other hand, social and enforcement authorities have a basically similar discourse on how to treat the phenomenon of prostitution. As all our Dortmund interviewees confirmed, the applications of the regulations differ by institution, but the set of values, problematizations, and goals of regulatory practices are basically similar.

In Leipzig it becomes apparent that most measures taken by police, revenue officers, and public order authorities aim at the repression, exclusion, and diminution of openly visible forms of sex work and its concomitant features. Prostitution might be perceived as an unavoidable phenomenon, but it is best located at the fringes of society. Street prostitution is forbidden here within the city centre, and only a few brothels are properly registered as '(brothel-like) establishments' (*Bordellähnliche Betriebe*). These are situated in remote districts.[5] This practice is absolutely at odds with the logics of the prostitution law (and local officials describe it as a 'double standard' or 'absurdity,' even if they do not support legalization of sex work). But it is backed by the *Land* administration. According to the interpretation given by the interior ministry of Saxony, the new prostitution law does not explicitly state that prostitution is no longer 'immoral.' As prostitution from this point of view continues to be immoral, a person who promotes prostitution by providing the conditions for it (for example, providing a licensed bar where contacts can be made) ceases to be 'trustworthy' in terms of trading. So she or he loses the license as well (see Wohlfarth, 2004, p. 128).

Although prostitution is not recognized as a trade, which means that self-employed prostitutes cannot register as tradeswomen[6] and that brothels are formally never registered as brothels in the trade register (but as saunas, erotic massage parlours, etc.), all those involved in sex work have to pay taxes, independently from the legal status of their business. The Leipzig tax revenue office generally treats the sex economy as a special economic branch with a tendency to criminality. The local revenue office has a special unit to investigate (hidden) brothels, massage parlors, apartments used for sex work and so on for suspected tax evasion. This special unit organizes raids on suspected sex work establishments in cooperation with police forces and public prosecution office. The raids are carefully prepared and carried out by a staff of thirty to forty persons at 'prime time,' namely, Friday or Saturday night. As a side effect they look for migrant sex workers without work or residence permits, and try to find out about women generating income by sex work while officially being on welfare and so on. According to this tax office task force, those subject to their raids – sex workers, sometimes brothel owners and pimps – are basically deviant. Although it is acknowledged that people might have their own (economic) reasons to work as prostitutes, pimps, etc. (improving their income, for instance), and although the internal revenue officers do not see it as their task to exercise moral judgement over these persons, prostitutes were categorized during the Leipzig interviews into groups including 'housewives,' 'hedonistic prostitutes,' ethnicized 'exotic creatures' including 'Thais,' who switch between cities like 'migratory locusts,' or 'the black race' (generally admired as 'cherry on the cake'[7]).

In Dortmund, the trade control and revenue offices try to register brothels, clubs, and apartments used for sex work; police forces are interested in having as much and as broad access to the sex trade as possible. There are still inspections of brothels and nightclubs, but they no longer have the character of raids. Controls are realized regularly as part of a routine; the legal status of the persons working in establishments is checked (work permit, work contract, or contract as a self-employed person), and the trade office controls hygiene standards required for the bar license. Only two persons are necessary to carry out the controls, and a police officer described this form of control as very efficient. According to him, the relationship with brothel owners is relaxed and cooperative:

The way it was before an inspection was very formal, very disciplined, no one talked to us, they all felt they could incriminate themselves; while today I can do an inspection with just two people! So, if I go to a brothel today, of the size, I don't know, of maybe twenty women, a club, a swingers' club or something, I might go with just one colleague! Because I know for sure: there won't be any notable incidents. I know there will be about fifteen, twenty women there; so I control their papers to see if they are all there, whether they have a work permit if they are foreigners, or whatever – well, and then I am done and there is usually a big to-do, how are you doing, any news, that sort of thing.

All these measures aim at normalizing the relationship between the sex industry and public authorities.

Concerning the social order authorities, the two different modes of regulation (reduction of visible prostitution by dispersion into invisible spaces and pathologization versus control by spatial concentration, legalization, and empowerment) correspond to different kinds of knowledge about, and constructions of, the nature of the subjects involved. Within Dortmund's empowerment model, sex workers and brothel keepers are imagined as 'normal' subjects with smallish deficits caused by lack of knowledge, lack of discipline, lack of good parenting; police, trade officers or internal revenue officers are not interested in the deeper deficiencies of sex workers. This is reflected in the narratives of the interview partners who scarcely concentrate on the personalities or characteristics of sex workers. Special information brochures (for example, 'Tax Laws Guide for Erotic Service Providers') explain general tax and legal rules applying to all service providers, and targeted information meetings show that the subjects of prostitution are considered to have certain knowledge deficits. It is presumed that sex workers, brothel managers, and the like have a lack of information concerning when and how to register properly with the trade supervisory office or the internal revenue office. But generally, sex workers (as well as their employers) are regulated and perceived in the first place as rational economic subjects, as employers, employees or self-employed, and the same rules count for them as for anyone else.

A sex worker is considered a 'woman like any other woman' according to a police officer (although this could be a back-handed compliment, this is not a statement imaginable within the Leipzig context). It is conceded, though, that sex workers may be members of especially vulnerable occupation groups. This becomes apparent in police officers' preoccupation with involuntary prostitution. They often point out that the distinction between voluntary and forced prostitution is not simple: many Eastern European women working from apartments, even if these women have a legal status and earn well, may be considered victims of trafficking in the technical sense, as they have been helped by organized groups to enter the country and have to pay back their debts to them.

In contrast to the public order authorities, social authorities and NGOs in Leipzig and Dortmund show a similar approach and a similar view on the individuals involved. Social workers' knowledge about sex workers is obviously more complex and concentrates on the personality, history, and supposed common characteristics of each sex worker. The central aim is the empowerment of the personality of sex workers, that is, the focus is on the social and psychological aspects of the sex worker's personality and situation, instead of on economic aspects or the unfolding of a criminal character.

All NGO projects, health authorities, and social organizations have strategies of empowerment and view women working in the sex industry as basically rational and in principle autonomous subjects in need of empowerment. All consider sex work a (more or less) legitimate occupation, a job not an identity, although there are differences concerning evaluation of prostitution as a job. Generally, staff members of all social authorities do not speak of 'prostitutes,' but of 'women/girls who work in prostitution,' who 'work on the street,' or 'who prostitute themselves.' All interview partners in the social sector distinguish between drug-addicted women and girls (on the one hand), and other sex workers (on the other hand). The former are deemed to be in need of more complex help structures. Social workers see their main task in supporting the subjects of their target group (prostituting women in search of support), with differing tools that apply to the respective groups, and differing views on whether and to what degree these women are (helpless) victims or agents of their lives who took a deliberate decision to work in the sex industry.

This perception is clearly distinct from the criminalizing point of view represented by public order authorities in Leipzig. However, it is also distinct from the idea of the sex worker as an enterprising self. The social workers do not consider sex work, in particular street prostitution, as the sort of job an enterprising person would choose deliberately. Rather, the narratives focus on women driven into outdoor prostitution by economic pressures. Two reasons are given for women being under such extreme economic pressure. First, drug addiction leads to prostitution for drug procurement. Second, poor formal education is often given as an explanation, particularly in the case of full-time street prostitutes.

> We have seen a dramatic increase of street workers in comparison to two or three years ago, simply because the street has become mainstream, so to speak. And because poverty is generally on the increase. So a lot more people are forced to take on jobs that they wouldn't otherwise have engaged in. And many women who work the street didn't graduate from high school, haven't got any vocational training, and are quite right in their assessment that they will have trouble finding a job. It's just really difficult for them. And of course if you have a bad job you don't earn anything really, or very little, anyway. It's just that in the long term on the street you don't really earn more either, so it's difficult to say how reasonable it is as an option. Those are their principal reasons, I think. And some women are dragged there by their boyfriends.

Whether because of lack of education, lack of social or emotional skills, or because of drug addiction, the consensus is that these women thus 'need support': the drug addicts need to be stabilized and supported in fulfilling their basic needs, the others need support in organizing their lives and in eventually perhaps taking the decision to leave the sex work sector. Here again the situation is specific to the two municipalities. While in Dortmund, street prostitution contains both drug addicts and other disadvantaged social groups, in Leipzig, where there is much less prostitution in general, only drug addicts are found on the street.[8] The fact that these persons engage in prostitution is seen as part of a generally problematic situation: drug abuse, experiences of (sexualized) violence and/or a bad childhood. In contrast to 'professional' sex workers or women prostituting occasionally, these persons are represented as being subjected to strong causalities such as the economic changes in Germany post-1990 or drug dependency.

One reason for pathologizing sex workers and their clients might be that it helps to justify a politics aimed at repressing visible forms of prostitution, a politics of exclusion. As openly moral grounds no longer count as a valid argument, others must be found: a threat to public order and public security, mental illness caused by drug addiction, and so on. This does not necessarily mean that these officers had personally different (moral) ideas about prostitution from their colleagues in Dortmund; it is simply that the concentration on the 'deviant' instead of the 'normal' aspects comes into the focus because of the modes of regulation. There is a clear correlation between the discourse on the subjects – as enterprising, more or less rational people – and a mode of regulation that is empowering, trying to induce self-regulation without analyzing the alleged causes of prostitution.

In contrast to street work, apartment prostitution in Liepzig is not really regulated in practice. The revenue offices are scarcely interested so long as it is not suspected that women in apartments work for well-earning 'bosses' or 'big fishes.' In Leipzig, the police know about approximately eighty (private) flats exclusively used for sex work, but say that they have little insight into what is happening within this area. Apartment prostitution is viewed as a self-regulating market or economy beyond the reach and responsibility of the police, according to one municipal officer:

> There may be a few shifts now and then, but whenever some [new people] push onto the market, they are disciplined by the other groups who claim their territory. So it does not come to our attention much. They don't report each other; they arrange it all among themselves. Which leads to quite a number of offences not becoming known. For example, they might destroy an apartment used for sex work if it is in their territory.

Because (self-employed) sex work is not accepted as an official trade, the legal status of these apartments is the same as that of any other privately rented flats; neither police nor public order officers may control these rooms without a search warrant. Controls are imposed only on demand, that is, in response to neighbors' complaints.

In Dortmund, on the other hand, all authorities combine their efforts in helping to 'normalize' the sex trade: the sex industry is considered a 'normal' (or almost normal) feature of society, a commercial branch like others, and the trade as well as its subjects therefore need to be included into societal life. This view is reflected in the forms of regulation: Dortmund has an established and officially recognized red-light district: There is a closed street with a number of officially registered brothels and – a little further away from the city centre – a street prostitution area. A street work café, run by a non-governmental aid organization, is located directly in this street. Police patrol the area, but their presence, as well as the street workers' café, is meant to serve to increase the security of sex workers (and their clients). Occasionally, the police also offer consultation hours for sex workers at the café, which, according to one social worker, is well accepted among the women.

The police consider the physical concentration of outdoor sex workers in a limited area to pose great advantages: regulation is much easier and more effective. For example, legal sex workers report anyone in that area who is younger than eighteen years old or without a work permit, in order to get rid of these additional competitors. At the same time, sex workers who offer their services on streets within the 'negative zone' (which means: somewhere in the central area outside the official street prostitution territory) if caught by police, are first warned and informed about the legal situation, and fined if caught there again. Because of the trouble they risk if staying within the negative zones, those who can work legally as prostitutes generally prefer working within the official street prostitution area.

In contrast to Leipzig, Dortmund has taken measures to implement the new law: there have been workshops, publications, pamphlets, journal articles in the local press, all with the aim of introducing sex workers to practices common to the legal economy. At the beginning of 2002, when the new law on prostitution came into force, revenue office, trade office, and police offered special orientation meetings where legal requirements and rules were explained to brothel owners, and employed and self-employed sex workers. Changes were introduced after the new law on prostitution had passed. Authorities in Dortmund decided that now brothel operators could obtain bar licenses because their business is no longer considered to be immoral, and started an information campaign. An information brochure designed in cooperation by several authorities provides basic information on a variety of topics, including a map of the areas in town where prostitution is permitted and where it is not allowed, information on alien law, and on taxation, aid organizations and their contact points. For each topic a contact person is named, for example at the local revenue office, where the contact person in charge is not located at the commission for investigation of suspected tax evasion, but at the department for income tax. Most of the laws in question do not apply specifically to the sex industry, but the brochure was designed exclusively for this target group.

Women working in the sex business are thus in some cases also seen as victims in need of empowerment, be it because they are victims of trafficking, or because (male) brothel owners or managers exert economic control over the women working for them. Labor standards and rights formulated in the prostitution law as well as information on legal requirements, and a regulation system that allows women to work legally and therefore to inform the police if their rights or personal integrity are violated (for example, by economic exploitation or rape) are used as means of empowerment.

In Leipzig, the category that comes closest to normality is the 'housewife,' often described as a part-time prostitute; she works mainly from her flat or a small brothel. She doesn't attract the authorities' attention because she is invisible in public, does not evade taxes insofar as her income probably stays within the tax-free amount, and she participates in the health insurance system via her husband. Her relative normalcy, together with her inconspicuousness, makes her un-interesting to the authorities. The same goes, for example, for 'students who want to supplement their student income.' What the officials are much more interested in (whether personally or professionally is not always clear), are the somehow deviant cases that might appear to be disgusting or especially appealing, such as 'exotic strangers,' as already described above. At the extreme end of the scale is the drug-addicted, irrational prostitute, mainly to be found on the street in Leipzig. Street sex work is said to attract a particularly difficult set of characters: as police controls in the street are rather strict and frequent, no sex worker who has the chance to get in contact with reliable clients in another way will be staying on the street waiting for clients. Police officers' descriptions of these women are not favorable and express the distance they feel for the street sex workers: for example, 'they look dirty, well, scruffy and cockish, I mean, degenerate.'

Their presence in a public area is perceived to pose not only an aesthetic, moral, and financial nuisance. 'Normal' women passing the same area might in consequence be treated as prostitutes by hopeful clients; children might perceive what they shouldn't; the real-estate values might be negatively affected; and used syringes and condoms produce public health problems. Thus, in the narratives of public servants in Leipzig, street prostitution (and its most visible protagonists, mainly sex workers) is connected to a whole host of undesirable social interactions for 'innocent' women and children, and this threatens the public order, which in turn is used to justify means against (visible) sex workers and to refuse a 'positive regulation' in the sense of an organized street prostitution area or a policy of normalization.

The civil servants we interviewed in Leipzig showed a great interest in categorizing sex workers, talking about their alleged personality structures and their motives of engaging in sex work. Women working on the street are particularly carefully observed. Public order officers patrol daily eight hours in this area, and whenever they happen to see a woman identified by them as a sex worker talking to a man in a car, this is documented in official minutes. The police try to identify sex workers by posing as potential clients and asking for sexual services. One officer hoped he could help towards 'healing' women from their willingness to engage in prostitution:

> We would have liked it if she had been away for four weeks or so, in jail, just so she has four weeks to get off drugs. Or just so she has four weeks to think, maybe also, maybe this is an illusion, maybe also to pay tribute to her dignity as a woman, in situations in which she can talk to innocent women.

In contrast with Dortmund, the links between the construction of the subjects involved and the mode of dealing with 'prostitution' are not so clear-cut in Leipzig. It is not at all self-evident why policemen, staff members of the public order office, or of the local revenue office are so interested in the personalities and the nature of women working in the sex industry; the strategies of displacement into invisible and non-controllable spaces operate at the surface, too, only in another way than in Dortmund, because of the fact that the aim is not inclusion, but exclusion. The measures taken do not aim at influencing underlying causes of prostitution.

These ambivalences become visible when the police officer talks about the absurdity of the impossibility of registering brothels as normal businesses, while at the same time refusing the idea that the city might allow for an organized street prostitution area; or when two internal revenue officers talk about women who according to their own testimonies prostitute for pleasure: 'They are girls who follow their proclivities.' As one of the internal revenue officers comments: 'The worst videos, everything.'

Accordingly, the clients of the social workers in Leipzig are not represented only as victimized girls in need of basic help, but sometimes are claimed to be normal, albeit particularly poor, working women, whose situation is not so much defined by sex work as by their economic situation. Whereas in Dortmund, the agency, autonomy and strength of women working in prostitution is stressed by both social authorities involved and for all types of sex workers identified, with a tendency to identify victims in the area of street prostitution and autonomous agents in other areas of sex work, this is clearly different in Leipzig.

To summarize, it might be said that in the case of the social authorities' regulation, empowerment is the key issue. However, the focus is not on the empowerment of economic and citizen subjects, but of psychologically, economically, and socially disadvantaged types. The subjects concerned are neither irrational, nor enterprising selves, but autonomous persons excluded from society because of their social status, who have great deficits and need support. In this sense, they are 'poor girls.'

Differing realities

As a result of different perceptions and modes of regulation, what is perceived as the socially relevant subject matter concerning 'prostitution' is different in the two cities. In Leipzig, sex workers in the perception of the public authorities and as an effect of their regulatory practices exist at the fringes of society and are confined to the periphery. In Dortmund, sex work is perceived as an already regular business, whereas all efforts are aimed at changing it into the legal, 'clean,' and easily controllable trade imagined as already existing. Within these different settings, the position of social workers becomes distinct in the two cities, although the basic approach in both might be similar. For example, social workers deal with street prostitution in Dortmund, and with drug addiction linked to street prostitution in Leipzig. The subjects concerned are sex workers in the first case and drug-addicted women and girls in the second.

As we have shown, the regulation of prostitution does not simply reflect German law on sex work, and nor is it uniform throughout Germany. Written law does not tell us much about actual practices of regulation, and so we cannot identify a 'German model' with respect to the regulation of sex work/prostitution.

Differences exist in the identification and construction of the subject matter ('prostitution'), the problem(s) this subject matter poses, the (groups of) subjects involved, and appropriate strategies of regulation. On the reasons for the specific forms of regulations and subject constructions evident in the two cities under study here, we can only speculate. In Leipzig, the conservative political frame of the Saxon government might contribute a lot to the interpretations that local interfering agencies make of the laws; but then, this does not explain the very different attitudes the caring entities of Leipzig have, because their views and practices differ sharply from the ministerial guidelines and also from the views presented at the local health authorities in the next middle-sized city in the same state. In Dortmund, on the other hand, a recently introduced reform aims at changing local administrations from interfering agencies to administrations that orient themselves more to the model of service provider, following the liberal logics of an activating state. However, other cities in this state have made the same reforms, but still handle the sex work trade very differently.

Variations in subject construction and regulating approach are not only or even primarily the result of differing institutional logics of police, public order office, social work, and so on. Nor are differences only a result of locally homogeneous models of regulation, where institutional distinctions do not have any influence. What we have found for the German case might apply in more general terms to most countries: how prostitution is governed is thus not only a matter of law, or perhaps not a matter of law at all. It is above all a matter of how it is regulated within a context of the specific knowledge of local authorities and how these make use of their leeway within the legal framework.

It becomes fairly quickly apparent that there is an epistemological gap between different public discourses, including national laws and internal administrative discourses. That is why an analysis of regulatory mechanisms (and of the attending effects) does not have as its object so much the national frameworks (see Outshoorn, 2004), but the directly regulating administrative bodies (Rose & Valverde, 1998, p. 546; Rose & Miller, 1992, p. 184). Because public administrators participate in public debates only exceptionally, the inherent or resulting logics, definitions of situations, classifications, and productions of realities cannot be reconstructed by using common discourse-analytical methods. That is why Valverde for instance researches court protocols: they represent the speech acts of administrators and — sometimes — of people being regulated, even though the arrangement of these discourses is somewhat formalized. Ultimately, Valverde has shown that positive law may follow a unique logic (although this assumption is already questionable), but implementation does not.

> However, what people do when invoking the law or facing legal difficulties is never law as such. People interact with, and help to maintain and transform, various legal complexes — ill-defined, uncoordinated, often decentralized sets of networks, institutions, rituals, text, and relations of power and of knowledge that develop in those societies in which it has become important for people and institutions to take a position vis-à-vis law. Unlike law, which hovers beyond the reach of those who act in its name, legal complexes can be empirically investigated. (Valverde, 2003, p.10)

NOTES

1 The law has not been changed, however, since 2005, when the Christian Democrats came into power – once in government, the party developed other priorities.

2 This topic has been developed in greater detail in Dölemeyer (2009).

3 See Frederick Schauer's *Profiles, Probabilities and Stereotypes* (2006) for a concise discussion of how this is deemed to be legitimate even when the officer is wrong: stereotyped policing is basically more efficient. Our point here, however, is not to assess the adequacy of the classifications and correlative legitimizing strategies, but to develop the logics of classification and the regulatory implications.

4 The female pronoun is used not in order to imply that the provision of sexual services is among the predominantly feminized occupations (statistics are scanty and notoriously unreliable), or because the legal vocabulary is gendered, but because the enforcement of these laws targets virtually only female prostitutes. Although we consistently asked public servants responsible for regulating prostitutes about their attitudes concerning sex workers, our respondents only talked about female sex workers unless specifically prompted about men. Though admitting, as a rule, that they knew of male prostitution, they emphasized that they 'did not like going there.' Their classifications of sex workers were thus always already gendered, and results presented here are only relevant to the feminized version of sex work.

5 On the other hand, there are quite a few establishments that are not registered as brothels but serve similar purposes in the guise of being nightclubs or bars with an enclosed building where rooms are let for commercial purposes.

6 Which does not mean that working as a prostitute would be illegal. It is just not regulated as a regular trade, but it is a legal job. This fairly odd status is somewhat contradictory and provides a confusing legal situation for those who have to enforce the law.

7 In German: *Sahnehäubchen*; these expressions were used by our interview partners at the police and at the internal revenue office in Leipzig.

8 Two reasons are often adduced for the relatively low levels of prostitution in Leipzig. First, the general level of income is significantly lower. Second, many Saxon residents make use of services (hairdressing, dentistry, car repair and also sexual services) that are cheaper across the Polish or Czech borders.

12   Sex Work, Communities, and Public Policy in the UK

Maggie O'Neill and Jane Pitcher

National policy and dominant discourses on prostitution in the UK tend to focus on the 'harm' caused by prostitution to local communities, with diversion and rehabilitation of sex workers currently being proposed as a solution to neighborhood problems. At a more local level, however, there have been diverse responses, some of which include sex workers as well as other community members in consultation processes, leading to a more holistic approach to resolving conflict. Within the context of the national socio-legal environment we draw on two research studies which involved street-based sex workers in research and consultation processes to argue that more inclusive consultation is required to bring about sustainable solutions to problems and more coherent local policy development.

The socio-legal context in the UK

The contemporary situation in the UK is marked by a changing regulatory framework underpinned by a shift from enforcement policing alone to 'multi-agency' welfarist responses that are predominantly police-led, in part as a consequence of new forms of governance (Scoular & O'Neill, 2006; Matthews, 2005; Matthews & O'Neill, 2003). The dominant discourses operating in academic, social policy, feminist and governance research are situated along a binary (or bifurcation) of prostitution as violence, or prostitution as work (O'Neill, 2001, Scoular & O'Neill, 2006). Prostitution as violence or abuse against women is currently the dominant discourse in the UK – a discourse used by both the Home Office and the Scottish Executive (Home Office, 2006; Scottish Executive, 2005).

A more recent focus on the 'harm' to communities has led to moves to exert stronger control over the movements of street-based sex workers through measures such as Anti-Social Behaviour Orders (ASBOs).[1] Such responses, however, have mainly served to displace street-based sex workers to other areas that may be less safe for working or where problems may arise for communities in new areas (Campbell & Hancock, 1998; Hubbard & Sanders, 2003; Pitcher et al., 2006). Current policy pays little attention to the fact that many street-based sex workers are not likely to be able to move to off-street locations in a safe working environment unless other problems they experience are addressed. Some women prefer to work on the street rather than indoors because of what they perceive as the relative autonomy of this form of working. ASBOs if breached can lead to imprisonment and further disadvantage through criminalization for an offence that previously was relatively low-level and would not have led to imprisonment. Criminal Anti-Social Behaviour Orders (CRASBOs) can be tacked on to the back of a criminal conviction and have sometimes been used with no consultation with projects (although it is suggested that consultation should take place in principle).

In response to a review of prostitution legislation (the first for fifty years) the Home Office published 'A Coordinated Prostitution Strategy' in January 2006. This document sets out the government's proposals for a coordinated strategy that focuses upon: prevention of involvement; fostering routes out; and protecting communities from street-based sex markets. Prostitution is defined as 'commercial sexual exploitation,' and the strategy seeks to address this issue by: tackling demand; ensuring justice; and tolerating off-street prostitution where two to three women are working together. To ensure the strategy is actioned there is a focus upon partnerships, the coordination of welfarist policing and the enforcement of the law to divert, deter, and rehabilitate those women who do not choose to exit as the most 'responsible' option (see Scoular & O'Neill, 2006 for full discussion of responsibilization to exit). The strategy does not propose to stop the use of ASBOs, but to introduce a new Intervention Order to run alongside them to 'provide those in prostitution with a further route into support services' (Scoular & O'Neill, 2006, p. 40). The issue of resourcing for support services is not addressed in the strategy, however, and given that continuation funding is a challenge for many projects, it is difficult to see how such measures could be effective, particularly as rehabilitation schemes which are not based on voluntary participation may serve to penalize rather than help vulnerable people (Melrose, 2007).

Phoenix and Oerton (2005) argue that the official discourse on prostitution 'consolidates moral authoritarianism ... through the criminalization and "reform" of women and children in prostitution' (p. 77); and that the problem of prostitution, which once was understood as a victimless crime, has shifted to a crime that victimizes the women and children involved and 'threatens to destroy individuals, families and communities' (p. 86). The authors argue that this new discourse 'locates individual women as being responsible for the social problems they encounter, thereby justifying a punitive response, when, despite the best efforts of support agencies around them, they continue with their involvement in prostitution' (p. 100). Similarly, Scoular and O'Neill (2006) argue that in promoting multi-agency responses that pivot around exiting and the responsibilization of sex workers, the state continues to privilege and exclude certain forms of citizenship, thus serving to support the ongoing hegemonic moral and political regulation of sex workers. To counter the existing ideological paradigm, they examine the extent to which the contestations and conflicts around prostitution reform in 2005 and 2006 offer routes to 'understanding' and negotiating inclusion' that may usher in 'real change.' They argue that such change requires a renewed research agenda that in focusing upon a politics of inclusion requires a more critical and holistic understanding of a social justice that coalesces around discourses of rights, redistribution, and recognition (Fraser, 1997; Bauman, 2000; O'Neill et al., 2004).

It is within the context of the current socio-legal environment and a renewed research agenda that focuses upon a more critical and holistic understanding of social justice that we address the contentions over the spaces in which street-based sex work takes place through our separate and joint research. While community responses to street-based sex work have been a major policy driver nationally, with national policy tending towards a view that prostitution is by its very nature 'harmful' to local neighborhoods, at local levels there has been a diversity of approaches. In some areas, local partnerships have tended to prioritize the interests of 'communities' or groups of local residents against those of sex workers, with projects and sex workers having a minor voice in comparison with statutory agencies and sometimes those seen as representing their community. In other partnerships, however, local sex work projects play a major part and these partnerships may take an alternative perspective, considering approaches that avoid punishment for sex workers where possible and encompassing a more holistic view of solutions which ensure that the interests of sex workers have a primary place in responses (Pitcher & Aris, 2003; Aris & Pitcher, 2004). In some localities, there has been active commissioning of research to inform local policy responses. The research that we have undertaken in two localities, both individually and jointly, illustrates how 'sex workers and community residents can come together ... to establish ways to introduce effective urban policy that is neither punitive, moralistic nor biased' (Sanders, 2004c, p. 1715).

Beyond binaries: creative consultation, project-led multi-agency approaches, and social justice

In this section, we draw on two research projects undertaken in the West Midlands, UK, which involved street-based sex workers in the design and delivery of the research and in consultation processes arising from the research.

The first study, commissioned by the Health Action Zone in Walsall used participatory action research (PAR) principles (O'Neill & Campbell, 2002).[3] The purpose of the research was to: assess present policy; consult all those involved and affected by prostitution; produce a strategic action plan; consider the possibility of 'safety zones,' and improve community safety. O'Neill and Campbell trained a group of community co researchers who helped them to conduct the research (see Safety Soapbox, 2009; O'Neill et al., 2003). The research team interviewed people in focus groups, in their homes, on the street, and in local businesses. A sex worker survey was conducted with 45 women, and 12 women participated in in-depth interviews. Ethnographic field research made contact with 81 women in total. Residents and sex workers also took part in the arts-based consultation that formed one strand of the research methodology. Creative consultation involves collaboration between participatory research and participatory arts that 'aims to incorporate the voices and views of communities directly into the process of policymaking and service delivery' (O'Neill & Webster, 2005, p. 2). In the process, our understanding of sex work is enriched by the experiences and ways of seeing of all those involved – residents; statutory and voluntary agencies; women and young people involved in sex work. The arts have a vital role in processes of regeneration, mediation and creating safe spaces for communication.

Some fourteen residents, young people resident in the area and seven sex workers took part in a series of seven art workshops (making a total of twenty-one workshops in total). Residents' views on prostitution represented diverse attitudes and values towards prostitutes and prostitution that exist in society more generally. The key issues for residents were: community safety, associated crimes, drugs, pimping, and the need to explore possibilities for an area where street prostitution could be regulated away from residential communities and in a manner that promoted the safety of sex workers. Ultimately all agreed that we have to work together to create change. This was evident most clearly in the images that emerged from the creative consultation – 'Safety Soapbox: Sharing Our True Colours' (documented at Safety Soapbox, 2009).

The second study was a community engagement research (CER) project focusing on the service needs of both street-based and off-street sex workers (Galatowicz et al., 2005). The research was undertaken by volunteers working with a local sex work project in the West Midlands, led by a more experienced researcher, with additional training and support provided by the commissioning body, the University of Central Lancashire. Although participation in the research was sought both from within the project's volunteer base and from sex workers who were service users, only project volunteers came forward to participate in the fieldwork. Researchers ensured that there was representation from a former service user on the steering group, however, and input from sex workers/service users into the research design and the opportunity to comment on report drafts. Key agencies such as the Drug Action Team and local authority housing department were also represented on the steering group and in the research design.

The researchers interviewed 37 women working on the streets and indoor locations to ask them about issues such as routes into sex work, their working practices and experiences, drug and alcohol use, their use and experience of services, and issues impacting on their lives such as housing problems, violence, and experience of the criminal justice system. They were also asked about how services could be made more accessible and whether they had suggestions for other improvements. In addition, two open days took place as part of the research process, giving the opportunity for interaction between sex workers and staff from local agencies. During the course of the research, a 'process mapping' day for services to sex workers took place, organized by the local sex work project, and involving representatives from a range of agencies (including police services, the local authority, health services, other members of the Community Safety Partnership, and voluntary organizations) and sex workers who used the project services. The researchers also attended and were able to participate in collaboration with other agencies towards a common goal for the sex work project and its service users. The research was presented to local agencies and service commissioners in order to inform future policies to ensure that they reflected the needs of working women.

Participatory research involving sex workers: problems and issues

As we have argued earlier, it is important to engage sex workers in research and consultation around policy developments likely to impact upon their lives. Such engagement is not a straightforward issue, however, and there are certain considerations to be taken into account when designing approaches to research and consultation.

One such consideration is access to women working in the sex industry. Access is often obtained by researchers through 'gatekeepers' such as sex work projects, which help to introduce them to service users and enable them to become familiar with working locations (Shaver, 2005; Sanders, 2006). It may take some considerable time for researchers to become accepted amongst the sex working community; this needs to be built into the research.

Involvement in research as a co-researcher can require a substantial amount of commitment and take time out of someone's working life, and thus this can be a disincentive to participating. Many research projects are also relatively short-term because of funding constraints and there is often not the time required to build up confidence and expertise through extensive training and research practice.

In the case of research with local residents, relations with street sex workers may be antagonistic (sometimes with hostility resulting in violence towards women working on the street – see Sanders, 2004c and Pitcher et al., 2006, for further discussion on this issue). Similarly, women have encountered lack of sympathy from representatives in service agencies, as detailed below. In such situations, it might be problematic for sex workers to become involved as co-researchers, if they are likely to encounter antipathy from other research participants. The environment has to be conducive to involving sex workers in research or consultation and it may take years to build up relations to a point at which sex-working women feel comfortable in attending meetings with researchers, service representatives, and residents, and feel that they will be treated with respect as equals.

Nonetheless, within our research there were positive examples of interactions between sex workers and local residents, or representatives from agencies such as the police. These had arisen through an incremental process, including mediation activities undertaken through sex work projects, to enable the development of understanding between different groups. For example, in the meetings and process mapping day outlined above, by taking discussions away from the street setting, where the different groups tended to be locked in conflict, it became possible for sex workers, police, other agency staff, and community representatives to engage with one another on a more equal basis and for them to exchange views and develop a greater understanding of one another's positions. Such a process then starts to create a climate in which it becomes accepted practice to hear the voices of sex workers when planning policy. It should be noted, however, that there may be frequent changes of personnel within the different agencies (and, for example, in the local area where the CER research took place, it was policy to move police officers to different geographical areas on a regular basis), and thus relationship development becomes an ongoing need to be addressed.

Local service provision and policy: reflecting the views of sex workers

The 'Working Together To Create Change' project created a space where sex workers' and residents' voices could come together to examine the issues and develop recommendations for policy and practice in relation to street sex work in residential spaces. O'Neill and Campbell (2002, p. 86):

> ... do not see sex workers as submissive victims. Nor do we dismiss those women in Walsall who stress the choice they actively make to work in the sex industry in the context of their skills, available employment opportunities and job preferences. Experiences of selling sex are diverse; sex workers exercise different degrees of power and control over the conditions they work under (see O'Connell Davidson, 1998).

The findings evidenced that a disproportionate number of women sex workers had experienced local authority care; homelessness; drug use and offending behavior; and violence against them.

He hadn't got no money, he pulled a big cleaving knife, he said, 'I've got no money but I'll still do business with you,' so I managed to talk my way out of it, he give me the knife, I talked to him, quietened him down and everything, he gave me the knife, I just left it at that.

I was six months pregnant, I was only doing oral and he punched the whole side of my face in. All I did was cover my stomach. He tried to run me over after I got out of the van. I gave him back his £20. It was not worth getting killed over.

To the police we're prostitutes so what. We get raped so they won't catch whoever's done it or ... you don't know what to do. Go back out on the street and get raped again. (O'Neill & Campbell, 2002, pp. 114–15)

National and international research indicates that violence against women and young people involved in prostitution is endemic. The most commonly reported source of violence in the Walsall study was client violence: 56 percent (n=25) of women had experienced violence from punters. This was followed by: violence from a partner/ boyfriend 42 percent (n=19); then pimp violence 33 percent (n=15); passersby 31 percent (n=14) of respondents. We asked respondents to indicate what types of violence they had experienced from clients. 47 percent (n=21) had been threatened with a weapon, 33 percent (n=15) had been raped, 29 percent (n=13) had been robbed, 31 percent (n=14) had been physically assaulted, 22 percent (n=10) had been sexually assaulted, and 13 percent (n= 6) had been kidnapped or abducted.

The authors asked respondents who had reported incidents to the police how satisfied they were with the response they received. Of those who responded the majority were not satisfied. Of the 16 women who had reported an attack, 1 was very satisfied, 5 were satisfied, 2 were unsatisfied and 8 were very unsatisfied. Women and young people involved in prostitution are very loath to take crimes of rape and assault to the police, because of the illegal nature of their activities and the social stigma involved in selling sex.

In terms of broader service provision, sex workers were asked to identify which services they felt were needed. The most requested were:

- 73 percent (n=33) condoms to be distributed more frequently

    Yeah, and if you don't, it's like, how much do you want, how much do you want to do it without Durex, and then I'll start going on, will you give me another life if you've got AIDS or anything.

I always start lecturing them, I always give them a lecture. (O'Neill &
Campbell, 2001, p. 124)

- 53 percent (n=23) drop-in service on or near the beat
- 49 percent (n=22) testing for sexually transmitted diseases (STDs) at
  GUM (Genito-Urinary Medicine) clinic that comes to us
- 44 percent (n=20) housing advice and support
- 38 percent (n=17) self defence and safety training information
- 36 percent (n=16) legal advice
- 33 percent (n=15) outreach needle exchange
- 33 percent (n=15) education/training advice and guidance
- 31 percent (n=14) better drug info and treatment
- 29 percent (n=13) better access to Hepatitis B injections
- 24 percent (n=11) outreach contraceptive service

Women were invited to make any further comments they wished about
services for sex workers. They recommended the need for: debt advice;
personal alarms that if lost can be replaced; asking the police if they can
allow the girls to use personal alarms; more help to keep the underage
prostitutes off the streets; something to be done about the violence and
attacks; more than one day a week of the outreach project; the involvement of sex workers through peer education work in provision and
policy making; getting support to find a job.

The key issues for change that women identified were: address safety
and violence; provide more outreach support; develop a drop-in;
develop better drug support and treatment; develop better health care
provision; provide education and training; develop an options initiative
and exit through sex worker outreach; provide a minimal enforcement
area away from residences, where women can work safely. These points
alongside findings and recommendations from residents were incorporated into a strategic action plan.

The CER study emphasized the diversity within the sex industry,
particularly between the experience and service needs of indoor-based
and street-based workers. It was also able to counter popular
misconceptions about reasons for working and routes in to sex work,
and some women were keen to participate because they could help
'correct some of the stereotypes about sex work.' Although economic
need was cited by many women as a reason for becoming a sex worker
(including debt, needing money to live or support children, or to buy
'extras' for the family from time to time), and some street-based sex

workers stated that they were working primarily to support their drug use, for some women, particularly indoor-based workers (and contrary to the current discourse of sex work as abuse), sex work was a matter of choice. For example, women talked of becoming a sex worker because 'I wanted a change of job,' or 'in response to an ad in a magazine.' Some women had worked in low-paid work previously (such as sales or service occupations) and apart from the issue of the 'terrible pay' of some of these jobs, had also left because of the conditions (including long hours, exploitation, and in some cases harassment from employers). Contrary to popular assumptions, it was clear from the research that most indoor-based workers did not use drugs.

One of the main reasons for the research was to explore the experiences of sex workers in relation to their access to services and their service needs. Some women felt 'let down' by services, particularly housing and social services. Many felt they were not listened to and had experienced patronizing attitudes from some staff. For example, one woman spoke of a health service being 'judgmental because I'm a single parent.' In comparison, the local sex work project was appreciated by many because 'they don't talk to you like [you're] crap and don't look down on you.'

All of the street-based workers who participated in the research had experienced homelessness or were currently homeless. This was often as a result of circumstances beyond their control, for example needing to move out of their home because of harassment, domestic violence, or relationship breakdown. In some cases women were made homeless because of a combination of a build-up of rent arrears and administrative error. 'Housing and housing benefits backlog of payments cause arrears – when you get arrears it's often not your fault because you moved house. You get evicted as a result and get court costs that housing don't pay' (Galatowicz et al., 2005, p. 28).

For many, the rent arrears were relatively minor (below £1,000), yet this debt still prevented them accessing housing. Some women had been in prison, often for minor offences such as non-payment of fines or breach of an order, which had compounded their problems. Because they were often in prison for a short period, little help was offered on release. For example, one woman who had been in a short while before she was interviewed stated that she had 'nowhere to stay, no money, no clothes' on release. Another spoke of 'no safety nets, no contact numbers, so nothing to help you out of the lifestyle.'

Suggestions for improvements to services included more outreach activities to help street workers to access services, more help with housing, greater flexibility in service provision, and services coming together in a 'one-stop shop.' One worker commented that 'agencies need to communicate more with one another.' One of the main points made by research participants was in relation to national rather than local policy: the need for decriminalization in order to make their work safer (Galatowicz et al., 2005, p. 30).

> I would like to see a change in the legislation and not penalizing street workers – more help for problems and also more safety for women on the street.

> They should legalize it. I'm coming out of the profession, but they should make the girls and clients feel safe and help them get their problems sorted out.

> This field of work should be legalized. It's not going away. It's a service girls provide and they shouldn't be penalized ... We should be heading for safety. It's a lot less safe on the streets now.

The value of participatory and collaborative methods of research: outcomes from the two studies

The creative consultation research in Walsall involved partnership working across a number of groups and agencies: the researchers; residents and representatives of Caldmore and Palfrey local committees; Walsall Community Arts team, and Walsall Youth Arts. The research report contained an action plan with over fifty recommendations separated into four key (interrelated) categories: Multi-agency responses; Policing; Sex worker services; and Children and young people. The authors stressed that the recommendations were part of a holistic package which advocated multi-stranded responses, there being no pretence that there was an easy 'solution' to the issues. Although some of the recommendations have been actioned, many have not, and one of the researchers articulated that it feels like 'One step forward: One step back.' The research did have some impact on policy. Local residents remained active and ensured that the issue was kept on the local agenda, they have been involved in further initiatives, and they have tried to be part of the multi-agency working group. Local residents have produced a leaflet to disseminate findings from the research and provide service contacts for residents. There was some further investment in the sex worker support service and some improvements in liaison between sex work projects and the police regarding documenting and disseminating 'ugly mugs', and regarding violence against street sex workers. The arts project Our Bodies Our Selves continued the use of arts as a mechanism for giving sex workers a voice. Our Bodies Our Selves is a collaboration between the local sex work project and Walsall Youth Arts.

Other outcomes included a report, 'Working Together to Create Change'; an art exhibition 'Safety Soapbox'; and a pamphlet 'What you told us about prostitution,' published by the community for the community, ensuring that the outcomes of the research are not shut away in a drawer, but kept alive and on the local agenda.

Recommendations emerging from the research and highlighted in the pamphlet produced by the residents included the following:

- a tolerance zone away from residential areas and businesses;
- opportunities for better education, prevention, and reduction of risks for the women involved;
- a stronger focus on deterring men who pay for sex and on the pimps;
- a program for young women to reduce the numbers going into prostitution;
- more help for drug users;
- more outreach support on and off the street;
- all agencies to join together to overcome the difficulties experienced by residents.

An action group was formed to take the recommendations forward, and since the research was completed this group has worked consistently to raise the issues wherever it can. It now has a representative on Walsall Prostitution Action Forum, and it raised the money to produce and distribute a leaflet summarizing the outcomes of the research to local residents. A website was developed where the images can be viewed alongside the final report and the leaflet.

Finally, community members recommended continued use of PAR as a means of giving women and young people a voice. This was actioned through collaboration between local public agencies and Walsall Community Arts. The project, called Sex, Lies and Love, was an anti-grooming arts initiative based upon the principles of PAR and techniques of peer empowerment such as forum theater (see Campbell & O'Neill, 2004). The project worked with peer educators and young women participants to produce an information leaflet and a series of images.

The website and pamphlet were developed by residents to provide feedback on the findings and the actioning of recommendations so far. This gave a clear message to the responsible authorities (local authority, public health department, police) that campaigns for the remaining recommendations would continue to put pressure on the responsible authorities to act, and in a fair way based on principles of mutual recognition – not just for residents but for sex workers and sex worker residents too.

On the other hand, the multi-agency forum did not welcome a residents' subgroup, nor were sex workers included other than being represented by the outreach organization. There was no coordinated strategic approach to the management of street prostitution, and no shared strategy that all stakeholders have signed up to. Moreover, the recommended regional strategy was not developed.

O'Neill and Campbell (2002) concluded that the richness of the findings and the inclusion of sex workers' voices and involvement highlighted the important role that PAR has to play in consulting and including all those involved and affected by street prostitution. Moreover, policies on prostitution must address both the safety and the rights of sex workers and of communities affected.

The community engagement research discussed earlier has also helped to promote the interests of sex-working women in the planning and delivery of local services. Representatives from local agencies such as the Drug and Alcohol Action Team and the local authority who participated in the steering group received regular feedback on the research. Where there were gaps in provision or problems with particular services, a dialog was encouraged between projects, the Community Safety Partnership supporting the projects and these services. The sex work project continues to represent the interests of sex workers in response to ongoing policy development. Where local communities, agencies, projects, and sex workers work closely together to address issues of concern, a more holistic response can be promoted. For example, through a lessening in community complaints and some residents speaking up for sex workers, the use of measures such as ASBOs in the local area has decreased in favor of alternatives (including a voluntary court diversion scheme).[4] Another example concerns antisocial behavior hotlines promoted by the Home Office – in the city where the CER project took place the sex work project is the designated agency responding to any concerns raised regarding street prostitution and thus is able to ensure a measured response that takes into account the interests of sex workers as well as community members, with a strong focus on mediation. In response to suggestions that emerged from the research about further outreach, staff from different service agencies locally (including drug and health services) accompany staff from the sex work project on outreach, enabling them to have direct access to street-based sex workers. Discussions have also been taking place concerning mechanisms for addressing the housing problems of people with small amounts of rent arrears. The need for peer education was also raised as an issue by some research participants, and one of the drugs services locally started a peer education project, involving people who have in the past been drug users, including former sex-working women.

A further impact of the research has been to raise the profile of the needs of sex-working women locally and to promote the important work that support projects are undertaking, thus helping them with accessing further funding for the longer term.

Many of these changes have been small, and within the national policy climate it becomes ever more difficult for sex workers and support projects to get their voices heard. As a result of the research initiatives discussed here, however, discussions on joint working initiatives to meet the needs of sex workers are ongoing, and small steps are being taken to build relationships between some agencies that previously had not worked together. Much of the change is incremental, but nonetheless any work that brings together sex workers, projects working with them, and other agencies, and which starts to build bridges and mutual understanding represents an important beginning to the process of policy change locally.

Ultimately, however, the lack of a coordinated strategic approach to prostitution in many areas at a local and at a regional level means that responses will always be piecemeal and unsustainable. This reflects the reality of a limited national strategy and lack of guidance on prostitution.

> Various research projects indicate overwhelming dissatisfaction with many existing polices and laws on prostitution which fail to address violence against sex workers; residents' and community concerns; and contribute to adverse circumstances for sex worker services addressing drugs, health and safety needs. (O'Neill and Campbell 2004; Pitcher et al., 2006; Sanders 2004c: Sagar 2005)

Many existing 'traditional' policies for the management of street prostitution do not appear to be based on evidence of effectiveness.

There is a need for an evidence-based approach to policy and legislation. Residents and sex workers and agencies involved in the management of street prostitution are asking for change and new approaches. Sadly, the recent Home Office national strategy does not answer this call by the residents and sex workers who took part in the studies described here.

Conclusion: the importance of genuine participation and inclusion in public policy research and safe spaces for dialog and knowledge production

Our collaborative research projects have demonstrated that it is possible to bring together agencies and sex workers in order to have constructive discussions on the future planning and delivery of services. By working with local residents and community groups, sex work projects have been able to develop an ongoing dialog that takes into account the interests of different members of local communities, including sex workers, and ensures that the needs of sex workers are reflected in community responses to national and local policy initiatives.

As argued by O'Neill and Webster (2005) participatory methodologies take *people* as the starting point and engage with individuals, organizations and neighborhoods 'to move out of old, rigid ways of doing things and look for new solutions' (p. 2) that are fundamentally about change. 'Not only do local people feel listened to ... It is a methodology which aims to overcome the problems associated with many traditional non-participatory research models which often have difficulty in engaging with "hard to reach" groups and result in documents containing recommendations neither supported nor endorsed by the communities they are intended to benefit' (p. 2).

Participatory methodologies should include the voices of women, other residents, and businesses, and respect their expertise/experience (based upon mutual recognition). Placing sex workers at the heart of participatory methodologies goes someway to acknowledge the women (and men) who sell sex both as members of neighborhoods and communities and as voices to be recognized and included as equal citizens. Such methodologies are also instrumental in helping to create safe spaces for these issues to be raised and dialog to take place across the divides between residents, responsible authorities, and sex workers. Thus they help to challenge dominant discourses and hopefully feed into public policy at local, regional, and national levels.

On a practical level, it is also important to establish mechanisms to enable research to be linked in with future policy-making processes, in order that the vital messages do not become lost. Ongoing collaborative working with practitioners and policy makers also helps ensures that the findings from research and evaluation can inform future policy (Pitcher, 2006a). Such collaboration enables the voices of sex workers to be heard in a wider policy arena and ensures that their views are fed into policy consultation and planning. We have argued in relation to the examples provided in this chapter that such participatory approaches are not only possible but can have real impact. Within current UK policy, however, there is little scope for involving sex workers in decisions relating to their lives. By treating sex work as essentially problematic, particularly when it is street-based, current government policy has effectively prohibited this kind of approach, leading to the likelihood of increased polarization rather than the development of understanding through dialog and joint working towards common aims.

NOTES

1 These are civil orders that aim to protect neighborhoods from anti-social behavior that causes distress and harassment. An ASBO might prohibit a sex worker from entering a specific area, for example.

2 The authors use 'understanding' methodologically, in the sense intended by Bourdieu (1996, pp. 22–3).

3 Participatory action research (PAR) is a methodology that encompasses social research, action or intervention and the production and exchange of knowledge. PAR has a better chance of developing solutions with communities or groups because it includes the very people who have a stake in the issue or problem being researched – community members, including in this case sex workers (O'Neill & Webster, 2005).

4 Voluntary court diversion schemes offer services to sex workers who have been arrested for loitering or soliciting, in place of penalties such as fines or ASBOs. Court diversion schemes are based on voluntary involvement, with the only condition being that the sex worker should attend a minimum number of appointments with a support project, with no expectations about continuing engagement at the end of that involvement (Pitcher, 2006b). Projects have found that this process helps to link sex workers with services after the minimum requirement for attendance has been met (Sanders, O'Neill and Pitcher, 2009). With the recent changes to the law regarding prostitution in the UK, however, it is not clear how existing voluntary schemes will be affected.

E   Organizing Beyond Divides

13 Sex Workers' Rights Activism in Europe: Orientations from Brussels

Giulia Garofalo

In October 2005, the European Conference on Sex Work, Human Rights, Labor and Migration was held in Brussels with the intention of building a movement led by sex workers and capable of challenging the 'trafficking' debate from a perspective of human, labor and migration rights. Around two hundred people from thirty countries in Europe participated, the majority of them sex workers. The participants' presence inside the building of the European Parliament on the third day of the conference was fundamental, as well as the colorful demonstration in the city center, with red umbrellas as a renewed symbol of sex workers' struggles.[1] The most important outcome of the conference was the production of two documents: the Sex Workers in Europe Manifesto (hereafter Manifesto; see ICRSE, 2005b), and the Declaration of the Rights of Sex Workers in Europe (hereafter Declaration; see ICRSE, 2005a).

The initiative to organize the conference was originally taken in 2003 by a small, courageous group of sex workers and sex work activists in the Netherlands. Following their call to activists across Europe, an organizing committee was created and started meeting at the offices of Mamacash, a grant organization for women based in Amsterdam.

Prior experiences and political approaches varied remarkably within the group. Some identified as sex workers; others were allies from feminist, anti-trafficking, or migrants' movements; others were in the process of developing one or more of these identities. Some had been active in international sex work politics for longer periods of time – such as Ruth Morgan Thomas from UK Network of Sex Work Projects, Marjan Sax who was involved in the first and second World Whores Conferences in 1985 and 1986, or Licia Brussa from the TAMPEP International Foundation (European Network for HIV/STI Prevention and Health Promotion among Migrant Sex Workers). Others had been playing an important part in the sex work debate in Europe, such as Laura Agustín; or Marjan Wijers, Marieke van Doorninck, and Marianne Jonker (*De Roode Draad*) from the Netherlands. Still others were relatively new to the movement, such as myself;[2] or had been active in national grassroots contexts, such as ROSEA in Sweden, Infoshare in Russia, Maggie's in Canada.[3] As part of its work, the group decided to found the International Committee on the Rights of Sex Workers in Europe (ICRSE) to compile some of the aims and responsibilities related to the conference and its political project.

To me, relatively young and new to sex work politics, being part of the organizing committee over the course of two years proved to be an unforgettable political experience. The following are reflections on the conference that I have developed through ongoing dialog with fellow activists and conference participants.[4]

The Conference

The Brussels conference was divided into three days of work: the first was dedicated to sex workers only; allies joined in on the second day; and on the third day events were all hosted inside the European Parliament where, thanks to the invitation of the Greens/European Free Alliance, the participants had the opportunity to present in the presence of a few members of parliament the three documents participants had developed during the conference: the Manifesto, the Declaration, and the Recommendations. The Declaration was then endorsed by an Italian member of the European Parliament, Vittorio Agnoletto (European United Left). The official closing of the conference was marked by a passionate reading of parts of the Manifesto by ten sex workers.

From there, almost all of the conference participants along with a number of activists from local feminist and migrants' organizations and a few more sympathetic sex workers from Brussels went on with a fun and well-attended march starting from Place de La Bourse (location of the stock exchange). The entire group was made beautifully visible by the red umbrellas, a symbol of resistance to attacks of many kinds.[5]

For the purpose of the conference, being a sex worker was based on self-definition: sex worker is whoever says s-he is. Politically this refers to anybody who is ready to speak from a position (also) based on work experience, no matter whether this experience is past or present, old or recent. However, self-definition does not necessarily coincide with being publicly out as a sex worker. Therefore, it was an important objective of the conference organizers to guarantee anonymity throughout the entire conference. Participants only met with the press if they wanted to. A public press conference was held at the European Parliament on the third day of the conference, by a group of about ten sex workers from different countries, alongside a few allies.

A conference report of collected recordings and documents was compiled by Andrew Sorfleet, a special-mission guest from Toronto, with particular attention to issues of (in)visibility. Although cameras were prohibited at the conference, hand-selected visual documentation was produced by an official conference photographer as well as inside a video booth, resulting in the video titled Ni *coupables ni victimes*.[6] However, despite these precautions and the general no-photo rule, many participants took pictures inside the conference venue. This leaves us with the question of how to negotiate and practice collective responsibility in a time that poses new challenges of (in)visibility because it is extremely easy to publish and distribute digital images. Although the majority of conference participants were in fact prepared to march in the street without covering their faces, the imperative not to compromise those who prefer anonymity remains.

Sex workers' self-organization and self-representation were among the guiding principles of the conference. In practice, this translated into the commitment to ensure that sex workers constituted the majority of participants, and into the decision to dedicate the first day to a sex-workers-only space. It also meant that the organizing committee did active outreach to sex workers and fully funded all sex worker participants, while at the same time developing a selection process to accept and fund allies.

During the process of inviting and selecting participants the organizing committee had two main concerns. First, we wanted to make sure that we had a wide variety of sex workers in terms of country of origin, working contexts, gender, and migration experiences. This variety is central to the value of the debate on sex work, and to the creation of political legitimacy too often denied to sex workers who speak out publicly ('you are an exception, you are not real prostitutes') – whereas sex workers who are ready (or forced) to present themselves as victims and who ask for help to change work become accepted as 'real prostitutes.' In practice, no applicant referring to her-himself as sex worker was refused, and instead an active outreach effort was made to include people who would not necessarily have applied. For instance, I personally went to Paris in August 2005 to involve sex workers from two different groups, ACT UP Paris and Femmes de Droits, Droits de Femmes. None of their members had previously known about the conference, and six of them were subsequently present in Brussels.

Furthermore, emphasis was put on involving participants from countries where sex workers' rights groups are not visible, in particular in Eastern Europe. Sex workers do not have autonomous organizations in many Eastern European countries, and the struggle for sex workers' rights is organized mainly either through gay and lesbian organizations (for example, the Nash Mir Ukraine gay and lesbian center), health projects (for example, La Strada Poland), or anti-trafficking groups (for example, the Anti-Trafficking Center in Belgrade).

Great effort was equally put in providing translations – while English was the main language spoken during the conference, translations into German, Russian, Spanish, and French were systematically provided during the organizing phase and throughout the conference.

Concerning allies, we aimed to include individuals and organizations who we believed would contribute to the conference by adding specific issues to the agenda as well as strengthening existing alliances and building new ones. In particular, we solicited individuals, organizations, and institutions organizing around human, labor, and migrants' rights, that we thought might be open to make sex workers' rights part of their agenda even if their professional and political activities were not centered on sex work. This included unions and labor rights' groups, such as Comisiones Obreras (Spain), the European Trade Union Federation (ETUC), and Global Labor Institute (Switzerland); and migrants' rights initiatives like GISTI (Groupe d'information et soutien des immigrés, in France), or Indymedia Estrecho in Spain. Relatively less attention was given to people who already play a well-established role in sex workers' rights issues, namely academics and the numerous health projects existing all over Europe. As a whole, these strategies reflected the intention to modify some of the legitimating mechanisms currently in place, which only grant certain actors the authority to speak about sex work: among them, allies (typically academics and health care or social workers) and sometimes sex workers, but limited to either the 'privileged' or the 'hopeless victims.'

Money for organizing and holding the conference came from a variety of grants and funds. The grant-giving organizations were mainly based in the Netherlands, supporting women's projects or more general philanthropic initiatives (e.g. Mamacash, Cordaid, Filia, Hivos, Haella, N(o)vib). In addition, the conference was sponsored by the Global Fund for Women, based in the US, and De Graaf Stichting, a Dutch foundation which has promoted sex workers' rights in the Dutch policy context for decades. Compared to other events centered on sex work, it is worthwhile mentioning that the organizations funding the conference had no particular focus on health issues, and that 'health' was not addressed as a subject *per se*. This choice was based on the awareness that a focus on health might prevent activists from elaborating critiques of national and European policies. Indeed, organizations providing health services often lack the financial autonomy and time to do so.

The first two days of the conference were dedicated to the discussion and revision of the Manifesto, the Declaration and the Recommendations. The first day centered around intensive work, by sex workers only, on the Manifesto; the work was organized in three separate groups, each dealing with different parts of the text: 'Introduction: Beyond Compassion'; 'Our Lives,' and 'Our Labor.' The Manifesto was eventually endorsed by a plenary assembly consisting of 120 sex workers. On the second day, a plenary of 200 people, composed of both sex workers and allies, discussed and subsequently endorsed the Declaration and the Recommendations.

It should be pointed out that both the Declaration and the Manifesto derived from a yearlong process involving the consultation of about thirty sex workers, sex workers' rights groups, and allies across Europe. Hence, the Manifesto and Declaration should be read in relation to each other, as part of a political project to create various tools for different political moments. The Manifesto, following the tradition of the World Charter for Prostitutes' Rights (1985), represents a more 'utopian' moment, and it is meant to express a collective 'vision of changes that are needed to create a more equitable society in which sex workers, their rights and labor are acknowledged and valued' (ICRSE, 2005b, 'Incipit'). Instead, the Declaration is meant as a tool for active engagement with existing laws. By listing both the rights everybody should enjoy under international legislation as well as the existing violations of rights of sex workers in Europe, it situates the struggle for sex workers' rights in an already (at least on paper) legitimate space. The Recommendations is a short document containing the main principles that should be followed for policy intervention both at the national and at the European level.

On days one and two, spaces were also created to think collectively about collaboration after the conference via a network, which subsequently came to be organized around the ICRSE's activist website (www.sexworkeurope.org).

A politics of alliances

The fundamental political project of the conference was a well-planned move out of the political isolation sex workers and sex work activists suffer from in their own local contexts but also, as a movement, on the national and international levels.

The urgency is real. According to the original statement of purpose of the conference:

> Repressive policies on migration, public order and morality have led to the increasing vulnerability of sex workers with all the negative consequences for their health and safety. Anti-prostitution and anti-migration policies negatively affect the rights of sex workers, whereas increasing emphases on citizens' security, law and order and closing borders have impeded the growth of rights movements in general. (ICRSE, 2004)

In this situation, '*sex workers' rights organizations decided to seek out and unite with new allies* concerned with human, labor, and migrants' rights' (ICRSE, 2004, emphasis is mine).

Indeed, as the Declaration explains,

> Practices [restricting the fundamental rights and freedoms of sex workers] occur across health and social care, housing, employment, education, administrative law and criminal justice systems. ... [T]here is not one country within Europe – including those with regulated sex industries – where sex workers have not reported discrimination and violations of their human rights ... [In the large majority of countries in Europe] it is illegal for sex workers to work together for their own protection without facing prosecution for 'pimping' one another ... A sex worker's child, upon reaching the age of majority, may be prosecuted with 'living off' the sex worker's earnings ... Sex workers lose custody of their children through social services or family courts solely because of their occupation, and not based on any specific evidence or harm or incapacity to parent. (ICRSE, 2005a, 'Why Do We Need a Declaration?')

A number of other policies are considered responsible for impairing sex workers' lives, work, and ability to organize, many of them related to migration issues. Consider for instance that:

> In Romania, ... sex work is illegal and the government has forbidden its citizens to engage in sex work. As a result of pressure from the Romanian government the Austrian government has terminated the permits of Romanian sex workers and women who have worked legally in Austria may face retribution on their return. (ICRSE, 2005a)

Sex work activists also exposed the fact that recent interventions legitimized as 'anti-trafficking actions' have had a negative impact on the living and working conditions of young migrants, through deportation and further restriction of their mobility. Not only do these interventions directly attack migrant sex workers, they also increase stigmatization of the whole industry and reinforce a climate of exploitation. In addition, the link being made between 'trafficking' and sex work is used to justify the cutting of public money to harm reduction projects that offer sex workers access to basic public services, such as TAMPEP – now being replaced by zero tolerance and forced rescuing operations. In some cases, these operations become law, as with the 1998 Crime and Disorder Act in the UK (O'Neill & Campbell, 2006), or with Sarkozy's Loi de Sécurité Intérieure (Home Security Law) in 2003 in France.

> In the United Kingdom, where street-based sex workers are criminalized, Anti-Social Behaviour Orders are used to restrict freedom of movement and in some cities posters identifying sex workers with names and photographs have been printed and distributed in communities. (ICRSE, 2005a)

The French 'Sarkozy Law,' introduced in spite of organized opposition by sex workers of various nationalities, allows the police to deport street workers who are migrants immediately, and to threaten and criminalize all others. This kind of political climate may also contribute to the increase in violence from both the police and clients against sex workers.

At the same time, and somewhat ironically, these policies are increasingly accompanied by moral, administrative, and criminal condemnation of sex workers' clients – de facto applied to street clients only. Unfortunately the feminist arguments supporting these policies ignore the historical fact that more criminalization results in less power for women (and others) who sell sex, while handing more power to organizers, clients, and the police.

For example in Sweden, where buying sexual services became a criminal offence in 1999, 'politicians and policy makers have threatened to withdraw from public debates if sex workers are also to participate and sex workers have been systematically excluded from public debate' (ICRSE, 2005a). Similar exclusionary practices are not uncommon across Europe.

In such a suffocating policy context the challenge posed to the ICRSE has been to extend the efforts of sex workers' rights activists beyond a narrow focus on 'sex-work specific' injustices. To break the isolation of this workers' movement may require that sex work activists explicitly support other activist struggles even if their causes may at first seem rather distinct from theirs. In fact, sex workers and sex work activists have a lot to contribute to the fight against labor exploitation, for human rights and freedom of movement, and in turn can learn a lot from others. Furthermore, by actively taking part in these larger political issues, sex work activists may open important chances to gain the recognition and support of others.

In these respects, it is interesting to observe how sex work activists' political practices today differ from those of the organizers of the Second World Whores Congress, held in Brussels in 1986. As Gail Pheterson and Margo St James mentioned in their introductory speech on the second day of the conference, the absolute priority for the International Collective of Prostitutes (ICPR) at the time was 'giving voices to the whores' – probably for the first time in history. It seems that twenty years later, the focus of the struggle originally initiated by ICPR has shifted to strategic considerations of *what kind of* political voices(s) sex workers and sex work activists want to raise, and what kind of alliances they want to cultivate. The terminology 'alliances' and 'allies' – as opposed to the terms 'guests' or 'supporters' preferred in the past[7] – may in this context reflect a conscious effort to build a type of relation with people without sex work experience that isn't based on notions of 'help' and 'need,' but on political reciprocity.

Beyond 'helpers'

This explicit political move towards new alliances may represent a resort from what strikes me as two major paralyzing moments of the sex workers' rights movement.

First, limiting the demands of sex work activists' to 'sex-work specific' issues runs the risk of reproducing sex workers as a category of the 'weak' or 'victims' in need of protection – which might be an invitation for all kinds of 'helpers'[8] but is definitely not empowering for sex workers. In particular, it is crucial not to be naïve *vis-à-vis* a certain liberal democratic promise that would like us to believe that politicians and their institutions are ready to represent and help just anyone. In fact, if compared to the beginning of the movement in the 1970s, the present European political contingency may make it even more unlikely that politicians will spontaneously take on sex work activists' concerns. Therefore, it is important to be as strategic with politicians as one is with other potential allies; in other words, sex work activists may try to meet them in the context of larger political debates rather than look at them as some sort of delegates or 'helpers.'

Second, the practice of a politics of alliances may also shed new light on burning issues raised by sex workers' identity politics, or the politics of organizing among self-identified sex workers. While the model followed in Brussels gave central importance to sex-worker-only spaces, it also showed an awareness of their limits, by placing them among other political spaces. This is well illustrated by the conference programme which included a first day for sex workers only, a second day with allies, and a third day of both sex workers and allies expressing themselves together in public spaces.

Rather than defining sex workers' spaces as 'preliminary' political moments, this kind of organizing delineates them as being funda-mental moments in the making of a collective voice that is also *always* to be created through the presence of sex workers and sex work activists in larger political spaces and debates, as well as through communica-tion with sex workers who are not part of sex work activists' collective spaces.

However, if used as the only model for activism, a sex-workers-only political practice may become suffocating, for it does not solve prob-lems of political representation ('who speaks for whom?') and it can turn into an exclusionary space. Indeed, it proposes a model of public coming-out as sex worker that is simply not feasible and maybe not even desirable for most people working in the sex industry in contem-porary Europe.

Choosing allies, producing collective truth

In order to understand the politics of alliances that sex workers organizing in Europe are hoping to develop it might be useful to explore some parts of the Manifesto in more detail. Indeed, the Manifesto – like the Declaration and the Recommendations – is meant to be a tool for political communication, among sex workers as well as with other activists. Together, they represent a specific political moment in the positioning of the sex workers' movement, in relation to other movements and potential allies in Europe. The collective creation of these documents does not resemble an academic project of finding 'truth' but rather marks a process of 'taking control of the production of truth' (Hardt & Negri, 2000, p. 156), together, as a movement. And this process is central to a politics of alliances.

Therefore, the question may be asked what type of alliances the Manifesto wants to build. In the limited space of this chapter, I consider it important to focus on two political bridges: the alliance to feminist politics and the link to the politics of migrants' rights. Both constituted important points of debate at the conference and yet they were dealt with in opposite ways.

FEMINIST ALLIES?

One may notice the absence of explicit feminist arguments in the Manifesto. And yet, arguably, many members of the organizing committee and many conference participants consider themselves feminists and have been part of feminist movements. How, then, is one to understand this explicit disconnection from feminist politics?

The answer can be found in history. In 1986, at the Second World Whores Congress, feminists were seen as attractive, if not natural allies. French feminist groups had supported prostitutes occupying churches in France in 1975 (Carthonnet, 2004), and feminists of Lotta Femminista from Italy met COYOTE in the 1970s (Busi, 2006). Also, it is within a French materialist feminist tradition[9] that prostitutes and non-prostitutes together produced the sharpest critique of the division of sex labor, both paid and unpaid (for example, Pheterson, 1996; Tabet 1991, 2004). Sex was identified as one of the services women are traditionally supposed to provide for men in a patriarchal society, often as part of unpaid, informal, invisible exchanges. From this perspective, the crucial issue is the struggle for better working conditions, both within marriage and in prostitution.

230

In contemporary Europe however, the most visible and powerful feminists have a very different view on these matters. The part of feminism that has become institutionalized appears to have done so by protecting the distinct interests of middle-class European women, who arguably tend to support themselves through activities such as marriage, party politics, and other well-paid 'straight' jobs. This kind of feminism is strongly abolitionist, as well demonstrated by the action of the Women's European Lobby in Brussels, or the case of Sweden, where the popular neo-prohibitionist law was largely pushed forward by female members of parliament. Also, this strand of contemporary feminism often ties into (if not contributes to) certain discourses on migration that – in increasingly racist and Islamophobic ways – establish second-class citizenship for migrants. In France, for instance, main campaigns led by institutionalized feminists in recent years have advocated simultaneously the elimination of prostitution, especially migrant prostitution, and the banning of Muslim women's headscarves from public spaces.[10]

NextGENDERation, a feminist network serving as a point of connection for young and non-institutionalized feminists who support sex workers' struggles in Europe, has denounced these tendencies:

> The queue of political leaders and public figures who affirm 'the equality of men and women' as a fundamental value of European civilization is getting longer and longer these days. This appeal to 'women's emancipation' is particularly popular among political leaders and parties who advocate 'integration' intended as assimilation of communities of migrant origins. This integration goes hand in hand with closure of borders and restriction of immigration into Europe as well as re-invention of Europe in terms of a homogeneous white civilization, a process which once again denies the obvious multi-ethnic, multi-cultural and multi-religious realities of Europe. (NextGENDERation, 2004)

In particular, current analyses of 'trafficking' proposed by institutionalized feminism appear to be limited and short-sighted. By focusing on 'bad men' exploiting 'poor women,' they point away from states' responsibilities in preventing people from legally migrating to or within Europe, in preventing all sex workers from working safely and organizing for their rights, and in fostering divisions between migrant and local sex workers. Instead, these analyses seem to give legitimacy to increasing deportations by advocating migrants' repatriation 'for their own good' since 'they did not want to come here in the first place.' This has to be considered in relation to the fact that in all European countries, including Germany and the Netherlands where prostitution is legal, it is illegal for migrants from outside the EU to work in the sex industry (Danna, 2003). Considering their policies on immigration and sex work, European states in fact may be producing deportable, second-class citizens who are available for exploitation in a variety of sectors, including the sex industry.[11]

What in the Manifesto seems like a silence regarding feminist issues should be understood as a moment of strategic political subtraction of the sex workers' movement. Indeed, aiming to minimize its reliance on any particular feminist analysis appears to be the best strategy, given the difficulty of divorcing feminist accounts from essentially anti-sexwork and anti-migration nexuses through which they are sustained in Europe today.

SEX WORK MOVES

During the conference, and as expressed in the Manifesto, a clear link was made between sex workers' and migrants' rights.

> The trafficking discourse obscures the issues of migrants' rights. [It] reinforces the discrimination, violence and exploitation against migrants, sex workers and migrant sex workers in particular ... The lack of possibilities to migrate puts our integrity and health in danger. (ICRSE, 2005b, 'The Right to Mobility')

In the past decade, the dominant trafficking discourse has established as its fundamental belief the view that *all* migrant women who work with sex are victims of organized crime and violent men who force them to come to Europe and to work as sex workers against their will – note that men and transgender people who sell sex are not really taken into consideration by such a deeply gendered analysis.

This view persists even though there is an increasing amount of evidence showing that the realities of migrant sex workers in Europe are multiple and in many respects reflect the difficult situation of all migrants – characterized by a general dependence on mediators and on one particular employer for travel, work, housing, visa, and so on. There certainly are workers who find themselves in situations that researchers have defined as 'slavery-like' conditions. For instance, estimates produced for street work in Italy (Carchedi, 2000), have indicated that 10 percent of workers are subjected to violence and/or the threat of violence, and confiscation of legal documents; they also have no freedom of movement. This situation is unfortunately not limited to the sex industry, but also exists in agriculture, domestic work, construction, and other sectors, and also applies to men and transgender people. In fact, slavery-like conditions may be a consequence of being forcibly transported to a foreign country but, as Wijers (1998) demonstrates, they may be a consequence of recruitment without coercion too. The point is that despite the serious but small risks of slavery-like situations, most people stay with the decision to work in the sex industry since despite the difficult and often unexpected conditions, it often appears to be the fastest way to realize their projects: to pay their migration debt, and to send money home.[12]

'Anti-trafficking' state interventions typically target migrant women in the sex industry, through forced 'rescuing operations.' The problem with these operations becomes clear when looking at their result: most 'rescued' workers refuse to denounce their traffickers and/or to declare themselves as being victims of trafficking. Consequently, rescuing operations are *de facto* criminalizing actions that result in the deportation of 'rescued victims.' In a few cases – if a migrant woman declares herself to be a victim of 'trafficking,' and if her story is close enough to the official definition of trafficking – in many EU countries she will have access to alternative treatment. In most European legal systems this treatment consists of a coordinated intervention of state and international agencies, police, immigration, and non-governmental organizations (NGOs) that provide victims with shelter and a rehabilitation program, lasting from a few weeks up to several months (Associazione On the Road, 2002). During this time the 'trafficked victim' is not allowed to work and she is encouraged, sometimes forced, to give evidence against her 'traffickers.' After that, she is offered 'voluntary repatriation': in other words, she is deported back home.[13] Most repatriated women, whether they have been part of an 'anti-trafficking' program or not, will try to come back to Europe – even if they have gone through heavy exploitation and abuse. They will start looking for another facilitator and start their migration process over again – they will be, as authorities say, 're-trafficked.' Often, however, being identified as ex-trafficked women and as coming from so-called 'countries of origin of trafficking,' they will find extra restrictions on their visa procedures, making their travel even more difficult.

'Anti-trafficking' interventions have unique consequences in an industry that is mainly shaped by an abolitionist agenda, that is, where most (sex) work is illegal anyway. Abolitionist policies create a dual level of criminalization for migrant sex workers and worsen the situation of the rest. This is peculiarly done through the mobilization of a powerful rhetoric: the rhetoric of 'choice' versus 'force.' Indeed, by the very same gesture that classifies all migrants *a priori* as 'trafficked victims' or 'sex slaves,' the rest of the workforce – namely, EU citizens, preferably white, middle-class, and Western European – are *a priori* classified as 'free workers,' or 'sex workers' (Doezema, 1998), or those who have 'chosen' this type of work. In the process of being distinguished from the 'victims,' the voluntary, consensual workers – or workers with agency – get to be defined *a priori* as never needing protection. Fundamentally, as the ICRSE put it:

> The abuses sex workers may undergo in the course of their work are [in this framework] considered to be the natural consequences of their willingness to work as prostitutes, meaning it is their own fault … This reinforces the classic dichotomy between 'innocent,' who deserve of protection, and 'guilty' women, who can be abused with impunity. (ICRSE, 2004)

Finally, not only in work practice, but also politically, these policies and discourses have furthered the divide between migrant and non-migrant workers in the sex industry, and prevented common organizing. However, the Brussels conference marks a change of orientation. The right to migrate and to remain were explicitly added to the agenda of sex workers in Europe: 'We demand that sex work is recognized as gainful employment, enabling migrants to apply for work and residence permits and that both documented and undocumented migrants be entitled to full labor rights' (ICRSE, 2005b, 'Our Labor'). This would indeed represent an improvement for all those working in the sex industry, whatever the conditions they work in, for a long or a short time, whether they identify as 'sex workers' or not.

Questions for the future

The Brussels conference demonstrates the immense power of common space, and of collective action. Two hundred activists together for three days – in a hotel, at a party, inside the European Parliament, marching in the streets – directly create a powerful political event. In events such as these the mobilizing of responsible and visible collective energy remains and reproduces itself beyond what is technically planned. Some examples after Brussels were the creation of the new group Les Putes in Paris soon after the conference, which organized the first of many Putes Pride in Paris in March 2006; and the creation of x:talk in early 2006, a London project to provide English classes for sex workers by sex workers. Also, the ICRSE itself has become part of a lively initiative in Central and Eastern Europe and Central Asia, the Sex Workers' Advocacy Network (SWAN).

However, amongst the proliferation of new actions, critical questions on future strategies at a European level of mobilization remain to be addressed. Namely, some ask what follows today from the Brussels conference, what is the future of the ICRSE and its network, what are its goals and targets. Many activists also wonder how a project can develop across a variety of national and regional contexts so different in language and in traditions of policies and resistance. These are not only legitimate but also fundamental questions. Yet they may become tricky to the extent that they already assume part of the answer they seem to be asking.

The main point is that, *at least in its best intention*, the political project beyond the Brussels conference is fundamentally *open and contestable*. The very way it came about, and the way it is developing at the moment of writing, speaks about its nature. It started with the organization of a very large meeting, and it consists of spaces or infrastructures – meetings, mailing lists, common initiatives, common documents –to strengthen and enlarge alliances around sex workers' rights in Europe. ICRSE thus remains open and contestable to the extent that the groups involved and the ways to create alliances are meant to keep changing. For instance, the Manifesto and the Declaration were designed to be rewritten at other European conferences to be organized in the future.

The political debate around sex work is increasingly unified in Europe, especially since migration (and thus 'trafficking') issues are in the competence of the European Union. However, a variety of different strategies and recipes are needed across Europe. Indeed, different legal cultures exist, and the traditions of organizing in the industry vary widely. For instance, issues in the Netherlands and Germany are connected to the state recognition of sex work as work, in a context where sex workers' organizations have a long history, also of institutionalization. In Greece, the presence of licensed brothels is in no way a guarantee of workers' rights, and the sex workers' organization has not yet begun to address migrants' issues. In France, the criminalization of street workers is accompanied by a strong move towards abolitionism within the left. And so on.

The Manifesto and the Declaration make clear that an important unity exists in the demands for policy change. In particular they ask for 'decriminalization' of sex work, including of organizing third parties, and for its partial 'legalization,' at least to include working permits for migrants. However, the way to go about these changes is not settled within the ICRSE project. The idea is that diversity cannot and should not be erased on a European level of resistance, and that is why the actual contents and strategies of ICRSE must remain open and contestable over time. This makes an important difference for questions of the future.

An important implication is that if there are people organizing actions or taking a position as ICRSE, potentially there will also be other people in different contexts organizing actions and taking other positions as ICRSE. In other words, different political strategies should not be seen as competing with one another. Lobbying members of parliament and struggling for legal change; focusing on self-organization among workers; putting visibility and sex workers' positive identity at the center; trying to build political practices that do not require personal exposure; these are all examples of different and potentially divergent strategies that are used by people involved in the project.

Concretely, ICRSE is a name that can be used by anyone who chooses to affiliate with it, by endorsing and promoting the Sex Workers in Europe Manifesto and the Declaration of the Rights of Sex Workers in Europe. The official aims of the project are to promote communication and collaboration among sex workers' rights groups and allies – including potential and new allies – in Europe and to promote the ideas contained in the Manifesto and the Declaration. This is being done through the Network mailing list, and the ongoing creation of new online spaces on the ICRSE interactive website (ICRSE, 2009). Until now this has meant that content and news are being uploaded by a number of different people. Meetings working on specific alliances have also taken place.[14] The Manifesto and the Declaration have been circulating until now in English, Russian, German, French, Spanish, Italian, Greek, Slovenian, Macedonian, and Norwegian, and they have been disseminated already in innumerable contexts in Europe and outside.

NOTES

1 Red umbrellas were first used in Venice in 2002 for a march organized by the Committee for Civil Rights of Prostitutes, a prostitutes' rights organization existing in Italy since 1983.

2 Since 1995 I have been active in autonomous feminist and queer politics in Italy. With Sexyshock (Bologna) we collaborated with the Committee for Civil Rights of Prostitutes (Pordenone, Italy) and with the MIT (Movimento Identità Transessuale [Movement of Trans Identity], Bologna, Italy), which is how I became involved in sex work politics in 2000 and subsequently heard about the organization of the conference. At this same time I had also started doing research on the political economy of prostitution.

3 For a complete list of the organizing committee members, see: www.sexworkeurope.org/site/index.php?option=com_content&task =view&id=34&Itemid=75 (accessed 20 May 2009).

4 Namely, I discussed the contents of this article with Jesper Bryngemark. Thanks to Camille Barbagallo of the International Union of Sex Worker and to Antonia Levy for their strong engagement with this text. Thanks also to Denise Rinehart for her generous editing skills.

5 For an explanation of the 'red umbrella' campaigns, see: www.sexworkeurope.org/site/index.php?option=com_content &task=view&id=25&Itemid=195 (accessed 20 May 2009).

6 This slogan comes from French activists and literally means 'neither guilty nor victims.' The video is available on the ICRSE website: www.sexwork europe.org/site/index.php?option=com_content&task=view&id=188&It emid=223 (accessed 20 May 2009).

7 Compare the instructions given to those enrolled in the World Whore Congress in Brussels 1986: 'All prostitutes and ex-prostitutes are welcome to participate actively in all sessions of the congress. Non-prostitute advocates are invited to listen and to contribute information or experiences when asked to so do by the prostitutes/ex-prostitutes; if you are not working or have never worked as a prostitute (meaning sex worker in any part of the industry), then you are a guest' (Pheterson, 1989, p. 48; italics are mine).

8 On 'helpers' in the European sex industry, see the work of Agustín (2004, 2005a).

9 The name 'French materialist feminists' was proposed in the 1990s by sympathetic Anglo-American authors (in particular Adkins & Merchant, 1996) to indicate a group of theorists who started working around the journal Questions Féministes that was founded in Paris in 1977 and had Simone de Beauvoir as its director. Some of the most well-known authors involved are Christine Delphy, Monique Wittig, Nicole-Claude Mathieu, Colette Guillaumin, Monique Plaza, Paola Tabet, and, in particular on prostitution, Gail Pheterson.

10 *Femmes publiques* is a feminist group that has reacted against this double political strategy promoted in France by institutionalized feminists.

11 On this issue see the work of Andrijasevic (2003) and of the Frassanito Network (2009).

12 According to research done in Italy, France, Austria, and Spain (Cabiria, 2004) the migration debt was in average 10,000 euros from Eastern Europe, and 70,000 euros from Africa.

13 In that sense, article 18 of Italian Immigration Law 40/1998 represents a famous exception for it includes the possibility of converting the temporary residence permit for victims of trafficking into a renewable work permit. Enforcement of article 18 is, however, very partial, arbitrary, and diverse across Italy, for its enactment depends on local police headquarters.

14 Among the many examples, the closest to me is the seminar at the European Social Forum in Athens in 2006. The seminar, co-organized by ICRSE with Frassanito Network and NextGENDERation, was titled 'What is Wrong with the Current European Anti-trafficking Policies?' It was considered a success in terms both of participation (about eighty participants) and of discussion. For more information, see the NextGENDERation website: www.nextgenderation.net/agenda.html (accessed 20 May 2009).

14 Conclusion: Pushing Boundaries in Sex Work Activism and Research

Melissa Hope Ditmore

Outside their work, sex workers participate in the same variety of roles and relationships as most people within family, among friends, and in their communities. Sex workers are not treated with the same respect as other members of society because they are thought of as sex workers first and foremost, rather than as people having the same human needs and wants and rights as others. This book offers a sophisticated overview and introduction to the sex work policy and theory, based on the understanding that sex workers are members of society rather than adjacent to society.

The chapters in this book expand on the literature to include new perspectives and ways of examining sex work, including money matters, personal relationships, relationships with the state, and organizing. This volume includes contributions from strong activists. The pieces included here and the recent efforts described below offer a compass for the future directions of sex workers' rights activism.

Sex worker advocates and activists remain active because there is still a great deal to do to improve the lives and working conditions of sex workers everywhere. Sex worker activism is necessary because sex workers suffer disproportionate violence and discrimination, which in turn has effects on their education, social mobility, occupational opportunities, quality of life, and health. Some people erroneously presume that sex worker rights activists are all 'happy hookers' who are thrilled with their work and have no suggestions for ways to improve it. The presumption that activists are cheerleaders for sex work demonstrates a lack of comprehension of the arguments made in favor of improving conditions for sex workers. Activists and advocates campaign for rights not because they have an idealized or unrealistic view of sex work, but because they know that sex workers still routinely experience rights violations, such as violence including rape and murder, inattention to violence by the authorities, disruption of family life when sex workers are denied child custody, and discrimination by health and medical professionals or educational institutions.

Vanguard campaigns for sex workers' rights are led by those most affected, for example, by violence, by the adverse effects of legislation, by unethical practices in research, by poor research, or by a lack of useful information. A myriad of reasons exist for sex workers to advocate for their rights themselves, and sex worker activists have made a number of important contributions in recent years. Garofolo describes the 2005 meeting in Brussels for the International Committee on the Rights of Sex Workers in Europe and the useful rights-oriented documents produced. This was followed by two meetings in Africa (Abuja, Nigeria, in December 2005 and Johannesburg, South Africa, in February 2009), both leading to the development of networks of advocates for the rights of sex workers, by the meeting of academics and sex workers and students in 2006 that led to this book, by the founding of the Paulo Longo Research Initiative in 2008, and by the formalization of the Global Network of Sex Work Projects, which replaced self-selected and informal groups of people working together on an ad hoc basis by a coordinated network. Sex workers in India campaigned to prevent further criminalization of sexwork-related activities. The Asia Pacific Network of Sex Workers and Women's Network for Unity documented human rights abuses in 2008, including the internment of sex workers in detention centres and the deaths of three sex workers in police custody. International protests over these documented abuses led to the release of detained sex workers. Sex worker activists and advocates continue this forward march.

Sex workers, whose campaigns are often unsupported and under-funded, have made considerable strides, but other influences have also gained ground. Every bit of progress is accompanied by a backlash from people and organizations who feel themselves or their agenda threat-ened by active sex workers. Weldon pointed out that some researchers may benefit richly by endorsing a specific view of sex work while using anti-trafficking rhetoric to resist any acknowledgement of sex work as work, precluding acknowledgement of the rights of sex workers such as good working conditions. This is the specific position expressed in the US government's 'anti-prostitution pledge' enacted under former President George W. Bush in 2002 and legislated in 2003, which states that organizations that acknowledge sex work as work are not 'appropriate partners' for US federal grants (Ditmore, 2007). This policy has been used to deny funding to specific programs and to sanction investigation of specific organizations. The worst effect of this policy has been that many organizations decline to work with sex workers, effectively or explicitly denying services to sex workers, because they fear jeopardizing their funding (*Taking the Pledge*, 2007). This was not an inadvertent or unintended consequence of the policy, but a deliberate goal. This state of affairs will not change without significant support among the US population for evidence-based aid and health programming of documented effectiveness. In order to bring about this policy change, sex workers will need to be active in diplomacy, advocacy, and fundraising initiatives.

UNAIDS has moved from a rights-based perspective on sex work in combating HIV/AIDS, where the goal is to reduce HIV transmission within sex work, to addressing sex work itself as something to be reduced. This is demonstrated in the draft Guidance Note on HIV/AIDS and Sex Work, which was released in 2007 and amended in 2009, Significantly, the Guidance Note did not include the specific inputs of sex workers provided during a global consultation held in 2006 (Ministry of Health of Brazil, UNAIDS & UNFPA, 2006) and subsequently expressed in protests following the release of the Guidance Note. The positive changes that were made to the amended Guidance Note, including addition of rights-based language, result from pressure applied by larger rights-oriented organizations including the Canadian HIV/AIDS Legal Network, the Open Society Institute, and the Human Rights Reference Group rather than sex worker groups. In May 2009, the new director of UNAIDS, Michel Sidibé, met with sex workers and advocates to propose ways to address the problems articulated by the Global Working Group on Sex Work and HIV Policy. Next steps include clarification of the ways to address these issues by including sex workers are being worked out.

Campaigns for sex workers' rights are undertaken by people affected today, but the results of such campaigns will affect sex workers of the future as well. We should applaud the visionary student who, during the Sex Work Matters conference, looked beyond the current situations discussed and asked about future generations of sex workers. Children of sex workers are a vital part of the movement for the rights of sex workers, and in parts of Asia are at the forefront of campaigns for their own rights alongside their parents' rights. In India and Bangladesh, the children of sex workers are actively involved and visible in programs and campaigns for the rights to education and health. It is common for people to grow up to work in the same economic sector as their parents, and sex work is no exception. This is particularly true in places where there are established communities of sex workers, with sex workers living and working in the same neighborhoods for generations. Whether you accept or deplore this state of affairs, it must be acknowledged, and the children of sex workers recognize that rights that are won or lost for their parents today will affect their own lives tomorrow.

This emerging movement of the families and children of sex workers and the mobilization of a diverse range of advocates, individuals, and organizations in support of the Global Working Group's efforts to improve UNAIDS guidance on sex work offer models for others working to support the advancement of sex workers' rights at local, national, and international levels.

Sex workers have made great strides, but a great deal more still needs to be done to ensure that they enjoy the full range of rights afforded others. So-called 'deviant' occupations represent only a small part of the lives of people in or associated with the sex industry. No one is a sex worker twenty-four hours a day, and sex workers have lives as diverse as anyone else's. An essential step towards ensuring that sex workers enjoy the same rights and conditions as anyone else is to acknowledge that they are a part of the community, both inside and outside of their work.

Organizations and groups that promote the rights of sex workers – some loose, some with strong structures and support – exist and continue to emerge around the world. Alliances formed across the many facets of people's lives – as family members, as workers, as neighbors, as associates – are critical to advancing sex workers' rights. Efforts to promote the rights of sex workers can make progress only with support from a broader cross-section of our societies.

Policy decisions affecting sex workers are often made without consulting sex workers. Viewed as simply 'part of the problem' – or as passive victims to be 'rescued' – their input is considered to be of no value. The results of such decisions are predictably ruinous: for the sex workers, for the communities in which they live, and for larger programs such as efforts to control HIV/AIDS. Decisions taken in a vacuum are disastrous not simply because they ignore the rights of sex workers as members of society, but because they also disregard their unique knowledge of the issues that affect their lives, and of their real needs and the conditions in which they live and work.

The way forward is to listen to sex workers and ask what would truly be of use to them – whether in law reform, research or any other area – to offer suggestions, and to support the needs of sex workers without imposing another agenda.

Contributing authors

Laura Agustín is the author of *Sex at the Margins: Migration, Labor Markets and the Rescue Industry* (2007). For the past fifteen years, her research has focused on the connections between migration, informal economies, the sex industry, and the large social sector dedicated to helping and saving migrants and prostitutes. She blogs at 'Border Thinking' on migration, trafficking, and commercial sex.

Mindy S. Bradley-Engen is assistant professor of sociology and criminal justice at the University of Arkansas. She is currently a National Institute of Mental Health Postdoctoral Fellow at the Sheps Center for Health Services Research at UNC-Chapel Hill, specializing in mental health and substance abuse services and systems. Her research focuses on justice policy and criminal justice responses to non-traditional offenders. She is also the author of *Naked Lives: Inside the Worlds of Exotic Dance* (2009).

Barbara G. Brents is an associate professor in the Department of Sociology and affiliate of the Women's Studies Department at the University of Nevada, Las Vegas. She studies sexual commerce and politics and is involved in projects studying sustainability in Las Vegas, globalization, tourism, and indoor sex work. She is currently working with Crystal Jackson and Kate Hausbeck on a book, *The State of Sex: Nevada's Legal Brothels*. The team has also published articles on violence in legal brothels and the marketing of brothels.

Anne Dölemeyer studied political science, sociology, and economics at Leipzig University, where she received an MA in political science. Her research interest concerns administrative epistemologies and the production of subjectivity through state actors. Her PhD thesis is on the civil struggles to rebuild New Orleans.

Giulia Garofalo has been involved in sex workers' rights activism, feminist and queer groups in Italy, the UK, the Netherlands, and France. As a researcher, her background is in economics, gender, and social sciences. She is currently completing her PhD on the political economy of sex work in Europe at the University of East London.

Kathryn Hausbeck is senior associate dean of the graduate college at the University of Nevada, Las Vegas. Dr Hausbeck is an associate professor in the Department of Sociology and a faculty affiliate in Women's Studies, Cultural Studies and the Asian Studies program. With colleague and co-author Barb Brents, she studies the organization and expansion of the sex industry in the United States, 'the pornographication of everyday life' and America's only system of legalized prostitution: the Nevada brothels. Kate, Barb, and Crystal Jackson are finishing a book with Routledge Press on *The State of Sex: Nevada's Legal Brothels*. Kate also is involved in projects on trafficking and homeless youth.

Carrie M. Hobbs earned her BA degrees in both sociology and criminal justice with honours in 2006. She completed her MS in operations management at the University of Arkansas in 2009, and is pursuing a law degree at Seattle University. Her interests include legal policy/ management and issues of civil rights/ representation among stigmatized populations.

Mashrur Shahid Hossain is assistant professor of English at Jahangirnagar University, Bangladesh. He teaches communication, media, and literature. His areas of interest and expertise include postcolonialism, cultural studies, media, gender, and American literature. Recently he completed two papers; on the politics of power/ pleasure in the representation of women in violent films, and on the language and mode of expression in SMS and IM. He is currently working on queer films as well as subversive and subaltern discourses.

Kerwin Kaye is a PhD candidate in the Department of Social and Cultural Analysis at New York University. His 2003 essay 'Male Prostitution in the Twentieth Century: Pseudohomosexuals, Hoodlum Homosexuals, and Exploited Teens,' won a Best of Journal award from the *Journal of Homosexuality*. He is also the editor of *Male Lust: Pleasure, Power, and Transformation* (2000).

Patty Kelly is a professor of cultural anthropology at George Washington University. She is also the author of *Lydia's Open Door* (2008), an ethnographic account of a year she spent inside the Zona Galáctica, a legal, state-regulated brothel in Mexico.

Juline A. Koken is a social psychologist and advocate for sex workers' rights. Her research examines the coping strategies and resiliency of sex workers of all genders, and how their experiences are impacted by factors such as race, gender, class, and working environment. She hopes her next project will sample clients of sex workers. Juline is currently a project director at the Center for HIV/AIDS Educational Studies and Training (CHEST) as well as a post-doctoral fellow in Behavioral Science Training at the National Development and Research Institutes (NDRI) in the US.

Maggie O'Neill is senior lecturer in criminology and social policy in the Department of Social Sciences at Loughborough University. An interdisciplinary scholar and expert in participatory action research, visual and arts-based research methods, she has worked for two decades with sex workers, sex worker support services, and communities affected by street sex markets. Maggie has published extensively in this area and is committed to producing knowledge that impacts upon policy making. Her books include *Prostitution and Feminism: Towards a Politics of Feeling* (2001), *Sex Work Now*, co-edited with Rosie Campbell (2006), *Prostitution: A Reader*, co-edited with Roger Matthews (2002), and *Prostitution: Sex Work, Policy and Politics*, co-authored with Teela Sanders and Jane Pitcher (2009).

Rebecca Pates studied philosophy at Oxford and McGill universities and is professor of political theory at Leipzig University. She coordinated two research projects on prostitution and trafficking funded by the EU and the Saxon governments on Germany's eastern borders. Her current research interests focus on the anthropology of the state. In 2009, she published a book on the administration of prostitution in Germany, the Czech Republic, and Poland with Daniel Schmidt, *Die Verwaltung der Prostitution* (2009).

Melissa Petro is published in *Research for Sex Work*. Her creative nonfiction appears in *Post Road* and *Hos, Hookers, Call Girls and Rent Boys*, an anthology of writing by sex workers. She is currently writing a memoir.

Jane Pitcher is an independent social researcher, with more than 20 years' research and evaluation expertise in the academic, voluntary, and public sectors, with a particular focus on qualitative and collaborative methods and research that is policy-relevant. She has undertaken research and published on women working in the sex industry, services to sex workers, and communities and street-based sex work. Key publications include Living and Working in Areas of Street Sex Work: From Conflict to Coexistence, with R. Campbell, P. Hubbard, M. O'Neill, and J. Scoular (2006) and Prostitution: Sex Work, Policy and Politics, co-authored with Teela Sanders and Maggie O'Neill (2009).

Daniel Schmidt is a researcher in political science and the deputy equal opportunity commissioner at Leipzig University. Besides his numerous publications on the politics of statistics, on prostitution, and on moral panics with regard to demographic developments, he is currently coordinator of a research project on the construction of the European (The Past Future of Europe).

Jo Weldon has worked in the adult entertainment industry for over two decades. She is an advocate of sex workers' rights and an expert on exotic dance. As an activist, her focus has been on working toward a better understanding of sex workers' realities, and on defusing prejudices against sex workers. Currently she is a burlesque performer, producer, and photographer, as well as a teacher of burlesque dance. Her book The Pocket Book of Burlesque, with a foreword by Margaret Cho, was published in 2009.

Bibliography

ABC News (2004) 'Porn Profits: Corporate America's Secret: Corporate America is Profiting from Porn – Quietly,' *ABC News Primetime*, available at http://abcnews. go.com/Primetime/story?id=132370&page=1 (accessed 5 May 2009).

Abramovich, E. (2005) 'Childhood Sexual Abuse as a Risk Factor for Subsequent Involvement in Sex Work: A Review of Empirical Findings,' *Journal of Psychology and Human Sexuality*, Vol. 17, pp. 131–46.

Ackman, D. (2001) 'How Big is Porn?' *Forbes*, 25 May 2001.

Act Up Paris (2009), available at http://www.actupparis.org (accessed 5 May 2009).

Adamache, R., C. Culos & G. Otero (1993) 'NAFTA: Class and Gender Implications for Mexican Women,' paper presented at 40th *Annual Conference of the Rocky Mountain Council for Latin American Studies*.

Adkins, L. (2002) *Revisions: Gender and Sexuality in Late Modernity*, Open University Press, Buckingham and Philadelphia.

Adkins, L. & V. Merchant (1996) *Sexualizing the Social: Power and the Organization of Sexuality*, St Martin's Press, New York.

AdultVideo Entertainment Monthly (2001) 'Marketing Story-Driven Porn,' *AdultVideo Entertainment Monthly*, February 2001.

Agger, B. (1989) *Fast Capitalism: A Critical Theory of Significance*, University of Illinois Press, Urbana.

Agustín, L. (2003) 'A Migrant World of Services,' *Social Politics*, Vol. 10, No. 3, pp. 377–96.

Agustín, L. (2004) 'At Home in the Street: Questioning the Desire to Help and Save,' in E. Bernstein & L. Shaffner (eds), *Controlling Sex: The Regulation of Intimacy and Identity*, Routledge, New York, pp. 67–82.

Agustín, L. (2005a) 'Helping Women Who Sell Sex: The Construction of Benevolent Identities,' *Rhizomes*, Vol. 10, available at: http://www.rhizomes.net/issue10 (accessed 5 May 2009).

Agustín, L. (2005b) 'Migrants in the Mistress's House: Other Voices in the "Trafficking" Debate,' *Social Politics*, Vol. 12, No. 1, pp. 96–117.

Agustín, L. (2005c) 'Still Challenging "Place": Sex, Money and Agency in Women's Migrations,' in A. Escobar & W. Harcourt (eds), *Women and the Politics of Place*, Kumarian Press, Bloomfield (CT), pp. 221–33.

Agustín, L. (2005d) 'The Cultural Study of Commercial Sex,' *Sexualities*, Vol. 8, pp. 621–34.

Bibliography

Allen, D. (1980) 'Young Male Prostitutes: A Psychosocial Study,' *Archives of Sexual Behavior*, Vol. 9, pp. 399–426.

Allman, D. (1999) M *is for Mutual, A is for Acts: Male Sex Work and AIDS in Canada*, Canadian Public Health Association/Health Canada, Ottawa (ON).

Altink, S. (2000) 'Red Thread Prostitutes Rights Organization,' lecture, Amsterdam, 2 October 2000.

Andermahr, S., T. Lovell & C. Wolkwitz (1997) *A Concise Glossary of Feminist Theory*, Arnold, London.

Anderson, E. (1990) *StreetWise: Race, Class, and Change in an Urban Community*, University of Chicago Press, Chicago.

Anderson, E. (1999) *Code of the Street: Decency, Violence, and the Moral Life of the Inner City*, W.W. Norton & Co., New York.

Andrijasevic, R. (2003) 'The Difference Borders Make: (Il)legality, Migration and Trafficking in Italy among "Eastern" European Women in Prostitution,' in S. Ahmed et al. (eds) *Uprootings/Regroundings: Questions of Home and Migration*, Berg, Oxford, pp. 251–72.

Aris, R. & J. Pitcher (2004) *Evaluation of Coventry SWISH Arrest Referral Scheme for Sex Workers: Final Report*, Terrence Higgins Trust, London.

Arnot, A. (2002) *Legalisation of the Sex Industry in the State of Victoria, Australia: The Impact of Prostitution Law Reform on the Working and Private Lives of Women in the Legal Victoria Sex Industry*, Department of Criminology, University of Melbourne, Melbourne.

Ashcroft, B., G. Griffiths & H. Tiffin (2000) *Post-Colonial Studies: The Key Concepts*, Routledge, London and New York.

Associazione On the Road (2002) *Article 18: Protection of Victims of Trafficking and Fight against Crime (Italy and the European Scenarios)*, On the Road Edizioni, Martinsicuro.

Attwood, F. (2006) 'Sexed Up: Theorizing the Sexualization of Culture,' *Sexualities*, Vol. 9, pp. 77–94.

Barnard, M. (1993) 'Violence and Vulnerability: Conditions of Work for Street-working Prostitutes,' *Sociology of Health and Illness*, Vol. 15, pp. 683–705.

Barry, K. (1984) *Female Sexual Slavery*, New York University Press, New York.

Barry, K. (1995) *The Prostitution of Sexuality*, New York University Press, New York.

Bartky, S. L. (1990) *Femininity and Domination: Studies in the Phenomenology of Oppression*, Routledge, London and New York.

Bartlett, C. S. (2003) *Stripper Shoes*, First Books, Bloomington (IN).

Barton, B. (2006) *Stripped: Inside the Lives of Exotic Dancers*, New York University Press, New York.

Bauman, Z. (2000) *Liquid Modernity*, Polity Press, Cambridge (UK).

Bauman, Z. (2003) *Liquid Love: On the Frailty of Human Bonds*, Blackwell Publishers, Malden (MA).

Beck, U. & E. Beck-Gernsheim (1995) *The Normal Chaos of Love*, Blackwell, Cambridge (MA).

Becker, H. S. (1963) *Outsiders: Studies in the Sociology of Deviance*, Free Press, New York.

Bell, D. (1976) *The Cultural Contradictions of Capitalism*, Basic Books, New York.

Berman, J. (2003) '(Un)Popular Strangers and Crises (Un)Bounded: Discourses of Sex-Trafficking, The European Political Community and the Panicked State of The Modern State,' *European Journal on International Relations*, Vol. 9, No. 1, pp. 37–86.

Bernstein, E. (2001) 'The Meaning of the Purchase: Desire, Demand and the Commerce of Sex,' *Ethnography*, Vol, 2, pp. 389–420.

Bibliography

Bernstein, E. (2007a) 'Sex Work for the Middle Classes,' *Sexualities*, Vol. 10, pp. 473–88.

Bernstein, E. (2007b) 'Buying and Selling the "Girlfriend Experience,"' in M. B. Padilla et al. (eds) *Love and Globalization: Transformations of Intimacy in the Contemporary World*, Vanderbilt University Press, Nashville, pp. 186–203.

Bhabha, H. K. (1994) *The Location of Culture*, Routledge, London and New York.

Bourdieu, P. (1996) 'Understanding,' *Theory, Culture and Society* Vol. 13, No. 2, pp. 17–39.

Bourdieu, P. & L. Wacquant (1992) *An Invitation to Reflexive Sociology*, University of Chicago Press, Chicago.

Bourgois, P. (1996) *In Search of Respect: Selling Crack in El Barrio*, Cambridge University Press, Cambridge.

Brants, C. (1998) 'The Fine Art of Regulated Tolerance: Prostitution in Amsterdam,' *Journal of Law and Society*, Vol. 25, pp. 6211–35.

Brents, B. G. & K. Hausbeck (2005) 'Violence and Legalized Brothel Prostitution in Nevada: Examining Safety, Risk and Prostitution Policy,' *Journal of Interpersonal Violence*, Vol. 20, pp. 270-295.

Brents, B. G. & K. Hausbeck (2007) 'Marketing Sex: US Legal Brothels and Late Capitalist Consumption,' *Sexualities*, Vol. 10, No. 4, pp. 425–39.

Brents, B. G. & T. Sanders (2010) 'Mainstreaming the Sex Industry: Economic Inclusion and Social Ambivalence,' *Journal of Law and Society*, Vol. 37, No. 1, pp. 40–60.

Brents, B. G., C. Jackson & K. Hausbeck (2010) *The State of Sex: Tourism, Sex and Sin in the New American Heartland*, Routledge, New York.

Bresnahan, M. (1995) 'Taking It to the Streets: Outreach to Youth in Times Square,' in R. McNamara (ed.), *Sex, Scams, and Street Life: The Sociology of New York City's Times Square*, Praeger Publishers, Westport, (CT), pp. 107–16.

Brewis, J. & S. Linstead (2000a) '"The Worst Thing is the Screwing" (1): Consumption and the Management of Identity in Sex Work,' *Gender, Work and Organization*, Vol. 7, pp. 84–97.

Brewis, J. & S. Linstead (2000b) '"The Worst Thing is the Screwing" (2): Consumption and the Management of Identity in Sex Work,' *Gender, Work and Organization*, Vol. 7, pp. 168–80.

Brewis, J. & S. Linstead (2000c) *Sex, Work and Sex Work: Eroticizing Organization*, Routledge, London and New York.

Bristow, J. (2007) *Sexuality*, Routledge, London and New York.

Brock, D. (1998) *Making Work, Making Trouble: Prostitution as a Social Problem*, University of Toronto Press, Toronto (ON).

Bröckling, U., S. Krasmann & T. Lemke (2004) 'Gouvernementalität, Neoliberalismus und Selbsttechnologien. Eine Einleitung,' in U. Bröckling et al. (eds) *Glossar der Gegenwart*, Suhrkamp, Frankfurt a. M., pp. 7–40.

Brooker, P. (1999) *A Concise Glossary of Cultural Theory*. Arnold, London.

Bruckert, C. (2002) *Taking It Off, Putting It On: Women in the Strip Trade*, Women's Press, London.

Brumberg, J. J. (1997) *The Body Project*, Vintage Books, New York.

Bublitz, H. (2003) 'Diskurs und Habitus. Zentrale Kategorien zur Herstellung gesellschaftlicher Normalität,' in Jürgen Link et al. (eds) *'Normalität' im Diskursnetz soziologischer Begriffe*, Synchron Wissenschaftsverlag, Heidelberg, pp. 151–62.

Buchowska, S. (2000) 'Trafficking in Women: La Strada,' lecture, Warsaw, 31 October 2000.

Bibliography

Bundesgesetzblatt (2001) Vol. 1, No. 74.

Burana, L. (2001) Strip City: A Stripper's Farewell Journey Across America, Miramax, New York.

Burawoy, M. (1982) Manufacturing Consent, University of Chicago Press, Chicago.

Busi, B. (2006) 'Il lavoro sessuale nell'economia della ri(produzione) globale,' in T. Bertilotti et al. (eds) Altri Femminismi. Corpi, Culture, Lavoro, Manifestolibri, Roma.

Butler, J. (1999 [1990]) Gender Trouble: Feminism and the Subversion of Identity, Routledge, New York and London.

Cabiria (2004) Femmes et Migrations en Europe. Stratégies et Empowerment, Le Dragon Lune, Lyon.

Califia, P. (1988) Macho Sluts, Alyson Books, Los Angeles.

Campbell, R. & L. Hancock (1998) 'Sex Work in the Climate of Zero Tolerance: Hearing Loud Voices and the Silence of Dissent,' paper presented at Sex Work Reassessed, University of East London, 9 September 1998.

Campbell, R. & M. O'Neill (2004) Evaluation of Sex, Lies and Love, NACRO.

Cannon, J., T. Calhoun & R. Fisher (1998) 'Amateur Stripping and Gaming Encounters: Fun in Games or Gaming as Fun?' Deviant Behavior, Vol. 19, pp. 3-15.

Carchedi, F. (2000) I colori della note, Franco Angeli, Milano.

Carthonnet, C. (2003) 'Une Voix Publique, Entretien avec Claire Cartonnet,' Vacarme, Vol. 25. Available at http://www.vacarme.org/article1637.html (Accessed 10 August 2009).

Castle, S. (2006) 'Passports and Panic Buttons in the Brothel of the Future,' The Independent, 23 September 2006.

Caukins, S. E. & N. R. Coombs (1976) 'The Psychodynamics of Male Prostitution,' American Journal of Psychotherapy, Vol. 30, pp. 441–51.

Centro de Informacíon y Análisis de Chiapas (CIACH), Coordinación de Organismos No Gubermentales Por La Paz (CONPAZ), y Servicios Informativos Procesados (1997) Para Entender Chiapas: Chiapas en Cifras, CIACH, CONPAZ & SIPRO, Mexico City.

Chapdelaine, A., M. J. Levesque & R. M. Cuadro (1999) 'Playing the Dating Game: Do We Known Whom Others Would Like to Date?,' Basic and Applied Social Psychology, Vol. 21, pp. 139–47.

Chapkis, W. (1997) Live Sex Acts: Women Performing Erotic Labor, Routledge, London and New York.

Chudakov, B., K. Ilan, R. H. Belmaker & J. Cwikel (2002) 'The Motivation and Mental Health of Sex Workers,' Journal of Sex and Marital Therapy, Vol. 28, No. 4, pp. 305–15.

Clark, P., M. A. Bellis, P. A. Cook & K. Tocque (2004) Consultation on a Managed Zone for Sex Trade Workers in Liverpool: Views from Residents, Business and Sex Trade Workers in the City of Liverpool; Executive Summary, Centre for Public Health, John Moores University, Liverpool.

Clatts, M., D. Hillman, A. Atillasoy & D. W. Rees (1999) 'Lives in the Balance: A Profile of Homeless Youth in New York City,' in J. Blustein, C. Levine & N. Dubler (eds), The Adolescent Alone: Decision Making in Health Care in the United States, Cambridge University Press, Cambridge (UK), pp. 139–59.

Clemmitt, M. (2008) 'Prostitution Debate: Should the United States Legalise Sex Work?' CQ Researcher, Vol. 18, pp. 433–56.

Comella, L. (2008) 'it's sexy. it's big business. and it's not just for men,' Contexts, Vol. 7, pp. 61–3.

Comisiones Obreras (2009) available at http://www.ccoo.es/ (accessed 5 May 2009).

Comitato per i diritti civili delle prostitute (2009), available at http://www.lucciole.org/ (accessed 5 May 2009).

Cordaid (2009), available at http://www.cordaid.nl (accessed 5 May 2009).

Crawford, D., D. Feng, J. Fischer & L. K. Diana (2003) 'The Influence of Love, Equity, and Alternatives on Commitment in Romantic Relationships,' *Family and Consumer Sciences Research Journal*, Vol. 31, pp. 253–71.

Danna, D. (2003) 'Trafficking and Prostitution of Foreigners in the Context of EU Countries Policies on Prostitution,' paper presented at *NEWR Workshop on Trafficking*, Amsterdam, 25–26 April 2003.

Davis, J. A., T. W. Smith & P. V. Marsden (2006) *General Social Surveys, 1972–2004* [*Cumulative File*], vol. ICPSR04295-v2, National Opinion Research Center, Chicago (IL); Roper Center for Public Opinion Research, Storrs (CT) & Inter-University Consortium for Political and Social Research, University of Connecticut/Ann Arbor (MI).

Davis, L. J. (1995) *Enforcing Normalcy: Disability, Defenses, and the Body*, Verso, London.

Davis, L. J. (2001) 'From *Enforcing Normalcy: Disability, Defenses, and the Body*,' in V. B. Leitch (ed.), *The Norton Anthology of Theory and Criticism*, Norton, New York and London, pp. 2400–21.

De Roode Draad (2009), available at http://www.rodedraad.nl/ (accessed 5 May 2009).

Delacoste, F. & P. Alexander (eds) (1987) *Sex Work: Writings by Women in the Sex Industry*, Cleiss, Pittsburgh.

Della Giusta, M., M. Di Tommaso & S. Strøm (2008) *Sex Markets: A Denied Industry*, Routledge, London and New York.

Della Giusta, M., M. L. Di Tommaso, I. Shima & S. Strom (2006) 'What Money Buys: Clients of Street Workers in the US,' University of Oslo, Department of Economics, Memorandum No. 10/2006.

Deutscher Bundestag (2001) *Entwurf eines Gesetzes zur Verbesserung der rechtlichen und sozialen Situation der Prostituierten*, Drucksache 14/5958.

Dinitz, S., F. Banks & B. Pasamanick (1960) 'Mate Selection and Social Class: Changes During the Past Quarter Century,' *Marriage and the Family Living*, Vol. 22, pp. 348–51.

Ditmore, M. (2005a) 'Trafficking in Lives: How Ideology Shapes Policy,' in K. Kempadoo (ed.), *Trafficking and Prostitution Reconsidered: New Perspectives on Migration, Sex Work and Human Rights*, Paradigm Press, Boulder (CO).

Ditmore, M. (2005b) 'New US Funding Policies on Trafficking Affect Sex Work and HIV-Prevention Efforts World Wide', *SIECUS Report*, Vol. 33, No. 2, pp. 26–9.

Ditmore, M. H. (2006) 'Tenofovir,' in M. H. Ditmore (ed.), *Encyclopedia of Prostitution and Sex Work*, Greenwood, Westport (CT), pp. 475–6.

Ditmore, M. (2007) 'Sex Work and Development,' in A. Cornwall, S. Correa & S. Jolly (eds), *Development with a Body: Making Connections between Sexuality, Human Rights and Development*, Zed Books, London, pp. 54–66.

Ditmore, M. (2008) 'Sex Work, Trafficking: Understanding the Difference,' *RHRealityCheck*, available at http://www.rhrealitycheck.org/blog/2008/05/05sex-work-trafficking-understanding-difference (accessed 21 June 2008).

Doezema, J. (1998) 'Forced to Choose: Beyond the Free v. Forced Prostitution Dichotomy,' in K. Kempadoo & J. Doezema (eds), *Global Sex Workers: Rights, Resistance and Redefinition*, Routledge, London and New York.

Doezema, J. (2002) 'Who Gets to Choose? Coercion, Consent, and the UN

Trafficking Protocol,' *Gender & Development*, Vol. 10, pp. 20–7.

Doezema, J. (2006) 'Weiße Sklavinnen, arme Slawinnen. Das Melodram vom Frauenhandel,' *Osteuropa*, Vol. 56, No. 6, pp. 269–84.

Dölemeyer, A. (2009) 'Gendering Space and Spacing Gender: Die räumliche Regulierung von Sexarbeit,' in E. Donat et al. (eds), *Nie wieder Sex*, VS, Wiesbaden, pp. 149–84.

Dubeck, P. J. & K. Borman (eds) (1997) *Women and Work: A Reader*, Rutgers University Press, New Brunswick (NJ).

Dworkin, A. (1981) *Pornography: Men Possessing Women*, E. P. Dutton, New York.

Dworkin, A. (1997) 'Prostitution and Male Supremacy,' in A. Dworkin, *Life and Death*, Free Press, New York, pp. 139–51.

Economist (1998) 'Giving the Customer What He Wants,' *The Economist*, 14 February 1998.

Edin, K. & L. Lein (1997) *Making Ends Meet: How Single Mothers Survive Welfare and Low-Wage Work*, Russell Sage Foundation, New York.

Edlund, L. & E. Korn (2002) 'A Theory of Prostitution,' *Journal of Political Economy*, Vol. 110, No. 1, pp. 181–214.

Enck, G. E. & J. D. Preston (1988) 'Counterfeit Intimacy: A Dramaturgical Analysis of Erotic Performance,' *Deviant Behavior*, Vol. 3, pp. 369–81.

European Trade Union Federation (ETUC) (2009), available at http://www.etuc.org (accessed 5 May 2009).

Farley, M. (2005) 'Unequal,' paid editorial, *The Nation*, 30 August 2005.

Farley, M. & H. Barkan (1998) 'Prostitution, Violence, and Posttraumatic Stress Disorder,' *Women and Health*, Vol. 27, pp. 37–49.

Farley, M. & V. Kelly (2000) 'Prostitution: A Critical Review of the Medical and Social Sciences Literature,' *Women and Criminal Justice*, Vol. 11, No. 4, pp. 29–64.

Farley, M., I. Baral, M. Kiremire & U. Sezgin (1998) 'Prostitution in Five Countries: Violence and Post-Traumatic Stress Disorder,' *Feminism and Psychology*, Vol. 8, pp. 405–26.

Fawkes, J. (2005) 'Sex Working Feminists and the Politics of Exclusion,' *Social Alternatives*, Vol. 24, pp. 22-23.

Femmes de Droits, Droits de Femmes (2009), available at http://femmesdedroits. wordpress.com/ (accessed 5 May 2009).

Femmes Publiques (2009), available at http://www.agirprostitution.lautre.net (accessed 5 May 2009).

Fensterstock, A. (2005) 'How You Got There,' in D. Egan et al. (eds), *Flesh for Fantasy. Producing and Consuming Exotic Dance*, Seal Press, Seattle.

Fernández-Kelly, M. P. (1983) *For We Are Sold, I and My People: Women and Industry in Mexico's Frontier*. SUNY Press, Albany.

Filia (2009), available at http://www.filia-frauenstiftung.de (accessed 5 May 2009).

Fine, G. A. (1996) 'Justifying Work: Occupational Rhetorics as Resources in Restaurant Kitchens,' *Administrative Science Quarterly*, Vol. 41, No. 1, pp. 90–116.

Fischer, C. et al. (2007) *Vertiefung spezifischer Fragestellungen zu den Auswirkungen des Prostitutionsgesetzes: Ausstieg aus der Prostitution und Kriminalitätsbekämpfung und Prostitutionsgesetz*. Bundesministerium für Familie, Frauen, Senioren und Jugend (ed.), available at http://www.bmfsfj.de/bmfsfj/generator/BMFSFJ/Service/Publikationen/ publikationsliste, did=93302.html (accessed 5 May 2009).

Flax, J. (1995) *Disputed Subjects: Essays on Psychoanalysis, Politics and Philosophy*, Routledge, London and New York.

Bibliography

Foucault, M. (1979) *The Order of Things: An Archaeology of the Human Sciences*, Vintage, New York.

Frank, K. (2002) *G-Strings and Sympathy: Strip Club Regulars and Male Desire*, Duke University Press, Durham (NC).

Fraser, N. (1997) *Justice Interruptus: Critical Reflections on the 'Postsocialist' Condition*, Routledge, London and New York.

Frassanito Network (2009), available at http://www.noborder.org/ (accessed 5 May 2009).

Free Speech Coalition (2006) *Adult Entertainment in America: A State of the Industry Report*, Free Speech Coalition, Canoga Park.

Galatowicz, L., J. Pitcher & A. Woolley (2005) *Report of the Community-Led Research Project Focusing on Drug and Alcohol Use of Women Sex Workers and Access to Services*, SWISH, for University of Central Lancashire and Dept of Health, Coventry.

Galen, M. Gräfin v. (2004) *Rechtsfragen der Prostitution: Das ProstG und seine Auswirkungen*, C. H. Beck, Munich.

Gergen, K. J. (1991) *The Saturated Self: Dilemmas of Identity in Contemporary Life*, Basic Books, New York.

Gertler, P., M. Shah & S. Bertozzi (2005) 'Risky Business: The Market for Unprotected Sex,' *Journal of Political Economy*, Vol. 113, No. 3, pp. 518–50.

Getlen, L. (2005) 'Why We Lie About Money and Sex,' bankrate.com, 28 April 2005, available at http://www.bankrate.com/brm/news/financial-literacy2004/debt-psychology.asp (accessed 20 May 2009).

Giddens, A. (1991) *Modernity and Self-Identity: Self and Society in the Late Modern Age*, Stanford University Press, Stanford (CA).

Giddens, A. (1992) *The Transformation of Intimacy: Sexuality, Love, and Eroticism in Modern Societies*, Stanford University Press, Stanford (CA).

Giobbe, E., M. Harrigan, J. Ryan & D. Gamache (1990) 'Prostitution: A Matter of Violence Against Women'. Statement released by WHISPER (Women Hurt In Systems of Prostitution Engaged in Revolt), Minneapolis (MN).

GISTI (Groupe d'Information et de Soutien des Immigrés) (2009), available at http://www.gisti.org/index.php (accessed 5 May 2009).

Glauser, B. (1997) 'Street Children: Deconstructing a Construct,' in A. James & A. Prout (eds), *Constructing and Reconstructing Childhood: Contemporary Issues in the Sociological Study of Childhood*, Taylor and Francis, New York, pp. 145–64.

Gledhill, J. (1995) *Neoliberalism, Transnationalization, and Rural Poverty: A Case Study*, Westview Press, Boulder (CO).

Global Fund for Women (2009), available at http://www.globalfundforwomen.org/cms/ (accessed 5 May 2009).

Global Labor Institute (2009), available at http://www.global-labor.org/ (accessed 5 May 2009).

Global Working Group on Sex Work and HIV Policy (2007) *Inputs to the UNAIDS Guidance Note on HIV and Sex Work*, available at http://www.nswp.org/pdf/20070920-GWGInputsHIVAndSWPolicy.pdf (accessed 30 May 2009).

Global Working Group on Sex Work and HIV Policy (2009) *Timeline of Events Prior to and in Response to the United Nations Guidance Note on Sex Work and HIV*, available at http://www.nswp.org/downloads/2008/20080615-TimelineOfEvents.pdf (accessed 30 May 2009).

Goffman, E. (1959) *The Presentation of Self in Everyday Life*, Anchor, New York.

Goffman, E. (1961) *Asylums*, Doubleday, New York.

Goffman, E. (1963) *Stigma*, Prentice Hall, Englewood-Cliffs.

Goldman, E. (1917) 'The Traffic in Women,' reprinted in R. Drinnon (ed.) (1969), *Anarchism and Other Essays*, Dover, pp. 177–94.

Green, A., S. Day & H. Ward (2000) 'Crack Cocaine and Prostitution in London in the 1990s,' *Sociology of Health and Illness*, Vol. 22, No. 1, pp. 27–39.

Greens/European Free Alliance (2009), available at http://www.greens-efa.org/index.htm (accessed 5 May 2009).

GStringGirlsJournal (2009), available at http://gstringgirl.livejournal.com (accessed 20 May 2009).

Haella (2009), available at http://www.haella.nl/ (accessed 5 May 2009).

Hagan, J. & B. McCarthy (1998) *Mean Streets: Youth, Crime and Homelessness*, Cambridge University Press, Cambridge (UK).

Harding, S. (1991) *Whose Science? Whose Knowledge?: Thinking from Women's Lives*, Cornell University Press, Ithaca.

Hardt, M. & A. Negri (2000) *Empire*, Harvard University Press, Cambridge (MA).

Harris, M. B. (1990) 'Is Love Seen as Different for the Obese?' *Journal of Applied Social Psychology*, Vol. 20, pp. 1209–24.

Harvey, D. (1989) *The Condition of Postmodernity: An Enquiry into the Origins of Cultural Change*, Blackwell, Cambridge (MA).

Harvey, D. (2005) *A Brief History of Neoliberalism*, Oxford University Press, Oxford (UK).

Hausbeck, K. & B. G. Brents (2002) 'McDonaldization of the Sex Industries? The Business of Sex,' in G. Ritzer (ed.), *McDonaldization: The Reader*, Pine Forge Press, Thousand Oaks (CA), pp. 91–106.

Hausbeck, K., B. G. Brents & C. Jackson (2005) 'Sex Industry and Sex Workers in Nevada' in D. Shalin (ed.), *Social Health of Nevada*, Vol. 2006, Center for Democratic Culture, University of Nevada, Las Vegas, available at http://www.unlv.edu/centers/cdclv/healthnv/sexindustry.html (accessed 5 May 2009).

Hawkes, G. (1996) *A Sociology of Sex and Sexuality*, Open University Press, Philadelphia.

Health 24 (2007) 'Sex Workers – Who and Why?' available at http://www.health 24.com/mind/Other/1284-1303,20720.asp (accessed 5 May 2009).

Hecht, T. (1998) *At Home in the Street: Street Children of Northeast Brazil*, Cambridge University Press, Cambridge (UK).

Hester, M. & N. Westmarland (2004) *Tackling Street Prostitution: Towards a Holistic Approach*, Home Office Research Study 279, HMSO, London.

Hibbard, J. (2005) '"Cathouse" Not a Secret to Viewers: Sexy Series a Hit for HBO, Cable Mum on Adult Shows,' *TV Week*, 11 July 2005.

Hivos (2009), available at http://www.hivos.nl/ (accessed 5 May 2009).

Hochschild, A. R. (1983) *The Managed Heart: Commercialization of Human Feeling*, University of California Press, Berkeley.

Hochschild, A. R. (2003) *The Commercialization of Intimate Life: Notes from Home and Work*, University of California Press, Berkeley.

Holyfield, L. (1999) 'Manufacturing Adventure: The Buying and Selling of Emotions,' *Journal of Contemporary Ethnography*, Vol. 28, pp. 3–32.

Home Office (2004) *Paying the Price: A Consultation Paper on Prostitution*, HMSO, London.

Home Office (2006) *A Co-ordinated Prostitution Strategy and a Summary of Responses to 'Paying the Price'*, Home Office, London.

Hossain, A. (2006) 'They Swing Between Both Sexes: Hijras as "Asexual Others,"'

SSSST.Net, available at web.hku.hk/~sjwinter/TransgenderASIA/paper_ swinging.htm (accessed 5 March 2009).

Hubbard, P. & T. Sanders (2003) 'Making Space for Sex Work,' *International Journal of Urban and Regional Research*, Vol. 27, pp. 75–89.

Husain, S. A. M. (2005) *Tritiyo Prokriti: Bangladesher Hizrather Artho-Shamajik Chitro* (Hidden Gender: Socio-Economic Status of Hijra Community of Bangladesh), Shoro-writu, Dhaka.

ICRSE (International Committee on the Rights of Sex Workers in Europe) (2004) *Proposal for a European Conference*, available at http://www.sexworkeurope.org/ (accessed 5 May 2009).

ICRSE (International Committee on the Rights of Sex Workers in Europe) (2005a) *Declaration of the Rights of Sex Workers in Europe*, available at http://www.sexworkeurope.org/site/index.php?option=com_content&task=view&id=35&Itemid=77 (see 'Resources'; accessed 5 May 2009).

ICRSE (International Committee on the Rights of Sex Workers in Europe) (2005b) *Sex Workers' in Europe Manifesto*, available at http://www.sexworkeurope.org/site/index.php?option=com_content&task=view&id=24&Itemid=54 (see 'Resources'; accessed 5 May 2009).

Iglesias-Prieto, N. (1997) *Beautiful Flowers of the Maquiladora: Life Histories of Women Workers in Tijuana*, University of Texas, Austin.

Illouz, E. (1997) *Consuming the Romantic Utopia: Love and the Cultural Contradictions of Capitalism*, University of California Press, Berkeley.

Indymedia Estrecho (2009), available at http://www.estrecho.indymedia.org/ (see also http://www.noborder.org) (accessed 5 May 2009).

Infoshare (2009), available at http://www.infoshare.ru (accessed 5 May 2009).

Ingelhart, R. (2004) *European and World Values Survey Four Wave Integrated Data File, 1981-2004*, vol. v.20060423. European Values Study Foundation and World Values Survey Association, ASEP/JDS, and ZA.

Ingelhart, R. (2008) 'Changing Values among Western Publics from 1970 to 2006,' *Western European Politics*, Vol. 31, No. 1–2, pp. 130–46.

International Union of Sex Workers (2009), available at http://www.iusw.org/ (accessed 5 May 2009).

Jackson, S. & S. Scott (2004) 'Sexual Antinomies in Late Modernity,' *Sexualities*, Vol. 7, pp. 233–48.

James, J. (1982) *Entrance Into Juvenile Male Prostitution*, National Institute of Mental Health, Washington, DC.

Jameson, F. (1991) *Postmodernism, or, The Cultural Logic of Late Capitalism*, Duke University Press, Durham.

Jankowski, M. S. (1991) *Islands in the Street: Gangs and American Urban Society*, University of California Press, Berkeley (CA).

Janus, M.-D., A. McCormick, A. W. Burgess & C. Hartman (1987) *Adolescent Runaways: Causes and Consequences*, Lexington Press, Lexington (MA).

Jenness, V. (1993) *Making It Work: The Prostitute's Rights Movement in Perspective*, Aldine de Gruyter, New York.

Johnson, A. B. (2005) *Choosing Dates and Mates: College Student Ratings of Self and Potential Opposite-Sex Partners*, dissertation at the University of Oklahoma.

Johnson, E. (1983) *In Search of God in the Sexual Underworld: A Mystical Journey*, William Morrow and Company, New York.

Jones, P., P. Shears & D. Hillier (2003) 'Retailing and the Regulatory State: A Case Study of Lap Dancing Clubs in the UK,' *International Journal of Retail & Distribution Management*, Vol. 31, pp. 214–19.

Kaye, K. (2001) *Boy Prostitutes and Street Hustlers: Depicting Male Street Prostitution*, MA thesis at San Francisco State University (listed under Kerwin Brook).

Kaye, K. (2003) 'Male Prostitution in the Twentieth Century: Pseudo-Homosexuals, Hoodlum Homosexuals, and Exploited Teens,' *Journal of Homosexuality*, Vol. 46, No. 1/2, pp. 1–77.

Kelly, P. (2003) 'I Made Myself from Nothing: Women and Sex Work in Urban Chiapas,' in C. Kovic & C. Eber (eds) *Women of Chiapas: Making History in Times of Struggle and Hope*, Routledge, London and New York, pp. 81–97.

Kelly, P. (2008) *Lydia's Open Door: Sex Work and the Modernization of Mexico*, University of California Press, Berkeley (CA).

Kempadoo, K. (1999) 'Slavery or Work? Reconceptualizing Third World Prostitution,' *positions*, Vol. 7, pp. 225–38.

Kempadoo, K. & J. Doezema (1998) *Global Sex Workers: Rights, Resistance and Redefinition*, Routledge, London and New York.

Khanam, J. (2008) 'Hijra,' *Bangladeshi Women*, available at http://jainub-khanam.blogspot.com/2008/08/blog-post.html (accessed 6 August 2008).

Kincaid, J. (1998) *Erotic Innocence: The Culture of Child Molesting*, Duke University Press, Durham.

Kipke, M., S. Montgomery, R. Simon & E. Iverson (1997) 'Substance Abuse Disorders Among Runaway and Homeless Youth,' *Substance Use and Misuse*, Vol. 32, pp. 965–82.

Koken, J. A., D. S. Bimbi, J. T. Parsons & P. N. Halkitis (2004) 'The Experience of Stigma in the Lives of Gay and Bisexual Male Internet Escorts,' *Journal of Psychology and Human Sexuality*, Vol. 16, pp. 13–32.

Krassmann, S. (2003) *Die Kriminalität der Gesellschaft*, UVK, Konstanz.

Kruks, G. (1991) 'Gay and Lesbian Homeless/Street Youth: Special Issues and Concerns,' *Journal of Adolescent Health*, Vol. 12, pp. 515–18.

Kulick, D. (1998) *Travesti: Sex, Gender, and Culture Among Brazilian Transgendered Prostitutes*, University of Chicago Press, Chicago.

La Strada Poland (2009), available at http://www.strada.org.pl/ (accessed 5 May 2009).

Lash, S. & J. Urry (1994) *Economies of Signs and Space*, Sage, London and Thousand Oaks (CA).

Latour, B. (2005) *Reassembling the Social: An Introduction to Actor-Network-Theory*, Oxford University Press, Oxford (UK).

Leidner, R. (1996) 'Serving Hamburgers and Selling Insurance: Gender, Work and Identity in Interactive Service Jobs,' in V. A. Taylor, N. Whittier & L. Richardson (eds), *Feminist Frontiers IV*, McGraw-Hill, New York, pp. 234–46.

Leigh, C. (1994) 'Prostitution in the United States: The Statistics', *Gauntlet: Exploring the Limits of Free Expression*, Vol. 1, pp. 17-19.

Leigh, C. (1997) 'Inventing Sex Work,' in J. Nagle (ed.), *Whores and Other Feminists*, Routledge, London and New York, pp. 223–31.

Leonard, D. & L. Adkins (1996) *Sex in Question: French Materialist Feminism*, Taylor and Francis, London.

Les Putes (2009), available at http://www.lesputes.org/ (accessed 5 May 2009).

Lever, J. & D. Dolnick (2000) 'Clients and Call Girls: Seeking Sex and Intimacy,' in R.

Weitzer (ed.), *Sex for Sale: Prostitution, Pornography and the Sex Industry*, Routledge, London and New York, pp. 85–103.

Levitt, S. D. & S. A. Venkatesh (2000) 'An Economic Analysis of a Drug-Selling Gang's Finances,' *Quarterly Journal of Economics*, Vol. 115, No. 3, August, pp. 755–89.

Levitt, S. D. & S. A. Venkatesh (2007) 'An Empirical Analysis of Street-Level Prostitution,' preliminary draft presented at Annual Meeting of the American Economic Association, available at http://economics.uchicago.edu/pdf/Prostitution%205.pdf (accessed 13 February 2009).

Lewis, J. & E. Maticka-Tyndale (2000) 'Methodological Challenges Conducting Research Related to Sex Work,' in *Escort Services in a Border Town: Transmission Dynamics of STDs Within and Between Communities*. Report issued by Division of STD Prevention and Control, Laboratory Centres for Disease Control, Health Canada.

Lewis, J., E. Maticka-Tyndale, F. Shaver & H. Schramm (2005) 'Managing Risk and Safety on the Job: The Experiences of Canadian Sex Workers, *Journal of Psychology and Human Sexuality*, Vol. 17, pp. 147–67.

Leyla's Chayhane (2008), available at http://www.geocities.com/leylasuhagi/index.html (accessed 6 August 2008).

Lim, L. L. (1998) *The Sex Sector: The Economic and Social Bases of Prostitution in Southeast Asia*, International Labor Organization, Geneva.

Lipsky, M. (1980) *Street-Level Bureaucracy. Dilemmas of the Individual in Public Services*, Russell Sage, New York.

McClintock, A. (1993) 'Sex and Sex Workers,' *Social Text*, Vol. 11, No. 4, Winter, pp. 1–10.

McGeady, M. R. (1994) *'Am I Going to Heaven?' Letters from the Streets*, Covenant House, New York.

McGeady, M. R. (1996) *Are You There, God?*, Covenant House, New York.

MacKinnon, C. (1993) *Only Words*, Harvard University Press, Cambridge (MA).

McNair, B. (2002) *Striptease Culture: Sex, Media and the Democratization of Desire*, Routledge, London and New York.

McNamara, R. (1994) *The Times Square Hustler: Male Prostitution in New York City*, Praeger, Westport (CT).

Maggie's (2009), available at http://walnet.org/csis/groups/maggies/ (accessed 5 May 2009).

Majumdar, A. & N. Basu (1997) *Bharater Hijrah Samaj* (Hijrah Community in India), Deep Prokashan, Kolkata.

Majumdar, A. & N. Basu (1999) *Purush Jakhon Jounakarmi* (When Men are Sex Workers), Deep Prokashan, Kolkata.

Majumder, N. (2005) *Hizre Samaj: Manabik Anusandhan* (Eunuch Society: Humanitarian Approach), Sahitya Prakash, Kolkata.

Males, M. (1996) *Scapegoat Generation: America's War on Adolescents*, Common Courage Press, Monroe (ME).

Males, M. (1999) *Framing Youth: Ten Myths About the Next Generation*, Common Courage Press, Monroe (ME).

Malik, F. (1999) 'Queer Sexuality and Identity in the Qur'an and Hadith,' available at Born Eunuchs homepage and library, http://www.well.com/user/aquarius/Qurannotes.htm (accessed 10 March 2009).

Mallon, G. (1999) *Let's Get This Straight: A Gay- and Lesbian-Affirming Approach to Child Welfare*, Columbia University Press, New York.

Mamacash (2009), available at http://www.mamacash.nl/ (accessed 5 May 2009).

Mandel, E. (1975) *Late Capitalism*, Humanities Press, London.

Masenior, N. F. & C. Beyrer (2007) 'The US Anti-Prostitution Pledge: First Amendment Challenges and Public Health Priorities,' *Public Library of Science Medicine*, Vol. 4, No. 207, available at http://www.plosmedicine.org/article/info:doi/10.1371/journal.pmed.0040207 (accessed 7 July 2008).

Maslach, C., W. B. Schaufeli & M. P. Leiter (2001) 'Job Burnout,' *Annual Review of Psychology*, Vol. 52, pp. 397–422.

Matthews, R. (2005) 'Policing Prostitution Ten Years On,' *British Journal of Criminology*, Vol. 45, pp. 1–20.

Matthews, R. & M. O'Neill (2003) *Prostitution*, International Library of Criminology, Criminal Justice and Penology, Ashgate, Aldershot.

May, D. C. (1999) 'Tolerance of Nonconformity and its Effect on Attitudes Toward the Legalization of Prostitution: A Multivariate Analysis,' *Deviant Behavior*, Vol. 20, pp. 335–58.

Melrose, M. (2007) 'The Government's New Prostitution Strategy: A Cheap Fix for Drug-Using Sex Workers?,' *Community Safety Journal*, Vol. 6, No. 1, pp. 18–26.

Merge Magazine (1998) *Getting Real Facts About Prostitution*, August 1998, available at http://www.mergemag.org/1998/archives98.html (accessed 6 December 2005).

Milne, C. (2005) *Naked Ambition: Women Pornographers and How They Are Changing the Sex Industry*. Carroll & Graf, New York.

Ministry of Health of Brazil, UNAIDS, UNFPA (2006) *Global Technical Consultation on HIV and Sex Work*, July 2006, available at http://www.nswp.org/downloads/2006/20060714-ReportOfGeneralTechnicalConsultation.pdf (accessed 30 May 2009).

MIT (Movimento Identità Transessuale) (2009), available at http://www.mit-italia.it/ (accessed 5 May 2009).

Moffatt, P. & S. Peters (2004) 'Pricing Personal Services: An Empirical Study of Earnings in the UK Prostitution Industry,' *Scottish Journal of Political Economy*, Vol. 51, No. 5, pp. 675-690.

Mohanty, C. T. (2004) *Feminism Without Borders: Decolonizing Theory, Practicing Solidarity*, Duke University Press, Durham and London.

Money News (2006) 'American Savings Lowest Since Depression,' 1 February 2006, available at http://www.newsmax.com/archives/articles/2006/2/1/193305.shtml (accessed 20 May 2009).

Montemurro, B. (2001) 'Strippers and Screamers: The Emergence of Social Control in a Noninstitutionalized Setting,' *Journal of Contemporary Ethnography*, Vol. 30, pp. 275–304.

Murphy, A. (2003) 'The Dialectical Gaze: Exploring the Subject–Object Tension in the Performances of Women Who Strip,' *Journal of Contemporary Ethnography*, Vol. 32, No. 3, pp. 305–35.

Nagle, J. (ed.) (1997) *Whores and Other Feminists*, Routledge, London and New York.

Nash, J. (1994) 'Global Integration and Subsistence Insecurity', *American Anthropologist*, Vol. 97, No. 1, pp. 7–30.

Nash, J. (2001) *Mayan Visions: The Quest for Autonomy in an Age of Globalization*, Routledge, New York and London.

Nash, J. & M. P. Fernández-Kelly (1983) *Women, Men, and the International Divison of Labor*, SUNY Press, Albany.

Bibliography

Nash Mir Ukraine Gay and Lesbian Center (2009), available at http://www.gay. org.ua (accessed 5 May 2009).

Nathan, D. (2005) 'Oversexed,' *The Nation*, 29 August 2005, available at http://www.thenation.com (accessed 6 December 2005).

NextGENDERation (2004) *Not In Our Names*, available at http://www.next genderation.net (accessed 5 May 2009).

NextGENDERation (2009), available at http://www.nextgenderation.net/ (accessed 5 May 2009).

O'Connell Davidson, J. (1998) *Prostitution, Power and Freedom*, Polity Press, Cambridge (UK).

O'Neill, M. (2001) *Prostitution and Feminism: Towards a Politics of Feeling*, Polity Press, Cambridge (UK).

O'Neill, M. & R. Campbell (2002) *Working Together to Create Change*, report for Walsall South Health Action Zone, available at http://www.safetysoapbox.co.uk/ (accessed 5 May 2009).

O'Neill, M. & R. Campbell (eds) (2006) *Sex Work Now*, Willan, Cullompton.

O'Neill, M. & M. Webster (2005) *Creativity, Community and Change: Creative Approaches to Community Consultation*, Staffordshire and Loughborough Universities, available from the authors: m.oneill@lboro.ac.uk; m.webster@staff.ac.uk.

O'Neill, M., P. Woods & M. Webster (2004) 'New Arrivals: Participatory Action Research, Imagined Communities and "Visions" of Social Justice,' *Journal of Social Justice*, Vol. 32, No, 1, pp. 75–89.

O'Neill, M., R. Campbell, A. James, M. Webster, K. Green, J. Patel, N. Akhtar & W. Saleem (2003) 'Sex work, Strategy and "Community": Implications for Community Safety,' in D. Bell & M. Jayne (eds), *City Cultures*, Ashgate, Aldershot.

Ong, A. (1987) *Spirits of Resistance and Capitalist Discipline: Factory Women in Malaysia*, SUNY Press, Albany.

Outshoorn, J. (2004) *The Politics of Prostitution, Women's Movements, Democratic States and the Globalisation of Sex Commerce*, Cambridge University Press, Cambridge (UK).

Outshoorn, J. (2005) 'The Political Debates on Prostitution and Trafficking of Women,' *Social Politics*, Vol. 12, pp. 141–55.

Overall, C. (1992) 'What's Wrong With Prostitution? Evaluating Sex Work,' *Signs*, Vol. 17, No. 4, pp. 705–25.

Parsons, J. T. (2005) 'Researching the World's Oldest Profession: Introduction,' *Journal of Psychology and Human Sexuality*, Vol. 17, pp. 1–3.

Passaro, J. (1996) *The Unequal Homeless: Men on the Streets, Women in their Place*, Routledge, London and New York.

Pateman, C. (1988) *The Sexual Contract*, Polity Press, Cambridge (UK).

Pates, R. & D. Schmidt (2008) 'Wahrheiten über Opfer: Menschenhandelsdiskurse im Vergleich,' in *Der involvierte Blick. Zwansprostitution und ihre Repräsentation*, Bulletin Texte 35, HU Berlin Zentrum für transdisziplinäre Geschlechterstudien, pp. 90105.

Pates, R. & D. Schmidt (2009) *Die Verwaltung der Prostitution: Eine vergleichende Studie am Beispiel deutscher, polnischer und tschechischer Kommunen*, Transcript, Bielefeld.

Perle, L. (2006) *Money, A Memoir*, Picador, London.

Perry, J. (1999) *A Girl Needs Cash: How to Take Charge of Your Financial Life*, Three Rivers Press, New York.

Pheterson, G. (ed.) (1989) *A Vindication of the Rights of Whores: The International Movements for Prostitutes' Rights*, Seal Press, Seattle.

Pheterson, G. (1990) 'The Category "Prostitute" in Social Scientific Inquiry,' *Journal of Sex Research*, Vol. 27, pp. 397–407.

Pheterson, G. (1996) *The Prostitution Prism*, Amsterdam University Press, Amsterdam.

Philaretou, A. (2006) 'Female Exotic Dancers: Intrapersonal and Interpersonal Perspectives,' *Sexual Addiction and Compulsivity*, Vol. 13, pp. 41–52.

Phillips, M. M. & M. Moffett (2005) 'Brazil Refuses US AIDS Funds, Rejects Conditions,' *Wall Street Journal*, 2 May 2005.

Phoenix, J. & S. Oerton (2005) *Illicit and Illegal: Sex, Regulation and Social Control*, Willan Publishing.

Pickering, H. & H. Wilkins (1993) 'Do Unmarried Women in African Towns Have to Sell Sex, or Is It a Matter of Choice,' *Health Transitions Review*, Vol. 3, pp. 17–27.

Pitcher, J. (2006a) 'Evaluating Community Safety Programmes and Community Engagement: The Role of Qualitative Methods and Collaborative Approaches to Policy Research,' *Urban Policy and Research*, Vol. 24, No. 1, pp. 67–82.

Pitcher, J. (2006b) 'Support Services for Women Working in the Sex Industry,' in R. Campbell & M. O'Neill (eds), *Sex Work Now*, Willan Publishing, Cullompton.

Pitcher, J. & R. Aris (2003) *Women and Street Sex Work: Issues Arising from an Evaluation of an Arrest Referral Scheme*, Nacro Research Briefing, London.

Pitcher, J., R. Campbell, P. Hubbard, M. O'Neill & J. Scoular (2006) *Living and Working in Areas of Street Sex Work: From Conflict to Coexistence*, Policy Press, Bristol.

Plummer, K. (1995) *Telling Sexual Stories: Power, Change, and Social Worlds*, Routledge, London and New York.

Plummer, K. (2001) *Sexualities: Critical Concepts in Sociology*, Routledge, London and New York.

Plummer, K. (2003) *Intimate Citizenship: Private Decisions and Public Dialogs*, University of Washington Press, Seattle.

Prasad, M. (1999) 'The Morality of Market Exchange: Love, Money, and Contractual Justice,' *Sociological Perspectives*, Vol. 42, pp. 181–214.

Rao, V., I. Gupta, M. Lokshin & S. Jana (2003) 'Sex Workers and the Cost of Safe Sex: The Compensating Differential for Condom Use Among Calcutta Prostitutes,' *Journal of Development Economics*, Vol. 71, pp. 585–603.

Raskin, J. (2004) *American Scream: Allen Ginsberg's Howl and the Making of the Beat Generation*. University of California Press.

Raymond, H., R. Stall & M. Kennedy (1999) 'Tribes in the Urban Streets: Tribal Affiliations Among Street Youth and High Risk Behaviors for HIV Transmission,' paper written for UCSF Center for AIDS Prevention Studies and Larkin Street Youth Center, on file with Kerwin Kaye.

Reiss, A., Jr (1987 [1961]) 'The Social Integration of Queers and Peers,' in E. Rubington & M. Weinberg (eds), *Deviance: The Interactionist Perspective*, 5th edn, Macmillan, New York, pp. 352–60.

Research Triangle Institute (1994) *Youth With Runaway, Throwaway, and Homeless Experiences: Prevalence, Drug Use, and Other At-Risk Behaviors*. US Department of Health and Human Services, Administration on Children, Youth and Families (ACYF), Family and Youth Services Bureau (FYSB), Washington, DC.

Ritter, B. (1988) *Sometimes God Has a Kid's Face*, Covenant House, New York.

Riviere, J. (1929) 'Womanliness as a Masquerade,' *International Journal of Psychoanalysis*, Vol. 10, pp. 303–13.

Bibliography

Roberts, N. (1992) *Whores in History: Prostitution in Western Society*, Harper Collins, London.

Rojek, C. (1994) *Ways of Escape: Modern Transformations in Leisure and Travel*, Rowman & Littlefield, Lanham, MD.

Rojek, C. & J. Urry (1997) *Touring Cultures: Transformations of Travel and Theory*, Routledge, London and New York.

Romans, S. E., K. Potter, J. Martin & P. Herbison (2001) 'The Mental and Physical Health of Female Sex Workers: A Comparative Study,' *Australian and New Zealand Journal of Psychiatry*, Vol. 35, pp. 75–80.

Ronai, C. R. & C. Ellis (1989) 'Turn-Ons for Money: Interactional Strategies of the Table Dancer,' *Journal of Contemporary Ethnography*, Vol. 18, pp. 271–98.

Rose, N. & P. Miller (1992) 'Political Power Beyond the State: Problematics of Government,' *British Journal of Sociology*, Vol. 43, No. 2, pp. 172–205.

Rose, N. & M. Valverde (1998) 'Governed by Law?,' *Social and Legal Studies*, Vol. 7, No. 4, pp. 541–51.

Roseneil, S. (2000) 'Queer Frameworks and Queer Tendencies: Toward an Understanding of Postmodern Transformations of Sexuality,' *Sociological Research Online*, available at http://www.socresonline.org.uk/5/3/roseneil.html (accessed 5 May 2009).

Roxburgh, A., L. Degenhardt & J. Copeland (2006) 'Post-Traumatic Stress Disorder Among Female Street-Based Sex Workers in the Greater Sydney Area, Australia,' *BMC Psychiatry*, Vol. 6, pp. 24.

Safa, H. (1994) *The Myth of the Male Breadwinner*, Westview Press, Boulder (CO).

Safa, H. (1995) 'The New Women Workers: Does Money Equal Power?' in F. Rosen & D. McFadden (eds), *Free Trade and Economic Restructuring in Latin America*, Monthly Review Press, New York, pp. 39–43.

Safety Soapbox (2009), available at http://www.safetysoapbox.co.uk/menu.htm (accessed 5 May 2009).

Sagar, T. (2005) 'Street Watch: Concept and Practice', *British Journal of Criminology*, Vol. 45, No. 1, pp. 98–112.

Sanders, T. (2002) 'The Condom as a Psychological Barrier: Female Sex Workers and Emotional Management,' *Feminism & Psychology*, Vol. 12, pp. 561–6.

Sanders, T. (2004a) 'A Continuum of Risk? The Management of Health, Physical and Emotional Risks by Female Sex Workers,' *Sociology of Health & Illness*, Vol. 2, No. 5, pp. 557–74.

Sanders, T. (2004b) 'Controllable Laughter: Managing Sex Work through Humour,' *Sociology*, Vol. 38, pp. 273–91.

Sanders, T. (2004c) 'The Risks of Street Prostitution: Punters, Police and Protesters,' *Urban Studies*, Vol. 41, No. 9, pp. 1703–17.

Sanders, T. (2005a) '"It's Just Acting": Sex Workers' Strategies for Capitalizing on Sexuality,' *Gender, Work and Organization*, Vol. 12, pp. 319–42.

Sanders, T. (2005b) *Sex Work: A Risky Business*, Willan Publishing, Portland (OR).

Sanders, T. (2006) 'Sexing Up the Subject: Methodological Nuances in the Female Sex Industry,' *Sexualities*, Vol. 9, No. 4, pp. 471–90.

Sanders, T., M. O'Neill & J. Pitcher (2009) *Prostitution: Sex Work, Policy and Politics*, Sage, London.

Scambler, G. & A. Scambler (1997) 'Conspicuous and Inconspicuous Sex Work: Neglect of the Ordinary and Mundane,' in G. Scambler & A. Scambler (eds),

Bibliography

Rethinking Prostitution: Purchasing Sex in the 1990s, Routledge, London and New York.

Schauer, F. (2003) Profiles, Probabilities and Stereotypes, Harvard University Press, Cambridge (MA).

Schlosser, E. (1997) 'The Business of Pornography,' U.S. News & World Report.

Scott, R. (1999) 'A Brief Dictionary of Queer Slang and Culture,' in Rebecca's Dictionary, 12 November 1999, available at http://www.geocities.com/WestHollywood/Stonewall/4219/ (accessed 12 February 2009).

Scottish Executive (2005) Being Outside: Constructing a Response to Street Prostitution. Report of the Expert Group on Prostitution in Scotland, Scottish Executive, Edinburgh.

Scoular, J. (2004) 'The "Subject" of Prostitution: Interpreting the Discursive, Symbolic and Material Position of Sex/Work in Feminist Theory,' Feminist Theory, Vol. 5, pp. 343–55.

Scoular, J. & M. O'Neill (2006) 'Regulating Prostitution: Social Inclusion, Responsibilisation and the Politics of Prostitution Reform', paper presented at the British Criminology Association Conference, Leeds.

Seidman, S. (2003) Beyond the Closet: The Transformation of Gay and Lesbian Life, Routledge, London and New York.

Seppa, A. & C. Michelle (2003) 'Labor Violations and Discrimination in the Clark County Outcall Entertainment Industry,' MA thesis, Sociology, University of Nevada, Las Vegas.

Sex Work Matters (2005), available at sexworkmatters.net/program.htm (accessed 5 May 2009).

Sexyshock (2009), available at http://www.ecn.org/sexyshock/ (accessed 5 May 2009).

Shah, S. P. (2004) 'Prostitution, Sex Work and Violence: Discursive and Political Contexts for Five Texts on Paid Sex, 1987–2001,' Gender & History, Vol. 16, pp. 794–812.

Sharpe, E. (2005) '"Going Above and Beyond": The Emotional Labor of Adventure Guides,' Journal of Leisure Research, Vol. 37, pp. 29–50.

Shaver, F. M. (2005) 'Sex Work Research: Methodological and Ethical Challenges,' Journal of Interpersonal Violence, Vol. 20, pp. 296–319.

Shrage, L. (1994) 'Comment on Overall's "What's Wrong with Prostitution? Evaluating Sex Work,"' Signs, Vol. 19, No. 2, pp. 564–70.

Simon, W. (1996) Postmodern Sexualities, Routledge, London and New York.

Simons, R. L. & Whitbeck, L. B. (1991) 'Sexual Abuse as a Precursor to Prostitution and Victimization Among Adolescent and Adult Homeless Women,' Journal of Family Issues, Vol. 12, pp. 361–79.

Sims, C. R. (1999) When the Streets Are Home: The Ministry of Presence Within the Theological Constructs of Personalism and Harm Reduction, MA thesis.

Singer, L. (1993) Erotic Welfare, Routledge, London and New York.

Skipper, J. K. & C. H. McCaghy (1970) 'Stripteasers: The Anatomy and Career Contingencies of a Deviant Occupation,' Social Problems, Vol. 17, pp. 391–405.

Skipper, J. K. & C. H. McCaghy (1971) 'Stripteasing: A Sex-Oriented Occupation,' in J. Henslin (ed.), The Sociology of Sex, Appleton Century Crofts, New York, pp. 275–96.

Snell, C. (1995) Young Men in the Street: Help-Seeking Behavior of Young Male Prostitutes, Praeger, Westport (CT).

Solaiman, M. (2009) 'Hijra,' Banglapedia, available at http://banglapedia.search.com.bd/HT/H_0117.htm (accessed 10 February 2009).

South, S. J. (1991) 'Sociodemographic Differentials in Mate Selection Preferences,' *Journal of Marriage and the Family*, Vol. 53, pp. 928–40.

Spain, W. (2007) 'Strip Clubs Go Mainstream,' MSN *Money MarketWatch*, available at articles.moneycentral.msn.com/Investing/Extra/StripClubsGoMainstream. aspx. (accessed 29 August 2009).

Spanier, G. B. & P. C. Click (1980) 'Mate Selection Differential between Whites and Blacks in the United States,' *Social Forces*, Vol. 58, pp. 707–25.

Sparr, P. (ed.) (1994) *Mortgaging Women's Lives: Feminist Critiques of Structural Adjustment*, Zed Books, London.

Spivey, S. E. (2005) 'Distancing and Solidarity as Resistance to Sexual Objectification in a Nude Dancing Bar,' *Deviant Behavior*, Vol. 26, pp. 417–37.

Stacey, J. (1996) *In the Name of the Family: Rethinking Family Values in the Postmodern Age*, Beacon Press, Boston.

Storr, M. (2003) *Latex and Lingerie: Shopping for Pleasure at Ann Summers*, Berg Publishers, Oxford.

Stripper Web (2009) *Stripper Psychology*, available at http://www.stripperweb. com/forum/showthread.php?t=62416 (accessed 5 May 2009).

Suárez Findlay, E. (1999) *Imposing Decency: The Politics of Sexuality and Race in Puerto Rico, 1870–1920*, Duke University Press, Durham (NC).

Sweet, N. & R. Tewksbury (2000) 'Entry, Maintenance and Departure from a Career in the Sex Industry: Strippers' Experiences of Occupational Costs and Rewards,' *Humanity and Society*, Vol. 24, No. 2, pp. 136–61.

Tabet, P. (1991) 'Les dents de la prostituée: échange, négociation, choix dans les rapports économico-sexuels,' in *Sexe et Genre. De la hiérarchie entre les sexes*, CNRS, Paris, pp. 227–44.

Tabet, P. (2004) *La Grande Beffa. Sessualità delle donne e scambio sessuo-economico*, Rubbettino, Soveria Mannelli.

Taking the Pledge (2007), video, available at http://blip.tv/file/181155 (accessed 30 May 2009).

Tampep International Foundation (2009), available at http://www.tampep.com/ (accessed 5 May 2009).

Tewksbury, R. (1993) 'Male Strippers: Men Objectifying Men,' in C. L. Williams (ed.), *Doing 'Women's Work': Men in Nontraditional Occupations*, Sage Publications, Newbury Park (CA), pp. 168–81.

Thio, A. (1998) *Deviant Behavior*, 5th edn, Addison-Wesley, Boston.

Thompson, W. E. & J. L. Harred (1992) 'Topless Dancers: Managing Stigma in a Deviant Occupation,' *Deviant Behavior*, Vol. 13, pp. 291–311.

Thompson, W. E., J. L. Harred & B. Burks (2003) 'Managing the Stigma of Topless Dancing: A Decade Later,' *Deviant Behavior*, Vol. 24, pp. 551–70.

Thukral, J. & M. Ditmore (2003) *Revolving Door: An Analysis of Street-Based Prostitution in New York City*, report issued by the Sex Workers Project at the Urban Justice Center, available at http://www.urbanjustice.org/sexworkersproject (accessed 5 May 2009).

Thukral, J., M. Ditmore & A. Murphy (2005) *Behind Closed Doors: An Analysis of Indoor Sex Work in New York City*, report issued by the Sex Workers Project at the Urban Justice Center, New York, available at http://www.urbanjustice.org/sexworkersproject (accessed 5 May 2009).

Toffler, A. (1990) *Powershift: Knowledge, Wealth, and Violence at the Edge of the 21st Century*, Bantam Books, New York.

UK Network of Sex Work Projects (2009), available at http://www.uknswp.org (accessed 5 May 2009).

UNAIDS (2009) *Guidance Note on HIV/AIDS and Sex Work*, available at http://data. unaids.org/pub/BaseDocument/2009/jc1696_guidance_note_hiv_and_sexwo rk_en.pdf (accessed 30 May 2009).

UNICEF (2005) *Child Poverty in Rich Countries*, Innocenti Report Card no. 6, UNICEF Innocenti Research Center, Florence (Italy), available at http://www.unicef.org /irc (accessed 5 May 2009).

Urry, J. (2002) *The Tourist Gaze*, Sage, London and Thousand Oaks (CA).

Valverde, M. (1998) *Diseases of the Will: Alcohol and the Dilemmas of Freedom*, Cambridge University Press, Cambridge (MA).

Valverde, M. (2003) *Law's Dream of a Common Knowledge: The Cultural Lives of Law*, Princeton University Press, Princeton (NJ).

Van Doorninck, M. & R. Campbell (2006) '"Zoning" Street Sex Work: One Way Forward?,' in R. Campbell & M. O'Neill (eds), *Sex Work Now*, Willen, Cullompton, Devon.

Vanwesenbeeck, I. (1994) *Prostitutes' Well-Being and Risk*, V University Press, Amsterdam.

Vanwesenbeeck, I. (2001) 'Another Decade of Social Scientific Work on Sex Work: A Review of Research 1990-2000,' *Annual Review of Sex Research*, Vol. 12, pp. 242–89.

Vanwesenbeeck, I. (2005) 'Burnout Among Indoor Female Sex Workers,' *Archives of Sexual Behavior*, Vol. 34, pp. 627–39.

Venkatesh, S. (2000) *American Project: The Rise and Fall of a Modern Ghetto*, Harvard University Press, Cambridge (MA).

Visano, L. (1987) *This Idle Trade*, VitaSana Books, Concord (ON).

Wacquant, L. (1995) 'Pugs at Work: Bodily Capital and Bodily Labor Among Professional Boxers,' *Body and Society*, Vol. 1, pp. 65–95.

Wacquant, L. (2003) *Body and Soul: Notes of an Apprentice Boxer*, Oxford University Press, New York.

Weber, M. (1946) 'Politics as Vocation,' in H. H. Gerth & C. Wright Mills (eds), *From Max Weber: Essays in Sociology*, Oxford University Press, New York.

Weisberg, D. K. (1985) *Children of the Night: Adolescent Prostitution in America*, Lexington Books, Lexington (MA).

Weitzer, R. (1991) 'Prostitutes' Rights in the United States: The Failure of a Movement,' *Sociological Quarterly*, Vol. 32, pp. 23–41.

Weitzer, R. (2000) *Sex For Sale: Prostitution, Pornography, and the Sex Industry*, Routledge, London and New York.

Weitzer, R. (2005) 'Flawed Theory and Method in Studies of Prostitution,' *Violence Against Women*, Vol. 11, pp. 934–49.

Weitzer, R. (2007) 'The Social Construction of Sex Trafficking: Ideology and Institutionalization of a Moral Crusade,' *Politics & Society*, Vol. 35, pp. 447–75.

West, D. J. & de Villiers, B. (1993) *Male Prostitution*, Haworth Press, Binghamton.

Wharton, A. S. (2009) 'The Sociology of Emotional Labor,' *Annual Review of Sociology*, Vol. 35, pp. 213–34.

White, L. (1990) *The Comforts of Home: Prostitution in Colonial Nairobi*, University of Chicago Press, Chicago.

White, M., C. Salas & S. Gammage (2003) *Trade Impact Review: Mexico Case Study. NAFTA and the FTAA: A Gender Analysis of Employment and Poverty Impacts in Agriculture*, Women's Edge

Coalition, Washington, DC.

Whyte, W. F. (1943) *Street Corner Society*, University of Chicago Press, Chicago.

Wijers, M. (1998) 'Women, Labor and Migration: The Position of Trafficked Women and Strategies for Support,' in K. Kempadoo & J. Doezma (eds), *Global Sex Workers: Rights, Resistance and Redefinition.*, Routledge, New York, pp. 69–78.

Wijers, M. (2001) *Keep Your Women Home: European Union Policies on Trafficking in Women and Strategies for Support*, in G.M. Rossilli (ed.) *Gender Policies in the European Union*, Peter Lang, London.

Williams, C. L., P. A. Guiffre & K. Dellinger (1999) 'Sexuality in the Workplace: Organizational Control, Sexual Harassment, and the Pursuit of Pleasure,' *Annual Review of Sociology*, Vol. 25, pp. 73–93.

Williams, T. (1992) *Crackhouse: Notes from the End of the Line*, Penguin Press, New York.

Willman, A. (2008) 'Safety First, Then Condoms: Commercial Sex, Risky Behavior and The Spread of HIV/AIDS in Managua, Nicaragua,' *Feminist Economics*, Vol. 14, No. 4, pp. 37–65.

Willman, A. (2009) *What's Money Got to Do With It? Risky Behavior in Commercial Sex Work in Managua, Nicaragua*, VDM, Berlin.

Willman, A. (forthcoming) 'Risk and Reward in Managua's Commercial Sex Market: The Mediating Role of Workplace,' *Journal of Human Development and Capabilities*.

Wohlfarth, J. (2004) 'Rechtsfragen um die Prostitution,' *Verwaltungsrundschau*, Vol. 4, pp. 126–31.

Wolkowitz, C. (2006) *Bodies at Work*, Sage, London and Thousand Oaks (CA).

Women's European Lobby (2009), available at http://www.womenlobby.org (accessed 5 May 2009).

Wonders, N. A. & R. Michalowski (2001) 'Bodies, Borders, and Sex Tourism in a Globalized World: A Tale of Two Cities – Amsterdam and Havana,' *Social Problems*, Vol. 48, pp. 545–71.

Wood, E. A. (2000) 'Working in the Fantasy Factory: The Attention Hypothesis and the Enacting of Masculine Power in Strip Clubs,' *Journal of Contemporary Ethnography*, Vol. 29, pp. 5–31.

World Charter for Prostitutes' Rights (1985), available at http://www.bayswan.org/ICPRChart.html (accessed 5 May 2009).

Zelizer, V. A. (2005) *The Purchase of Intimacy*, Princeton University Press, Princeton (NJ).

Index